A
A P

With expert

course to romance, adventure, good health, or career op
portunities while gaining valuable insight into yourself
and others. Offering a daily outlook for 18 full months,
this fascinating guide shows you:

- The important dates in your life
- What to expect from an astrological reading
- How the stars can help you stay healthy and fit.
  And more!

Let this sound advice guide you through a year of heav-
enly possibilities—for today and for every day of 2012!

SYDNEY OMARR'S® DAY-BY-DAY
ASTROLOGICAL GUIDE FOR

ARIES—March 21–April 19
TAURUS—April 20–May 20
GEMINI—May 21–June 20
CANCER—June 21–July 22
LEO—July 23–August 22
VIRGO—August 23–September 22
LIBRA—September 23–October 22
SCORPIO—October 23–November 21
SAGITTARIUS—November 22–December 21
CAPRICORN—December 22–January 19
AQUARIUS—January 20–February 18
PISCES—February 19–March 20

IN 2012

SYDNEY OMARR'S®

DAY-BY-DAY ASTROLOGICAL GUIDE FOR

LEO

JULY 23–AUGUST 22

2012

by Trish MacGregor
with Rob MacGregor

A SIGNET BOOK

SIGNET
Published by New American Library, a division of
Penguin Group (USA) Inc., 375 Hudson Street,
New York, New York 10014, USA
Penguin Group (Canada), 90 Eglinton Avenue East, Suite 700, Toronto,
Ontario M4P 2Y3, Canada (a division of Pearson Penguin Canada Inc.)
Penguin Books Ltd., 80 Strand, London WC2R 0RL, England
Penguin Ireland, 25 St. Stephen's Green, Dublin 2,
Ireland (a division of Penguin Books Ltd.)
Penguin Group (Australia), 250 Camberwell Road, Camberwell, Victoria 3124,
Australia (a division of Pearson Australia Group Pty. Ltd.)
Penguin Books India Pvt. Ltd., 11 Community Centre, Panchsheel Park,
New Delhi - 110 017, India
Penguin Group (NZ), 67 Apollo Drive, Rosedale, Auckland 0632,
New Zealand (a division of Pearson New Zealand Ltd.)
Penguin Books (South Africa) (Pty.) Ltd., 24 Sturdee Avenue,
Rosebank, Johannesburg 2196, South Africa

Penguin Books Ltd., Registered Offices:
80 Strand, London WC2R 0RL, England

First Printing, June 2011
10 9 8 7 6 5 4 3 2 1

First published by Signet, an imprint of New American Library,
a division of Penguin Group (USA) Inc.

CONTENTS

CHAPTER 1

Paradigm Shift

There's more hype about December 21, 2012, than there was about the Y2K scare at the turn of the century. Depending on which Web site or book you read, the world will end on that day, the poles will shift, the aliens will land. In fact, there's been so much hype that in March 2007 *USA Today* ran an article titled "Does Maya Calendar Predict 2012 Apocalypse?"

"Maya civilization, known for advanced writing, mathematics and astronomy, flourished for centuries in Mesoamerica, especially between A.D. 300 and 900. Its Long Count calendar, which was discontinued under Spanish colonization, tracks more than 5,000 years, then resets at year zero," wrote G. Jeffrey MacDonald in the *USA Today* article.

It resets on December 21, 2012. It's the day that marks the winter solstice in the northern hemisphere. It's also the day that the sun will be aligned with the center of the Milky Way galaxy for the first time in nearly 26,000 years or, to be exact, in 25,625 years, what the Mayans considered to be a single galactic day. They divided that galactic day into five cycles of 5,125 years, and on December 21, that fifth cycle ends. So, what's that mean for us?

According to Mayan Indian elder Apolinario Chile Pixtum, it definitely doesn't mean the end of the world. He, in fact, says the doomsday theories spring from

Western, not Mayan ideas. "I came back from England last year and man, they had me fed up with this stuff."

Jose Huchin, a Yucatan Mayan archaeologist, says that if he went into Maya-speaking communities and asked people what was going to occur in 2012, they wouldn't have any idea. "That the world is going to end? They wouldn't believe you," he says.

A likely possibility for 2012 is a shift in paradigms. If 2011 was the year of transitions, then 2012 can be viewed as the year when people begin to embrace new ways of thinking about themselves, the society in which they live, and the world. With the meltdown in the financial and housing markets in 2008–2009, the election of the first African-American president, the bailouts of banks, rising foreclosures and unemployment, and the broken health-care system, a shift in belief systems seems inevitable.

As Daniel Pinchbeck wrote in *2012: The Return of Quetzalcoatl*: "If we were to conclude, after careful consideration, that our modern world is based upon fundamentally flawed conceptions of time and mind, that on these fatal defects we had erected a flawed civilization . . . then logic might indicate the necessity, as well as the inevitability, of change. Such a shift would not be 'the end of the world,' but the end of a world, and the opening of the next."

How You Can Adapt to the Paradigm Shift

Our lives are marked by transitions. We make the *transition* from adolescence to adulthood, from dependent to independent, from being single to being married, from youth to middle age to old age, from life to death. These transitions are often marked by rituals—diplomas, ceremonies—that recognize our rites of passage.

In astrology, we have similar transitions, but they are triggered by the movement of the outer planets—Jupiter, Saturn, Uranus, Neptune, and Pluto. These planets are the slowest moving, so they exert the most impact on our lives. The lineup in 2011 pushed us toward the paradigm shift that will occur in 2012.

So now you're asking, *How's it going to affect me?* That depends on the angles these slower-moving planets make to your sun sign—and on your attitudes and deepest beliefs. After all, the planets only depict possible patterns that may occur. *We're* the scriptwriters. We have free will, the ability to make choices. Astrology simply provides information that makes those choices easier. To be informed is to be empowered.

The planet to watch in 2012 is Neptune, which enters Pisces on February 3 and remains there until the end of March 2025. Neptune was in Pisces briefly in 2011—from April 5 to August 5—then turned retrograde and slipped back into Aquarius for a final time. Since it takes this planet fourteen years to transit a single sign, it won't be back to Aquarius for another 168 years!

Now let's take a closer look at what Neptune's transit may mean for each of us.

The Role of Neptune in 2012

Neptune is an elusive planet, so far away from the sun that it's one of two planets that can't be seen without a telescope. The temperature of its surface clouds is around -218 degrees Celsius. Its atmosphere is composed of hydrogen and helium, and its interior is mostly ice and rock.

When Voyager 2 flew past Neptune in 1989, it was discovered that Neptune had a dark area composed of gas that swirled violently with the force of a hurricane. They called it the Great Dark Spot and compared it to the Great Red Spot on Jupiter. In 1994, however, the Hubble telescope found that that spot had disappeared. So we know that Neptune, like Jupiter, has weather patterns.

To understand Neptune's influence in our lives and how it will impact us from 2012 to 2026, when it moves through Pisces, let's take a walk through a brief slice of history.

The planet was discovered in 1846—not because it was spotted through a telescope, but due to a disturbing characteristic in the orbit of Uranus. Astronomers suspected the erratic orbit was created by the gravitational pull of another planet. In a sense, then, the way in which Neptune was discovered is a metaphor for its elusive characteristics in astrology. It symbolizes imagination, spiritual and intuitive talents, psychic experiences, artistic inspiration. On the downside, it represents our illusions, our blind spots, and governs alcoholism, drug addiction, confusion, escapism of all kinds. Astrologer Steven Forrest calls Neptune "the planet of consciousness . . . the blank state."

Shortly after Neptune was discovered, the California gold rush began (illusions). The Romantic movement (inspiration) also started, a reaction against intellectualism, materialism, and the rigidity of social structures that protected the wealthy, the privileged. Then in 1848, just two years after Neptune's discovery, the Spiritualist movement was born in a small cottage in Hydesville, New York, where the Fox family lived.

John and Margaret Fox and two of their daughters, Margaret and Kate, had moved into the house in December 1847. The place was reputedly haunted and strange noises and rappings could be heard at night, which kept the family awake. On the night of March 31, about three nights after the family had moved into the house, young Kate heard the noises and responded by snapping her fingers and called out, "Mr. Splitfoot. Do as I do." She then clapped her hands several times.

The pattern of her clapping was instantly duplicated. Her sister then joined in and demanded that "Splitfoot" do what she did. Her four claps were immediately answered with four claps. Mrs. Fox asked the invisible guest to rap out the ages of all of her seven children, which it did, with a pause between each one to individualize them.

Mrs. Fox began to question the rapper. Was it a human being? There was no response. She then asked it to rap twice if it was a spirit. It rapped twice—and the spiritualist movement was born.

Twenty-nine years after Neptune's discovery, a medium named George Colby of Iowa was holding a séance at the home of a local resident, a fellow named Wadsworth. Nothing extraordinary had happened so far that night. Colby was already a successful medium, and he'd done the usual things that night—passed on messages from the dead to the living.

Then, suddenly, Colby received a message from his Indian guide, Seneca, instructing him to travel immediately to Eau Claire, Wisconsin, where he was to hook up with T. D. Giddings, a Spiritualist. Once he was in Wisconsin, Seneca said, further instructions would be given. Colby, being a product of a time when the Spiritualist movement was sweeping across the country, did the expected thing. The next morning he packed up and left for Wisconsin. He met up with Giddings, and at a séance shortly afterward Colby and Giddings were given instructions to leave Wisconsin and head to Florida.

Colby was only twenty-seven years old at the time, a single man ready for adventure. Giddings, however, had a family and took them along. Back then, steamboats and trains were the only route south, and this odd little entourage took both. They rode a train to Jacksonville, Florida, then traveled by steamboat down the St. John's River to a place called Blue Springs. This frontier town was supposedly in the general vicinity of their final destination.

Seneca had described the place they were going to settle as having hills and a chain of lakes. The only thing that lay beyond the borders of Blue Springs looked like dense, subtropical forest. But when Seneca made contact and told the two men to begin their trek into the woods and to follow his directions, they did so.

They made their way through dense growth and after several miles arrived at the spot where Seneca said the Spiritualist camp would be created. Everything—from the high bluffs to the lakes and the lay of the land— looked exactly as Seneca had described.

Colby built a house on the shores of Lake Colby, and Giddings and his family built a home nearby. Colby eventually obtained a government deed for seventy-four acres that adjoined the area where he and Giddings had settled. They were apparently the only people for miles around.

For eighteen years, Colby didn't do much of anything about establishing a Spiritualist community in the area. He adopted several orphans, however, and raised them. He also operated a dairy.

In 1893, a Spiritualist named Rowley showed up and decided to establish a Spiritualist center in either De-Leon Springs or Winter Park. He invited a number of prominent Spiritualists from the north to travel to Florida to check out the area. Two of these Spiritualists were women who were prominent in the Lily Dale Spiritualist camp in New York. They didn't particularly care for Rowley, but Colby won them over, and they decided to create a Spiritualist camp on his property.

In October 1894, twelve mediums signed the charter for the Southern Cassadaga Spiritualist Camp. According to the charter, the association was to be a nonprofit organization that would promote the Spiritualist beliefs in the soul's immortality, "the nearness of the Spirit World, the guardianship of Spirit friends, and the possibility of communion with them," as the charter reads.

Seneca, Colby's guide, apparently advised him to remain in the background during this time, so his name doesn't appear on the charter, and he didn't have much to do with the organization of the camp. However, in 1895, he deeded the association thirty-five acres of his land. The first meeting was held in late 1895 and lasted three days. A hundred people attended the event to meet and sit with the mediums who had been invited.

Within three years of that first meeting, eight cottages, a dancing pavilion, a lodging hall, and a library had been built on the association grounds. Wealthy mediums from the north were being enticed to move to Cassadaga on a more or less permanent basis. From the late 1800s to the early part of the twentieth century, not much is written about the town. The camp apparently flourished, however, because the Cassadaga Hotel was built in 1922 and so were most of the cottages that still stand today.

In the century plus since Cassadaga was established, the rest of central Florida has grown up around it. Just thirty minutes south of it on I-4 is a whole other kind of world—Disney World! But as soon as you turn off Interstate 4, memories of Dumbo and Epcot, Universal and MGM, give way to southern pine forests. A kind of presence infuses the still air. You can't help but feel that nothing is what it appears to be.

For years there wasn't even a sign for Cassadaga. It was almost as if the people who are supposed to find their way here did so in spite of the lack of directions. Even today Cassadaga is little more than a black dot on a map, a punctuation point in the vastness of the pine forest. Lake Helen is the nearest town.

But if you blink too fast, Lake Helen is already a memory. Just beyond the outer edge of the town, the road climbs and dips through a series of low hills and shallow valleys. The trees seem thicker and darker here, the Spanish moss sways in the breeze, and shapes eddy across the shadowed road. A hush lingers in the air. Stop your car, lower your windows, and you probably won't hear a sound.

7

About half a mile outside of Lake Helen, you'll see a sign announcing that you're now in Cassadaga. But it isn't until you come around the next sharp curve that you know you're there. A large two-story stucco building looms in front of you, the Cassadaga Hotel. Its Mediterranean architecture dates back to the 1920s, during the heyday of Spiritualism. Along the right side of the building stretches a wide porch filled with rocking chairs. At dusk some evenings, when the light plays tricks with perception, some of the empty chairs rock, creaking softly in the quiet.

Spirits enjoying the evening? One never knows for sure. But perhaps that's part of the lure and the mystique of Cassadaga.

Given the uncertainty of the times in which we live, it's not surprising that business in Cassadaga is flourishing. On any weekend, the hotel lot is jammed with cars, and everywhere you look, people are walking around in search of the right psychic. Both sides of the main street are lined with small buildings that have signs posted out front advertising the kind of reading available. Unlike the early days of Cassadaga, when it was mainly Spiritualists, today's psychic offerings are vast. You can find everything from astrologers, tarot readers, and Reiki healers. But the mediums are still the draw, the magnet. As one young woman explained to us during a recent trip, "Everything is changing so fast, life is moving at such a rapid clip, that people are turning more and more to spiritual and intuitive insights and guidance."

And that pretty much sums up a large part of what Neptune's transit through Pisces may bring for each of us.

Neptune in Pisces

We had a brief taste of Neptune in Pisces, the sign it rules, between April 3, 2011, and August 4, 2011. Then Neptune turned retrograde and slipped back into Aquarius. But on February 3, 2012, it enters Pisces again. For clues about how this transit may manifest itself for you, look back to those four months in 2011. What was going on in your life then? Did you feel more creative? Did you take up a new artistic hobby? Did your spiritual beliefs undergo some sort of transformation? Were you more intuitive? Were you called upon to give selflessly in some respect? Did you feel your life was confusing, your goals muddled? Did you indulge more frequently in alcohol and drugs?

All of these areas fall under the governance of Neptune. So now let's look specifically at each sign for possible shifts under Neptune's fourteen-year transit through Pisces.

Aries ♈

Cardinal, fire

You're the trailblazer of the zodiac, known for your fearlessness, impulsiveness, and well, yes, sometimes your recklessness. You enjoy anything that induces an adrenaline rush—from extreme sports to love affairs to high-wire creative projects. You think outside the box, aren't known as a team player, and would rather delegate than be delegated to. In love, your passions are often extreme, you can be jealous and possessive, but when you fall, you fall hard, with your entire heart.

You're like an action hero, always on the move, doing, figuring the angles. Even your strong intuition comes through action—mostly impulses and burning hunches

9

on which you act quickly. Your spiritual beliefs probably aren't traditional, i.e., not associated with a particular religion or church. It's more likely that you've pieced together your own beliefs over the years and are still adding to them.

During Neptune's transit of Pisces and your solar twelfth house, your intuition and spirituality will deepen, the scope will broaden, and chances are it will all begin in the privacy of your interior world. Your dream life will be more vivid, and it should be easier to recall your dreams and work with them. You should have greater access to your own unconscious, so that it's easier to recall past lives and understand your own motives and psyche. In fact, the more you work consciously with your intuitive abilities and spiritual beliefs, the easier this paradigm shift will be for you.

Since the twelfth house represents institutions, it's possible that you may have more contact with hospitals, nursing homes, even prisons. You might be an employee or volunteer in one of these organizations. In some way, this experience enables you to reach for the greater good rather than for what is good only for you.

Taurus ♉

Fixed, earth

Your stubbornness, patience, and resoluteness are legendary. You complete whatever you start and often end up completing what other people start as well. In other words, due to your resilience and endurance, you often win where others fail. Where Aries trailblazes, you cultivate—relationships, a beautiful home, a family, a career, a garden. You enjoy being surrounded by beauty but aren't necessarily an extravagant spender.

Some signs need drama to thrive, but you're not one of them. You're a romantic who enjoys a harmonious relationship in which creativity can flourish. You tend to keep things to yourself—not so much secretive as circumspect. You speak when you have something meaningful to say.

Once Neptune enters Pisces, the tide will turn more in your direction. Pisces is a water sign that's compatible with your earth-sign sun, and you'll find that it deepens your innate curiosity about the deeper mysteries in life—telepathy, precognition, psychokinesis, synchronicity, what makes the universe tick, communication with the dead, UFOs, crop circles. You may join groups that support these interests and get involved with charitable organizations that support ideals in which you believe.

The eleventh house symbolizes groups, friends, our wishes, hopes and dreams, the people you hang with, goals, your life plan. So during Neptune's transit through Pisces, groups will be a major theme for you. You may join online groups that support your ideals, interests, and goals. There may be a psychic or intuitive component to these groups. Perhaps you end up in England, investigating crop circles. Or you might join a ghost-hunting group, a writer's group, a theater group. You might teach yoga for meditation to groups. You get the idea. One way or another, through group participation, online or off, you learn to reach for the greater good, the higher inspiration, the greater spiritual ideal.

Gemini ♊

Mutable, air

You're the communicator of the zodiac and can talk circles around anyone, anywhere, at any time, on virtually any subject. Your knowledge may not always be deep, but it's broad. When you don't know something, you research and ask questions incessantly, until your burning curiosity is sated.

Because you're ruled by Mercury, the planet of communication, you tend to use your rational, intellectual mind to explore your world. Your rational analysis of everything—from ideas to relationships—probably drives you nuts at times. But when this characteristic leads you into an exploration of psychic and spiritual realms, you're more grounded. With Neptune's transit through Pisces, you're going to have plenty of opportunities for this kind of exploration.

Neptune will be transiting the career section of your chart for fourteen years, suggesting that your professional life will be the focus of subtle but important change. In some way, psychic and spiritual exploration will become part of your professional endeavors. Opportunities will present themselves in these areas. Your creative ventures during this time will have a deeply psychic and spiritual texture to them. Your own intuition should deepen considerably, and as long as you act upon that inner knowledge, you won't be disappointed.

If you're not satisfied with your profession when this transit starts, then you may change career paths. Don't worry about how this will come about. You'll recognize the choices you should make and will have a strong inner sense about when to make them. During this transit, you'll learn to trust this inner sense and through your profession will learn to reach for inspired creativity and for what is best for the larger good, not just for what is good for you.

Cancer ♋

Cardinal, water

You need roots, a place to call home, and it doesn't matter if that place is a camper, a palace, or a state of mind. Home is your harbor, your refuge, your retreat.

As a cardinal water sign, your intuition and perceptions are finely honed. Just about everything for you is filtered through a subjective lens, through your emotions and intuition. You may not always be able to explain to others why you make certain decisions, but you don't have an overpowering need to explain yourself. You do what you do because it feels right to you.

You're affectionate, passionate, and even possessive at times. Emotionally, you act and react the same way that a crab moves—sideways. It's how you avoid confrontation and revealing who you really are, deep within. You're often moody and changeable, but once you trust someone, you trust forever.

With Neptune in fellow water sign Pisces, transiting your solar ninth house, you'll be enjoying a prolonged period of psychic and spiritual development that your Cancer nature will love. Workshops and seminars on intuitive development are a possibility—you take them or teach them! Travel to foreign countries is likely, but it won't be strictly for pleasure. You could be on a spiritual quest of some kind, visiting sacred sites in different countries in search of answers, information, illumination.

In romance and love, any relationship that develops under this transit may have a deeply spiritual component to it. The person could be someone you have been with in past lives and now you're together again for this psychic exploration.

Leo ♌

Fixed, fire

Life is your stage, Leo. Your flamboyance and flair for drama infuse you with great magnetic appeal toward which others gravitate. You seek to succeed in everything you do and undertake, want to make an impact in every situation and usually do. Your generosity and loyalty are legendary, but not without strings! You expect to be the sun around which others spin like planets. Nothing short of center stage suits you. Perhaps this is why so many Leos enter the dramatic and creative arts. It's an area where they excel.

Your leadership abilities, fun-loving nature, and genuine compassion are much appreciated by your friends and loved ones. You bring passion and commitment to everything you do, and it's these qualities that enable you to tackle challenges head on. In love and romance, you're passionate and loyal.

During Neptune's transit through Pisces and your solar eighth house, you may find the boundaries between you and others blurring. It's as if you're being asked to move off center stage for a while so that you can give freely of your time, money, energy, to others. The eighth house represents shared resources—usually with a spouse, but it can be anyone with whom you share expenses, time, energy, expertise. So it's possible that your spouse or partner's income may be muddled or confused during this transit.

Since the eighth house also represents inheritances, there could be some confusion concerning a will. But however this transit unfolds for you in terms of specific events, the point is to heighten your spiritual and intuitive awareness so that you reach first for the greater good.

Virgo ♍

Mutable, earth

You're the perfectionist of the zodiac, something you probably consider both a blessing and curse. Your attention to detail is extraordinary—think Tony Shalhoub in *Monk*. The man walks into a room, and in a single sweeping glance the details leap out at him—the pencil aligned with due north, the faintest smudge of lipstick on a coffee mug, the rug slightly askew. Thanks to this attention to detail, you're able to penetrate deeply into any topic you study, any research you conduct. You dig and dig until you have all the information you need.

Like Gemini, you're ruled by Mercury, so your mind is lightning quick and you communicate your ideas with great authority. Duty and responsibility are important to you, and your focus is on doing your job, whatever it is, efficiently and well. There's no harder worker than you, Virgo.

Neptune's transit through Pisces and your solar seventh house means it will be opposed to your sun for fourteen years. Oppositions are like an itch you can't scratch; you just learn to live with it. During this period, your greatest lessons and challenges will come through business and personal partnerships. You may be called upon to place a partner's interests and well-being before your own. The best way to navigate this opposition is to develop your intuition and learn to rely on your inner guidance.

There may be some confusion around partnerships too. But if you continually strive to associate with upbeat, spiritual individuals, to seek out those of like minds and interests, you should do just fine. Any relationships in which you get involved are likely to have deep past-life connections.

Libra ♎

Cardinal, air

You're the mediator, Libra, the one who sees both sides of an issue because you can step into the other guy's shoes, zip yourself up inside his skin, understand how and why he feels the way he does. You're all about finding harmony and balance, the very quality that often eludes you. But seek it you must, as if it's your prime directive. In love, you're a romantic who flourishes in a committed, enduring relationship. But regardless of how long the relationship lasts, you still need to be shown and told that you are loved.

You excel in any profession that requires a balanced intellect and sensitivities. Music and the arts suit you, but so does the law, teaching, research, investigation. During Neptune's transit through Pisces, your daily work will take a decided turn toward the spiritual and psychic. You may begin to take time each day to meditate, practice yoga, or engage in creative work that develops and enhances your intuition.

You may find that the individuals who enter your daily work life during this transit are people you have known in past lives, and you're coming together again for a specific purpose. Perhaps you're going to join forces for some large-scale project that makes a difference in the world. Or maybe you meet up again simply to support each other. One thing is for sure: it's going to be an intriguing fourteen years. The best way to navigate it, Libra, is to pay close attention to synchronicities. They're your guides.

Scorpio ♏

Fixed, water

Intensely passionate, secretive, and downright psychic, you're one of the most strong-willed signs in the zodiac and certainly one of the most misunderstood. Like your fellow water signs Cancer and Pisces, you live in a world of feeling and intuition, filtering all your experiences through a subjective lens. But you're also vastly different from your brethren water signs. You're basically fearless, with a great capacity for endurance that rivals Taurus, and you don't know the meaning of the word "indifference." You live pretty much in a black and white world, where things are either right or wrong, without nuance.

You're the consummate investigator. Easy answers never suit you, so you dig deeper and deeper, connecting the dots the rest of us miss. You have a rich inner life, glean a lot of information through nontraditional means, i.e., psychically, and never apologize for it.

During Neptune's transit of Pisces and your solar fifth house, you're in for a treat, Scorpio. Your considerable intuition will deepen even more. You'll be so in tune with your muse that your creativity simply flows out of you. Since the fifth house also symbolizes love and romance, you can expect some intense relationships that are madly passionate and perhaps rooted in past lives. If you have a child during this transit, he or she will be intensely creative in some way, with some special talent. It will be up to you to help the child develop and nurture that talent.

Because Neptune blurs the boundaries between us and others, it's possible that you'll be called upon to give of yourself in a selfless way—to a lover, a child, a creative project. If you resist the urge to get lost in escapism—drugs, alcohol, sex—then this transit should prove beneficial in your evolution as a human being.

Sagittarius ♐

Mutable, fire

You're blunt, witty, nomadic. You're the seeker of truth, express what you feel and believe, and don't care if anyone agrees with you. You're after the big picture, the broad canvas of any issue, belief, situation, relationship. Mundane details bore you. Intellectually, you're logical and rational, like Gemini, your polar opposite. But there are some important differences. Gemini is focused on the here and now; you've always got one eye on the future, on the larger family of humanity, the planet, the universe.

You love your freedom, the ability to just take off on a whim, with a pack and your ATM card, and chafe at any restrictions others try to put on you. Yet, in a relationship, you're passionate though rarely possessive; attentive to your partner and yet careful to maintain your freedom.

Once Neptune enters Pisces and your solar fourth house, you may find that your natural interest in mysticism, metaphysics, and things that go bump in the night takes on a whole new meaning. Suddenly, but subtly, your home and family life could become a hub of psychic activity and spiritual exploration. Your quest involves your family, your emotions toward them and vice versa, and you may discover layers of meaning in these relationships that you simply didn't see before.

There can be confusion during this transit too. If you move, there could be confusion about the neighborhood, the house, the contract. Depending on your age, one of your parents may need additional help and support or may move in with you. However this part of the equation unfolds, you may have to give more than you receive. But ultimately, your intuition becomes your compass, and through giving without expectation of compensation, you learn to extend yourself for the greater good.

Capricorn ♑
Cardinal, earth

Any boss worth her job knows that if you give a task to a Capricorn, it gets done with a shocking efficiency, dedication, and understanding of the nuances involved. But it's not just work at which you excel, Capricorn. This is how you conduct everything in your life—you appraise the situation, event, or relationship, figure out a strategy, then set things in motion that are intended to reach the goal, whatever it may be.

You're industrious, disciplined, structured, and have so much common sense it sometimes works against you! When you need intuition, right-brain thinking, your left brain, your rational mind, hurls up blocks and urges you to rely solely on logic. But that's going to change under Neptune's transit through Pisces and your solar third house, Capricorn.

The third house governs communication, and during Neptune's fourteen-year transit through Pisces, your conscious mind becomes more intuitive, psychic, right-brain. It will be easier for you to grasp the larger picture of your goals, daily life, and relationships with siblings, friends, neighbors. Whereas before you might have been intent on a particular course, now you'll be urged to explore other options, to take interesting detours into unexplored realms.

You'll learn to rely more and more frequently on your gut feelings, your hunches, your initial sense about people, situations. Your intimate partnerships will have a richness and depth you haven't experienced before. The spiritual and psychic connections you feel in these relationships will be based on your genuine beliefs and not on something you've learned to believe from parents, peers, friends. You'll be operating on a whole different level and will learn to trust these feelings first and foremost.

Aquarius ≈

Fixed, air

You value freedom and individuality above all else, and it's evident in the way you think, your belief system, your passions, and interests. Others may sometimes see you as eccentric, but in truth you're the visionary of the zodiac. You believe that whatever you can imagine, can become tangible.

You're a conundrum to the people who know you. You're a nonconformist who conforms when it suits you and a passionate advocate for your causes, but from an intellectual rather than an emotional basis. Once you commit in a relationship, you still demand your freedom and space, and this is true for all facets of your life. You work best in avant garde fields—film, electronics, the arts, television, broadcasting.

Neptune's transit through Pisces and your solar second house will impact your finances and your values. For instance, you may become more cognizant of how you spend your money. Do you, for instance, buy products from a company that promotes ideals that are contrary to your own? Do you use your power as a consumer to make statements about your ideals and beliefs? Are you generous toward charities and nonprofit organizations whose causes are in line with your ideals? Is your profession in line with them?

You may find that you begin to value different qualities in your romantic relationships. You may be looking for a deeper spiritual or psychic connection with a partner. You may decide that the area where you live no longer feels right for you. There are many possible ways this transit can unfold for you. But you will certainly discover that you now seek the greater good for the collective—family, friends, community, world.

Pisces)(

Mutable, water

Like Scorpio and Cancer, you live primarily through your emotions and intuition. You also have a fantastic imagination that takes you places denied to the rest of us. Your inner world is rich, textured, alive with archetypal material, past-life memories, and connections to the collective unconscious. Your empathic nature makes you something of a psychic sponge, so it's important that you associate with positive, upbeat people.

With Neptune in your sign for the next fourteen years, there will be many subtle changes in your life. You may decide to change careers, to pursue a line of work that is more spiritual or psychic in nature. You may find yourself growing away from certain people in your life whose interests and beliefs aren't aligned with your own. It's possible, too, that you take up meditation, yoga, or other mind/body practices that enable you to stay grounded and attuned.

In romance and love, your needs and desires will shift. You'll want a partner whose ideals match your own and will need to feel a deep spiritual connection with anyone with whom you get involved. There can be confusion with this transit—Neptune often fogs the brain!—but as long as you resist escapism, you should do fine.

CHAPTER 2

Astrology 101

On the day you were born, what was the weather like? If you were born at night, had the moon already risen? Was it full or the shape of a Cheshire cat's grin? Was the delivery ward quiet or bustling with activity? Unless your mom or dad has a very good memory, you'll probably never know the full details. But there's one thing you can know for sure: on the day you were born, the sun was located in a particular zone of the zodiac, an imaginary 360-degree belt that circles the earth. The belt is divided into twelve 30-degree portions called signs.

If you were born between July 23 and August 22, then the sun was passing through the sign of Leo, so we say that your sun sign is Leo. Each of the twelve signs has distinct attributes and characteristics. Leos, for instance, love being the center of attention. They're warm, compassionate people with a flair for the dramatic. Virgos, born between August 23 and September 22, are perfectionists with discriminating intellects and a genius for details. Capricorns, born between December 22 and January 19, are the worker bees of the zodiac, serious-minded, ambitious, industrious.

How Signs Are Classified

The twelve signs are categorized according to element and quality or modality. The first category, element, reads like a basic science lesson—fire, earth, air, and water—and describes the general physical characteristics of the signs.

Fire signs—Aries, Leo, Sagittarius—are warm, dynamic individuals who are always passionate about what they do.

Earth signs—Taurus, Virgo, Capricorn—are the builders of the zodiac, practical and efficient, grounded in everything they do.

Air signs—Gemini, Libra, Aquarius—are people who live mostly in the world of ideas. They are terrific communicators.

Water signs—Cancer, Scorpio, Pisces—live through their emotions, imaginations, and intuitions.

The second category describes how each sign operates in the physical world, how adaptable it is to circumstances:

Cardinal signs—Aries, Cancer, Libra, Capricorn—are initiators. These people are active, impatient, restless. They're great at starting things, but unless a project or a relationship holds their attention, they lose interest and may not finish what they start.

Fixed signs—Taurus, Leo, Scorpio, Aquarius—are deliberate, controlled, resolute. These individuals tend to move more slowly than cardinal signs, are often stubborn, and resist change. They seek roots and stability and are always in the game for the long haul. They aren't quitters.

Mutable signs—Gemini, Virgo, Sagittarius, Pisces—are adaptable. These people are flexible, changeable, communicative. They don't get locked into rigid patterns or belief systems.

SUN SIGNS

Sign	Date	Element	Quality
Aries ♈	March 21–April 19	Fire	Cardinal
Taurus ♉	April 20–May 20	Earth	Fixed
Gemini ♊	May 21–June 21	Air	Mutable
Cancer ♋	June 22–July 22	Water	Cardinal
Leo ♌	July 23–August 22	Fire	Fixed
Virgo ♍	August 23–September 22	Earth	Mutable
Libra ♎	September 23–October 22	Air	Cardinal
Scorpio ♏	October 23–November 21	Water	Fixed
Sagittarius ♐	November 22–December 21	Fire	Mutable
Capricorn ♑	December 22–January 19	Earth	Cardinal
Aquarius ♒	January 20–February 18	Air	Fixed
Pisces ♓	February 19–March 20	Water	Mutable

The Planets

The planets in astrology are the players who make things happen. They're the characters in the story of your life. This story always begins with the sun, the giver of life.

Your sun sign describes your self-expression, your primal energy, the essence of who you are. It's the archetypal pattern of your Self. When you know another person's sun sign, you already have a great deal of information about that person. Let's say you're a Taurus who has just started dating a Gemini. How compatible are you?

On the surface, it wouldn't seem that you have much in common. Taurus is a fixed earth sign; Gemini is a mutable air sign. Taurus is persistent, stubborn, practical, a cultivator as opposed to an initiator. Gemini is a chameleon, a communicator, social, with a mind as quick as lightning. Taurus is ruled by Venus, which governs the arts, money, beauty, love, and romance, and Gemini is ruled by Mercury, which governs communication and travel. There doesn't seem to be much common ground. But before we write off this combination, let's look a little deeper.

Suppose the Taurus has Mercury in Gemini and suppose the Gemini has Venus in Taurus? This would mean that the Taurus and Gemini each have their rulers in the other person's sign. They probably communicate well and enjoy travel and books (Mercury) and would see eye to eye on romance, art, and music (Venus). They might get along so well, in fact, that they collaborate on creative projects.

Each of us is also influenced by the other nine planets (the sun and moon are treated like planets in astrology) and the signs they were transiting when we were born. Suppose our Taurus and Gemini have the same moon sign? The moon rules our inner needs, emotions and intuition, and all that makes us feel secure within ourselves. Quite often, compatible moon signs can overcome even the most glaring difference in sun signs because the two people share similar emotions.

In the section on monthly predictions, your sun sign always takes center stage, and every prediction is based on the movement of the transiting planets in relation to your sun sign. Let's say you're a Sagittarius. Between January 7 and February 4 this year, Venus will be transiting your sign. What's this mean for you? Well, since Venus rules—among other things—romance, you can expect your love life to pick up significantly during these weeks. Other people will find you attractive and be more open to your ideas, and you'll radiate a certain charisma. Your creative endeavors will move full steam ahead.

The planets table provides an overview of the planets and the signs that they rule. Keep in mind that the moon is the swiftest-moving planet, changing signs about every two and a half days, and that Pluto is the snail of the zodiac, taking as long as thirty years to transit a single sign. Although the faster-moving planets—the moon,

Mercury, Venus, and Mars—have an impact on our lives, it's the slow pokes—Uranus, Neptune, and Pluto—that bring about the most profound influence and change. Jupiter and Saturn fall between the others in terms of speed. This year, Jupiter spends the first six months in Taurus, then enters Gemini on June 11 and doesn't leave that sign until late June 2013.

In the section on predictions, the most frequent references are to the transits of Mercury, Venus, and Mars. In the daily predictions for each sign, the predictions are based primarily on the transiting moon.

Now glance through the planets table. When a sign is in parentheses, it means the planet corules that sign. This assignation dates back to when we thought there were only seven planets in the solar system. But since there were still twelve signs, some of the planets had to do double duty!

THE PLANETS

Planet	Rules	Attributes of Planet
Sun ☉	Leo	self-expression, primal energy, creative ability, ego, individuality
Moon ☽	Cancer	emotions, intuition, mother or wife, security
Mercury ☿	Gemini, Virgo	intellect, mental acuity, communication, logic, reasoning, travel, contracts
Venus ♀	Taurus, Libra	love, romance, beauty, artistic instincts, the arts, music, material and financial resources
Mars ♂	Aries (Scorpio)	physical and sexual energy, aggression, drive

Planet	Rules	Attributes of Planet
Jupiter ♃	Sagittarius (Pisces)	luck, expansion, success, prosperity, growth, creativity, spiritual interests, higher education, law
Saturn ♄	Capricorn (Aquarius)	laws of physical universe, discipline, responsibility, structure, karma, authority
Uranus ♅	Aquarius	individuality, genius, eccentricity, originality, science, revolution
Neptune ♆	Pisces	visionary self, illusions, what's hidden, psychic ability, dissolution of ego boundaries, spiritual insights, dreams
Pluto ♀ ♇	Scorpio	the darker side, death, sex, regeneration, rebirth, profound and permanent change, transformation

Houses and Rising Signs

In the instant you drew your first breath, one of the signs of the zodiac was just passing over the eastern horizon. Astrologers refer to this as the rising sign or ascendant. It's what makes your horoscope unique. Think of your ascendant as the front door of your horoscope, the place where you enter into this life and begin your journey.

Your ascendant is based on the exact moment of your birth and the other signs follow counterclockwise. If you have Taurus rising, for example, that is the cusp of your first house. The cusp of the second would be Gemini, of the third Cancer, and so on around the horoscope circle in a counterclockwise direction. Each house governs a particular area of life, which is outlined below.

The best way to find out your rising sign is to have your horoscope drawn up by an astrologer. For those of you with access to the Internet, though, there are several sites that provide free birth horoscopes. www.astro.com and www.cafeastrology.com are two good ones.

In a horoscope, the ascendant (cusp of the first house), IC (cusp of the fourth house), descendant (cusp of the seventh house), and MC (cusp of the tenth house) are considered to be the most critical angles. Any planets that fall close to these angles are extremely important in the overall astrological picture of who you are. By the same token, planets that fall in the first, fourth, seventh, and tenth houses are also considered to be important.

Now here's a rundown on what the houses mean.

Ascendant or Rising: The First of Four Important Critical Angles in a Horoscope

- How other people see you
- How you present yourself to the world
- Your physical appearance

First House, Personality

- Early childhood
- Your ego
- Your body type and how you feel about your body
- General physical health
- Defense mechanisms
- Your creative thrust

Second House, Personal Values

- How you earn and spend your money
- Your personal values
- Your material resources and assets
- Your attitudes and beliefs toward money
- Your possessions and your attitude toward those possessions
- Your self-worth
- Your attitudes about creativity

Third House, Communication and Learning

- Personal expression
- Intellect and mental attitudes and perceptions
- Siblings, neighbors, and relatives
- How you learn
- School until college
- Reading, writing, teaching
- Short trips (the grocery store versus Europe in seven days)
- Earth-bound transportation
- Creativity as a communication device

IC or Fourth House Cusp: The Second Critical Angle in a Horoscope

- Sign on IC describes the qualities and traits of your home during early childhood
- Describes roots of your creative abilities and talents

Fourth House, Your Roots

- Personal environment
- Your home
- Your attitudes toward family

- Early childhood conditioning
- Real estate
- Your nurturing parent

Some astrologers say this house belongs to Mom or her equivalent in your life, others say it belongs to Dad or his equivalent. It makes sense to me that it's Mom because the fourth house is ruled by the moon, which rules mothers. But in this day and age, when parental roles are in flux, the only hard and fast rule is that the fourth belongs to the parent who nurtures you most of the time.

- The conditions at the end of your life
- Early childhood support of your creativity and interests

Fifth House, Children and Creativity

- Kids, your firstborn in particular
- Love affairs, romance
- What you enjoy
- Creative ability
- Gambling and speculation
- Pets

Traditionally, pets belong in the sixth house. But that definition stems from the days when pets were chattel. These days, we don't even refer to them as pets. They are animal companions who bring us pleasure.

Sixth House, Work and Responsibility

- Day-to-day working conditions and environment
- Competence and skills
- Your experience of employees and employers
- Duty to work, to employees
- Health and the daily maintenance of your health

Descendant/Seventh House Cusp: The Third Critical Angle in a Horoscope

- The sign on the house cusp describes the qualities sought in intimate or business relationships
- Describes qualities of creative partnerships

Seventh House, Partnerships and Marriage

- Marriage
- Marriage partner
- Significant others
- Business partnerships
- Close friends
- Open enemies
- Contracts

Eighth House, Transformation

- Sexuality as transformation
- Secrets
- Death, taxes, inheritances, insurance, mortgages, and loans
- Resources shared with others
- Your partner's finances
- The occult (read: astrology, reincarnation, UFOs, everything weird and strange)
- Your hidden talents
- Psychology
- Life-threatening illnesses
- Your creative depths

Ninth House, Worldview

- Philosophy and religion
- The law, courts, judicial system
- Publishing
- Foreign travels and cultures

- College, graduate school
- Spiritual beliefs
- Travel abroad

MC or Cusp of Tenth House: The Fourth Critical Angle in a Horoscope

- Sign on cusp of MC describes qualities you seek in a profession
- Your public image
- Your creative and professional achievements

Tenth House, Profession and Career

- Public image as opposed to a job that merely pays the bills (sixth house)
- Your status and position in the world
- The authoritarian parent and authority in general
- People who hold power over you
- Your public life
- Your career/profession

Eleventh House, Ideals and Dreams

- Peer groups
- Social circles (your writers' group, your mother's bridge club)
- Your dreams and aspirations
- How you can realize your dreams

Twelfth House, Personal Unconscious

- Power you have disowned that must be claimed again
- Institutions—hospitals, prisons, nursing homes—and what is hidden
- What you must confront this time around, your karma, issues brought in from other lives

- Psychic gifts and abilities
- Healing talents
- What you give unconditionally

In the section on predictions, you'll find references to transiting planets moving into certain houses. These houses are actually solar houses that are created by putting your sun sign on the ascendant. This technique is how most predictions are made for the general public rather than for specific individuals.

Lunations

Every year there are twelve new moons and twelve full moons, with some years having thirteen full moons. The extra full moon is called the Blue Moon. New moons are typically when we should begin new projects, set new goals, seek new opportunities. They're times for beginnings. They usher in new opportunities according to house and sign.

Two weeks after each new moon, there's a full moon. This is the time of harvest, fruition, when we reap what we've sown.

Whenever a new moon falls in your sign, take time to brainstorm what you would like to achieve during the weeks and months until the full moon falls in your sign. These goals can be in any area of your life. Or, you can simply take the time on each new moon to set up goals and strategies for what you would like to achieve or manifest during the next two weeks—until the full moon—or until the next new moon.

Here's a list of all the new moons and full moons during 2012. The asterisk beside any new moon entry indicates a solar eclipse; the asterisk next to a full moon entry indicates a lunar eclipse.

LUNATIONS OF 2012

New Moons	Full Moons
January 23—Aquarius	January 9—Cancer
February 21—Pisces	February 7—Leo
March 22—Aries	March 8—Virgo
April 21—Taurus	April 6—Libra
*May 20—Gemini	May 5—Scorpio
June 19—Gemini	*June 4—Sagittarius
July 19—Cancer	July 3—Capricorn
August 17—Leo	August 1—Aquarius
September 15—Virgo	August 31—Pisces
October 15—Libra	September 29—Aries
*November 13—Scorpio	October 29—Taurus
December 13—Sagittarius	*November 28—Gemini
	December 28—Cancer

Every year there are two lunar and two solar eclipses, separated from each other by about two weeks. Lunar eclipses tend to deal with emotional issues and our internal world and often bring an emotional issue to the surface related to the sign and house in which the eclipse falls. Solar eclipses deal with events and often enable us to see something that has eluded us. They also symbolize beginnings and endings.

Read more about eclipses in the Big Picture for your sign for 2012. I also recommend Celeste Teal's excellent book, *Eclipses*.

Mercury Retrograde

Every year, Mercury—the planet that symbolizes communication and travel—turns retrograde three times. During these periods, our travel plans often go awry, communication breaks down, computers go berserk, cars or appliances develop problems. You get the idea. Things in our daily lives don't work as smoothly as we would like.

Here are some guidelines to follow for Mercury retrogrades:

- Try not to travel. But if you have to, be flexible and think of it as an adventure. If you're stuck overnight in an airport in Houston or Atlanta, though, the adventure part of this could be a stretch.
- Don't sign contracts—unless you don't mind revisiting them when Mercury is direct again.
- Communicate as succinctly and clearly as possible.
- Back up all computer files. Use an external hard drive and/or a flash drive. If you've had a computer crash, you already know how frustrating it can be to reconstruct your files.
- Don't buy expensive electronics. Expensive anything.
- Don't submit manuscripts or screenplays, pitch ideas, or launch new projects.
- Revise, rewrite, rethink, review.

In the Big Picture for each sign, check out the dates for this year's Mercury retrogrades and how these retrogrades are likely to impact you. Do the same for eclipses.

CHAPTER 3

Matters of the Heart in 2012

When you're in the throes of a paradigm shift, every area of your life may feel more vulnerable. You may notice a distinct change in what you want and expect in a romantic partnership. You may find yourself attracted to people who are different from people to whom you've been attracted in the past. Whether you're in a new or long-term relationship or are just looking, it's important to keep the channels of communication wide open.

There are, however, some constants to keep in mind with romance and love—which sun signs are most compatible with your own.

Astrology and Carl Jung

In 1950, Swiss psychologist Carl Jung undertook an astrological study about the compatibility of 180 married couples and used 50 aspects—or angles that planets make to each other. This was in the days before personal computers and astrology software that can erect a natal chart and compare several charts in just seconds. The study took several years, and the results were intriguing.

He found three aspects to be the best indicators for compatibility: a sun/moon conjunction, where one partner's sun sign is the same as the sign of the other person's moon; a moon/moon conjunction, where both individuals have their moons in the same sign; and a moon/ascendant conjunction, when one partner's moon is in the same sign as the other person's ascendant. In his book *Synchronicity, An Acausal Connecting Principle,* Jung noted that the first two aspects "have long been mentioned in the old literature as marriage characteristics, and they therefore represent the oldest tradition."

The sun/moon conjunction makes perfect sense astrologically. Your sun sign describes your overall personality; the sign of your moon describes your inner world, your emotions, what makes you feel secure. So if you're a Pisces involved with someone who has a Pisces moon, for example, then there's a beautiful give and take between you. You understand each other. If you have different sun signs, but your moons are in the same sign, then the emotional and intuitive connection is so strong you probably finish each other's sentences.

What about that third aspect, with the moon and ascendant in the same sign? This one also makes perfect sense. The ascendant is the doorway to your chart and describes, among other things, the persona you project to the outside world. So an individual with his or her moon in the same sign as your ascendant feels emotionally secure in your presence and sees the person behind the mask you wear.

Another compatibility aspect includes Venus, the planet that symbolizes love and romance. The most common I've seen are: Venus/sun, Venus/moon, Venus/ascendant; Venus/descendant cusp (cusp of the seventh house of partnerships); and Venus/Mars in the same sign. Another interesting connection I've noted is among couples who have "mirror" charts, where the sign of one partner's ascendant is the same as the other person's descendant. In other words, let's say you have Scorpio rising and your partner has Scorpio on the cusp of his or her seventh house. This aspect brings balance to the relationship.

But because one size doesn't fit all, you and your partner may have other aspects in your charts that make you compatible. For the purpose of this book, we're going to be looking only at sun-sign combinations for compatibility.

Your Best Matches

Aries

Your freedom and independence are paramount to your happiness, so you need a partner who understands and respects your space. But because you're a stranger to compromise, a vital part of any relationship, you may find intimate relationships challenging. Once you're involved, your passions are fierce and can easily topple into the dark extremes of jealousy, possessiveness, suspicion.

Your entrepreneurial and fearless spirit enjoys a partner who can compete with you on any level—on those long hikes into the wilderness, in the boardroom, in the classroom, in the garage out back where you're building your newest invention. You get the idea here, right, Aries? Boredom is your nemesis. So, which signs are good matches for you? Let's take a closer look at some of the possibilities.

Sagittarius. This fellow fire sign will give you all the freedom you crave—and then some. She'll match you joke for joke, drink for drink. If she's the physical type, and many of them are, she'll match you on those hikes. But for a Sadge, those hikes may be in some far-flung spot like Tibet. Like you, Sadge pushes herself, but she's more adaptable than you are. Sometimes she may come off like a know-it-all. But overall, this combination holds great promise.

Gemini. This air sign's wit, versatility, and ability to talk about virtually anything appeal to you. He's generally not possessive, either, a major plus when you're in one of your darker moods. His mind is sharp and lightning quick, and he probably has a vast, complicated network of friends and acquaintances. Also appealing. So what're the negatives? Gemini generally isn't as independent as you are and may spend more time with his friends than he does with you. But overall, this combination is lively, fun, and never boring.

Leo. Another fire sign. On the surface, it looks like a good match. Leo possesses an infinite capacity for enjoyment, which appeals to you. But she also loves having center stage—not just sometimes, but most of the time—and that can be a major turnoff for you.

Libra, Aquarius. Libra is your opposite sign. The match could be fantastic because you balance each other. Where you're the loner, she's the social butterfly. You're independent, she's a networker with more friends than a hive has bees. Whether this works or not depends on the signs of your natal moons, ascendants, and Venus. You and Aquarius could be a winning combination. His independence matches yours, he's as sharp as the proverbial tack, and he pulls no punches in expressing what he wants, when he wants it. Downside? He may not be as physical or competitive and lives much of his life in his head.

What about another *Aries*? Depends on the signs of your moons. Strictly on the basis of sun signs, you're both so independent the relationship may never get off the ground!

Taurus

Stable, dependable, patient. You bring these qualities to any close relationship, and once you commit it's usually for keeps. You aren't into drama, artifice, flamboyance—not for yourself and not in a partner, either. But you en-

39

joy a partner who is physically attractive or who has a particular artistic gift that you appreciate—music, art, a way with words, anything that appeals to your senses.

If you're a Taurus who is into sports and health, and many of them are, then a health-conscious partner is a major plus. But there's another side to you, too, an inner mystic, a quiet, observant Buddha who remains calm and centered, in tune with unseen forces. You would do well with a partner who possesses that quality as well.

Leo, Sagittarius, Aries. Unless you have a moon, rising, or Venus in one of those signs, the fire signs probably won't work for you. Too much drama, boisterous behavior, and anger to suit your tastes.

Virgo, Capricorn. Fellow earth signs. Virgo could be the ticket. She's as practical as you are and, in many instances, just as mystical. Capricorn is focused, as physical as you are, but may not be as mystically inclined.

Scorpio. Your opposite sign, so there may be a good balance. She's secretive and can be vengeful, but she's just as mystical as you are.

Gemini

In a romantic relationship, conversation and discussion top your list. In fact, any potential partner must seduce your mind first—with ideas, information, books, theories that connect seemingly disparate bits of whatever it is that rushes through your head 24/7. You're up front about what you feel, but those feelings could change at a moment's notice, a dichotomy that can be confusing to a partner. And to everyone else around you, for that matter. No wonder your sign is represented by the twins.

For you, everything starts with a single burning question: *Why?* You then set about to find out why, and in the course of your quest you may be distracted by a million other pieces of information that are eventually integrated into your journey. This means, of course, that your journey toward the why of the original question may not end in *this* lifetime! So you need a partner whose curiosity matches your own.

Sagittarius, Aries. Sadge is your opposite sign. He matches you in curiosity, but may not be up to snuff in other areas. With Aries, there's never a dull moment. She's a match for your quickness and wit, but may not have the curiosity you do about other people.

Libra and Aquarius. Usually compatible in that both signs value information and communication.

Water signs. Oddly, Pisces might be a good match because it's the only other sign represented by two of something, and his imagination will appeal to you.

Cancer

In romance, it's always about feelings first—not the mind, not even the body, but *emotions*. Your partner has to be as dedicated to her inner world as you are to yours, so that your inner worlds can, well, *merge*. That's the ideal. Yet, because you're a cardinal sign, like Aries, Libra, and Capricorn, there's a certain independence in you that demands emotional space. Contradictory, but not to you.

Despite your emotional depth, you tend to avoid confrontations. Like the crab that symbolizes your sign, you retreat into your shell at the first sign of trouble. Yet, how can you smooth out anything in a relationship if you can't discuss disagreements? It's as if you expect disagreements to be ironed out telepathically. So if that's true, then your best matches romantically are probably other water signs. Let's take a deeper look.

Pisces, Scorpio. Both signs are as psychic as you are, but in different ways. Pisces is the softer of the two signs, dreamier. Scorpio might overwhelm you, but gives you the emotional space you need.

Taurus. A good match. This earth sign helps you to ground yourself in the real world and gives you emotional space—maybe more than you need!

Capricorn, Virgo. Cappy is your opposite sign, so the possibility of balance is there. Virgo might be too picky for your tastes, but shows you how to communicate verbally.

Air signs? Fire signs? Not so good, unless you have a moon, ascendant, Venus, or Mars in one of those signs.

Leo

You've got enough passion for all the other signs in the zodiac—and then some. That passion is often linked to the attention of others, which probably explains why so many actors and actresses have a Leo sun, moon, or ascendant. Your life is about drama, and the higher the drama, the deeper your passion. But it's that passion that busts through obstacles, that burns a path toward where you want to go in both life and love.

Your compassion extends to anyone in a tough situation—or to any creature that needs love and reassurance that we humans aren't heartless. So, let's be real here. Your partner, whoever he or she is, probably has to love animals the way you do. Even if there are twenty strays in your back yard, your partner must be amenable to the idea that you feed the multitudes. Not an easy request, says the universe. But there are some strong possibilities.

Sagittarius, Aries, fellow fire signs. Sadge, symbolized by a creature that is half human and half horse, usually has animal companions—not pets, but *companions.* There's a big difference. She's your match in the compassion area. She understands your need to connect to an audience. But she may not stick around to be a part of that audience. The energy match with Aries is great. But unless you've got the moon, ascendant, or Venus in Aries, she may not shower you—or your animal companions—with enough attention.

Gemini, Libra. These two air signs could be excellent matches for you, Leo. You'll enjoy Gemini's lively intellect and Libra's artistic sensibilities.

Virgo

You're the absolute master of details. You collect massive amounts of information, sift through it all with an eye for what works and what doesn't, and toss out everything that is extraneous. Your quest for perfection is never compromised, and it's evident in the inner work you do, honing your own psyche, and in everything you take on in the external world. These qualities can make a romantic partnership somewhat challenging because your partner goes under the same microscope that everything else does.

You're a layered individual and benefit from a partner who understands that and knows how to peel away those layers without making you feel vulnerable or exposed. A partner who enjoys every single one of those layers. So who's your best match?

Taurus and Capricorn. Fellow earth signs. Taurus takes all the time the relationship needs to peel away the layers of your personality so she can find the gold at your core. She's patient, resolute, determined. Capricorn might consider the relationship as just one more challenge to be conquered, but could be a nice balance to your penchant for details.

Cancer, Scorpio. These two water signs complement you. Cancer grasps who you are emotionally, but may not be as willing as you are to discuss elements of the relationship. Since your sign is ruled by Mercury, the planet of communication, that could be a drawback. Scorpio's emotional intensity could be overwhelming, but he'll be delighted to peel away the layers of your personality!

Gemini. Even though air and earth aren't usually compatible, Gemini and Virgo share Mercury as a ruler. Communication in this combination is likely to be strong and fluid, with a constant exchange of ideas.

Libra

There's a certain duality in your psychological makeup that isn't mentioned very often. It's not due to a penchant for secrecy or deviousness, but to a reluctance to hurt anyone's feelings. As a result, you often find yourself paralyzed by indecision. *Who do I really love? A or B?* Since you don't want to hurt either person, you maintain both relationships and make yourself and everyone around you absolutely nuts.

You have a need for harmony and balance in relationships. You dislike confrontation and dissension, so all too often you surrender to your partner's wants at your own expense. So which signs are good matches for you?

Gemini, Aquarius. Fellow air signs understand your psychological makeup. Gemini experiences some of the same duality that you do, but for different reasons. He isn't bothered by dichotomies, since his own life is predicated on them. He appeals to that part of you who needs to communicate honestly. Aquarius may be a bit too rigid for you, insisting that you bend to his desires, but the depth and breadth of his vision attract you at a visceral level.

Sagittarius, Leo, Aries. Any of the fire signs could be an excellent match. Sagittarius never bores you and enjoys you for *who you are.* Leo may want more attention than you're willing to give, but her warmth and compassion will delight you. You and Aries, your opposite sign, balance each other.

Taurus, Virgo, Capricorn. Of the three earth signs, Taurus is probably the best match because you share Venus as a ruler. That means you have similar tastes in music and art and probably share some of the same attitudes and beliefs about money.

Scorpio

As the most emotionally intense sign of the zodiac and one of the most psychic, your powerful and magnetic personality can intimidate even heads of state. Your life patterns are about breaking taboos, digging deeper, looking for the absolute bottom line in whatever you do, in any relationship in which you become involved. You feel and intuit your way through life, and your partner must understand that.

All of this brooding and mulling takes place in the privacy of your own head. The side you show others is light and funny, with a dry wit that can charm, seduce, or spar with the best of them. Yet inside you're always asking, *What motivates him? What secrets does he have?* Given the complexities of your personality, which signs are most compatible with yours?

Pisces, Cancer. Of these two water signs, Pisces matches you in raw intuitive ability, but may be too indecisive to suit you long term. Cancer can be just as secretive as you, but unless you've got a moon or rising in Cancer, this sign could be too clingy.

Taurus, Virgo, Capricorn. The earth signs are compatible matches. Taurus, your opposite sign, brings sensuality to your sexuality and helps to dispel your suspicions about other people's motives. Her earthiness grounds your psychic ability. Virgo's discerning and gentle nature mitigates your emotional intensity. Capricorn's determination appeals to that same quality in you.

Fire signs? *Leos* and Scorpios are both fixed signs, and there seems to be something between them that is powerful. Look at Leo Bill Clinton and Scorpio Hillary.

Sagittarius

You're so multifaceted, with so many different talents, that a relationship presents certain dilemmas—namely, commitment to another person. It's so much easier to commit to, well, your own interests! Also, there's that little ole thing called personal freedom, which you value every bit as much as Aries.

Like Libra, there's a curious duality in your makeup,

best explained, perhaps, by the symbol for your sign—the mythological centaur. Half-horse, half-human, this figure might be defined as the wild woman (or man) versus the conformist. A part of you operates from gut instinct and the other part of you is acculturated. Which signs are your best matches?

Aries, Leo, Sagittarius. As remarked under the Aries section, a relationship with this sign may not go anywhere because you're both so independent. Aries might want to be in charge all the time, and you get fed up and hit the open road. Leo could be a terrific choice, particularly if one of you has a moon in the other's sun sign. Another Sadge would be intriguing.

Taurus, Virgo, Capricorn. Of these three earth signs, Capricorn is the best match. Even if she lacks your intuitive gifts, her focus, direction, and resolute determination equal yours. Taurus, your opposite sign, could also be a good match. You share a fascination with the paranormal, and your energies would balance each other.

Air signs? Water signs? Probably not, unless you have a moon, rising, or some other prominent planet in those signs.

Capricorn

You build relationships in the same careful way that you build everything else in your life—a brick at a time. A conversation here, a dinner there, a movie, a moonlit walk, an exchange of beliefs: you're methodical, consistent, disciplined. Pretty soon, the foundation is solid, the chemistry is exactly right, and you know exactly what you want.

A relationship, of course, involves the human heart—not mortar and bricks—and that's where it may get tricky. You could discover that your methodical approach doesn't work as well in a relationship as it does with your career. Your success will depend, to a certain extent, on your compatibility with your partner.

Taurus, Virgo, Capricorn. Taurus's solidity and dependability appeal to you, and he's as private as you are. But his still waters run deep, and he may not express his emotions as readily as you would like. Yet the match would be a good one. Virgo understands what drives you. Another Capricorn, i.e., type A personality, would wear you out!

Scorpio, Pisces. While either of these water signs is compatible with your earth-sign sun, Pisces may too ambivalent for you, too indecisive. Scorpio, though, is a strong match. All that intensity appeals to you at a visceral level, your sex lives would be fantastic, and you share a similar determination. *Cancer,* your opposite sign, might work if the Cancer has a moon or rising in your sign.

Fire signs? Air signs? Again, it depends on the distribution of fire- and air-sign planets in your natal chart.

Aquarius

In love and romance, as in life, your mind is your haven, your sanctuary, your sacred place. It's where everything begins for you. From your visionary, cutting-edge ideas to your humanitarian causes and interests in esoterica, you're a wild card, not easily pigeonholed. It doesn't make any difference to you whether your partner shares these interests, as long as he or she recognizes your right to pursue them.

There's a rebel in you that pushes against the status quo, and that's something your partner has to understand too. Your connections to people and to the world aren't easily grasped by others. Too weird, they think. Too out there. But that's fine. You understand who and what you are, and in the end, that's all you need. So, which signs are your best matches?

Gemini, Libra. Your air sign *compadres* are excellent matches. Gemini suits your prodigious intellect, causes, and ideas. Good communication usually is a hallmark of this relationship, and Gemini is supportive of your causes. With Libra, the focus is on relationships—yours and Libra's connection to five million others. But the right mix exists for a strong partnership. A relationship with another *Aquarius* could be challenging since you'll both insist you're right. But if you can move past that, you'll do fine. Another Aquarius may be like looking in the mirror 24/7. Not for the faint-hearted.

Aries, Leo, Sagittarius. With these fire signs, you enjoy the freedom to be your own person. Life with Aries is never boring and the conversation and adventures are stimulating, but he may not share your humanitarian and esoteric interests. Sagittarius loves your mind and insights, your idealism and rebellion against the establishment. Great compatibility overall. Leo is your opposite sign, suggesting a good balance between your head and his heart.

Earth or water signs? Only if you have prominent planets in either of those elements.

Pisces

It's true that your inner world is often more real and genuine to you than anything in the external world. The richness of your imagination, the breadth of your intuition . . . these qualities create a kind of seductive atmosphere that's tough to move beyond. But because you're a physical being, in a physical world, who has to eat and sleep, work and function, who loves and triumphs and yearns, you have to move beyond it. So you do.

But always there's an inner tension, a kind of bewilderment, a constant questioning. *Where am I going? What am I doing? Do I really want to do this or that?* Your head and your heart are forever at odds, so no wonder your sign is symbolized by two fish moving in opposite directions. In romance and love, this indecisiveness can be problematic. So which signs are most compatible for you?

Scorpio, Cancer. Scorpio's emotional intensity could overwhelm you, but he balances your indecisiveness with his unwavering commitment to a particular path. Intuitively, you're on the same page, a major plus. Cancer's innate gentleness appeals to you, and she appreciates you exactly as you are.

Taurus, Capricorn. These two earth signs appeal to you at a visceral level. Taurus's solid, grounded personality comforts that part of you that is so often torn between one direction and another. Her sensuality is also a major plus. Capricorn's singular vision and direction are a mystery to you, but there's much to learn from her. *Virgo*, your opposite sign, can bring balance.

Fire signs probably won't work for you unless you have a moon or rising in a fire sign. Of the air signs, *Gemini* is probably the most compatible for you. Since you're both symbolized by two of something—two fish, the twins—he understands your dichotomies.

CHAPTER 4

Your Career Choices in 2012

Despite how things may look in the job market, despite the grim statistics about the economy, the housing market, the banks, the plunging dollar, and all the rest of the depressing news that flows into our lives 24/7, many people flourish in economically difficult times. In fact, if you've been laid off from your job, the first thing you can do to turn things around is to look at it as an opportunity. The more positive and upbeat your attitude, the more frequently you view every challenge as an opportunity, the greater the chances that you'll turn things around.

Several years ago friends of ours, a married couple who are both writers, had pretty much hit rock bottom. The wife admitted that she was ready to start cleaning pools just to have a steady income. Then practically overnight everything turned around. Her husband sold a novel that became a popular cable TV show, a producer commissioned her to write a script, and suddenly their bank account fattened, they bought a second home, a new car and a boat, and the world opened up for them. It can open up for you, too.

We create our realities from the inside out. Everything you see around you is a manifestation of a belief that you hold. Some of our beliefs have been passed down to us by well-meaning family members, mentors, teachers, or friends, and we adopt those beliefs because we respect the people who handed them to us. But what do *you* believe about your abilities and talents and your ability to earn your living doing what you love? How do you handle stress? Change?

In 2012, when so much of the world seems to be shifting beneath our feet, we have a chance to delve into those beliefs and get rid of the ones we have adopted out of convenience. We can either go with the flow, change with the times, or we can offer up resistance. The more we resist, the more pain we experience. The more we go with the flow, the greater our capacity to discover where we should be. Which path will you take?

Inventory

One way to prosper professionally during good *and* bad times is to know what you want. So let's take an inventory.

1. Describe your dream job/profession

_____

_____

_____

2. Lay out a strategy for finding/attaining this dream job/profession. Do you need more education, time, additional skills? If so, include those things, and set a goal for attaining them.

_____

_____

_____

3. Set realistic professional goals. Choose a time frame—a month, six months, a year—whatever feels right to you. Ask yourself what you would like to be doing a year from now. Describe it in detail. Make it real!

_____

_____

_____

4. What kind of inner work can you do to make these goals a reality more quickly? Visualization? Take workshops or seminars? Develop your intuition? Describe in detail.

_____

_____

_____

5. What are your greatest strengths? Describe them. Then focus on the strengths you have—not your weaknesses.

_____

_____

_____

Using Synchronicity in 2012

The Swiss psychologist Carl Jung coined the term. It means: the coming together of inner and outer events in a way that can't be explained by cause and effect and that is meaningful to the observer. Or, it's a meaningful coincidence. When it happens to you, don't dismiss it as a random curiosity. A synchronicity can be a navigational tool, a confirmation, warning, or guidance.

For Frank Morgan, an actor who played five different parts in *The Wizard of Oz*, a stunning synchronicity served as confirmation that he was on the right professional track by accepting parts in the movie.

One of the parts he played was the disreputable Professor Marvel. For that role, the director and wardrobe man wanted him dressed in a "nice-looking coat, but tattered," said Mary Mayer, a unit publicist on the film. So they traipsed down to a second-hand clothing store and purchased a rack of coats. Then Frank, the director, and the wardrobe guy all got together and selected one of the coats.

Imagine his surprise when he turned the pocket of the coat inside out and found a name sewn into the lining of the coat: L. Frank Baum, the author of *The Wizard of Oz*. The additional synchronicity here is that both men who wore the coat were named Frank.

In times of stress or major transitions—marriage, divorce, birth, a move, career change or change in employment and income—synchronicities may occur more frequently. Decipher the message if you can, and know that synchronicities indicate we're in the flow, exactly where we're supposed to be.

Your Career Path in 2012

Regardless of what you do for a living, whether you love or detest it or merely tolerate it, you can maximize your strengths and talents to enhance your professional opportunities.

Aries

As a cardinal fire sign, your entire life is about movement, action, doing. You're the pioneer, the entrepreneur, the one who really does march to the beat of a different drummer. Your pioneering spirit is your most valuable asset for navigating any professional changes you encounter this year.

There is no such thing as a challenge for you. You simply rise to the occasion and banish the challenge. You also refuse to recognize defeat. What someone else might see as a setback, you view as an opportunity. In 2011, you learned to follow your passions, wherever they led, and in 2012 that faith starts paying off. Whenever a negative thought enters your mind, change it immediately to something upbeat and positive. Follow the methods that feel right to you.

Taurus

Your senses are so finely tuned that you hear the music of the spheres, poetry flows through your dreams, you have the heart and soul of a mystic. You're the most enduring, taciturn, and physical of the twelve signs. You always finish what you start unless it's just unbearable! In 2011, you learned that your resolute determination is your greatest asset for navigating professional changes. In 2012, you learn to trust your intuition.

Until June 11 this year, Jupiter remains in your sign, a positive and lucky transit that you should take advantage of. Jupiter expands whatever it touches, and every twelve years it touches your sun. You're in the right place at the right time with this transit, so take full advantage of it. Don't shy away from new opportunities that broaden your life.

You already know your own value. In 2012, everyone around you learns it as well, and you keep moving forward and never look back.

Gemini

You're the communicator, your mind buzzing constantly with information that you eagerly share with others.

Some people say you never shut up, that you talk just to fill the silence. Not true. Beneath your chatter lies an insatiable curiosity.

Your ability to multitask and your curiosity are your greatest assets for navigating any professional changes this year. In fact, in 2011 you learned to follow the impulses of your curiosity to see where they might lead, and they led some mighty strange places. But you were in the right place, at the right time. In 2012, your versatility and communication abilities enable you to navigate the paradigm shift that's underway.

Cancer

You're completely attuned to emotions—yours and everyone else's. It's easy for you to slip into someone else's skin and feel what they feel. You hurt as they hurt. You weep as they weep. You laugh as they laugh. Like fellow water sign Pisces, you're a psychic sponge, an empath. Your extraordinary memory is intimately linked to your emotions, and your intuition is remarkable. All of these traits helped you to successfully navigate the transitions of 2011. During the first six months of 2012, when Jupiter is in compatible earth sign Taurus, your hard work last year really begins to pay off. You meet people who not only share your interests, but who are helpful in some way professionally. Your professional options expand. Perhaps you launch a business, write a novel, have a photography exhibit. One way or another, you begin to achieve your dreams, Taurus.

Embrace whatever change comes your way, and trust that the universe works for your highest good.

Leo

You were born to express your creativity through performance. You love the applause, the recognition, the immediate gratification and feedback. Of course, not every

Leo is an actor or actress, but every Leo loves drama. So whether you're on the stage, in front of a classroom, or counseling a patient in therapy, your creative flair moves through you like a force of nature. In 2011, you learned how valuable this asset was in helping you to navigate any professional changes you experienced.

Now, in 2012, especially from June 11, 2012, to late June 2013, you're well positioned for seeing your dreams unfold. Jupiter will be in compatible air sign Gemini, and things should expand explosively for you. Join groups, engage your friends, and offer zero resistance to whatever comes your way.

Virgo

Your gift is details. Whether it's your own life that you're honing, sculpting, and shining like some fine gem, or a particular project or relationship, you can see the finished product in a way that others can't. You also have a particular gift or ability that you're always willing to provide to others, without thought of compensation. These traits carried you through professional changes you may have experienced in 2011.

The first six months of 2012, when Jupiter is in fellow earth sign Taurus, should be fantastic for you, regardless of any doom and gloom around you. Your worldview expands, you may have a chance to travel overseas, perhaps even a publishing opportunity presents itself. It's all preparation for Jupiter's transit through Gemini and your career sector from June 11, 2012, to late June 2013. Now *that* period, Virgo, is going to blow your mind. So prepare yourself for a wild, wonderful career ride.

Libra

You can work a room like a seasoned politician, spreading peace and harmony even among people who can't agree on anything. That's your magic. Yet the very qualities that you can instill in others often elude you. Not that any of us could tell by looking at you. Libra is a master of social camouflage. It seems that nothing ruffles you. But within, you're struggling to maintain harmony without compromising your principles. Your sphere is relationships. More than any other sign, you can see the many sides of an issue and understand that your truth may not be everyone's truth. But you can live with the paradox. It's your gift.

Any professional challenges you encountered in 2011 were undoubtedly overcome by your ability to connect with people. You're in for a real treat from June 11, 2012, to late June 2013, when expansive Jupiter transits fellow air sign Gemini. During this period, your professional opportunities should abound, taking you into new areas and new creative venues and bringing opportunities for foreign travel.

Scorpio

You're the emotional vortex of the zodiac, a spinning whirlwind of contradictions. You aren't like the rest of us, and that's the way you prefer it. You dig deeply into everything you do, looking for the absolute bottom line, the most fundamental truth, and then you excavate everything at the discovery site just to make sure you've gotten it all.

Professional challenges that you encountered last year were met with the fortitude and resilience for which you're known. In 2012, your best bet is to team up with a professional or romantic partner and launch a business or some other endeavor you've always wanted to try. The best time for this is from January 1 to June 11, when expansive Jupiter is in Taurus, your solar seventh house. Your intuition will be spot on during this period. Listen to it.

Sagittarius

You're the life of the party, just like your fellow fire sign Leo. But your approaches are different. Where Leo seeks recognition and applause, you're after the big picture, and it doesn't matter how far you have to travel to find it, how many people you have to talk to, how many books or blogs you must read. When your passion is seized, you're as doggedly relentless as Taurus. One part of you operates from raw instinct; the other part of you is acculturated, aware of how to work the system.

In 2011, the year of transition, you realized that you don't recognize professional challenges. You learned that any bump in a road simply means you take an alternate path to get to where you want to go. Between June 11, 2012, and late June 2013, expansive Jupiter will be in Gemini, in your solar seventh house. To maximize this beautiful transit—and to get the most out of it professionally—team up with a partner, romantic or professional, and try some entrepreneurial venture that suits your soul, Sadge.

Capricorn

You're the achiever, the builder, the classic type A personality whose focus is so tight that everything and everyone becomes part of your journey toward . . . well, the top of the hill, the pinnacle of whatever you're attempting to reach. You can build anything, anywhere. A fictional world, a belief system, an invention, a concept, a family, a video world. Name it, and you can build it.

Any professional challenges you encountered in 2011 were undoubtedly tackled the same way that you have tackled any other challenge in your life—by finding a way around it. Or through it. As a cardinal earth sign, you value what is tangible, practical, efficient, and your journey through any obstacle reflects it. In 2011, you learned how not to fear, and that got you through every professional challenge you encountered. In 2012, particularly until June 11, when Jupiter is in fellow earth sign Taurus, your muse is so up close and personal that your creativity soars. Use it to navigate the shifting sands in your world.

Aquarius

You're not easy to pigeonhole. Sometimes you seem to be the paragon of independence. Yet you enjoy the company of groups who share your passions. You're the one who thinks so far outside the box that people close to you may accuse you of communication with aliens, ghosts, goblins, elves. Even if it's true, you just laugh and continue on your journey into the strange, the unknown, on into the heart of the universe.

Any challenges you encountered professionally in 2011 were no major thing for you. You always managed to work your way around the challenge by continuing to explore what interests you. Between June 11, 2012, and late June 2013, Jupiter transits fellow air sign Gemini and your solar fifth house. This should be a huge bonus for you, Aquarius. Your creativity becomes your most valued asset for navigating the paradigm shift. And regardless of how out of the box your professional ideas are this year, you come through it all in great shape.

Pisces

Dreamer, healer, mystic: all these adjectives fit you, Pisces. You live within a rich, inner world that is both a buffer and a conduit to deeper experiences. You don't need anyone else to tell you this. At some level you already know it, appreciate it, embrace it. While it's true that you're a sucker for a sob story, an attribute that can turn you from hero to martyr in the space of a single breath, there's no concrete evidence that you're more of a victim than any other sun sign.

Any professional challenges that came your way during 2011 were met with your powerful intuition, your prodigious imagination, and your unique way of dealing with adversity through faith in your role in the larger scheme of things. The tentacles of your psychic abilities were active 24/7, at your disposal, and awaited your instructions. In 2012, especially until June 11 when Jupiter transits compatible earth sign Taurus, your communication abilities shine. Everything that swirls through your head, in your imagination, can be expressed in ways that others understand. Professionally, this talent alone puts you well ahead of the pack.

CHAPTER 5

Family Stuff

Our birth family is like a mini world. It's with them that we develop psychologically, emotionally, spiritually and intellectually. It's with them that we develop our defenses, needs, expectations, belief systems. They encourage certain behaviors and discourage others. We learn to rebel or conform or just fit in. Family, then, is where it all begins, which is probably why many books and movies deal with dysfunctional or eccentric families.

The paragon of dysfunctional families is probably the Corleones, in the *Godfather* movies. So much drama, violence, and emotion. The emotion is equally intense in *My Big Fat Greek Wedding*, where a young Greek woman falls in love with a non-Greek man. She tries to convince her family to accept him while she struggles to come to terms with her cultural identity. And it's all couched in comedy.

Jeanette Walls, in her memoir, *The Glass Castle*, recalls her bizarre childhood with an alcoholic father and a mother who abhorred domesticity. Jeanette and her siblings gradually made their way to New York. Their parents followed them but chose to be homeless.

Brokeback Mountain, based on a short story by Annie Proulx, is about a forbidden passion between two cowboys in the early sixties and how their love for each other impacts their families.

Your Family

Take a look at your own family. What are the dynamics? Does everyone get along? Are there certain issues that surface time and again? If you have siblings, do they each seem to have different roles in the family? One might be the rebel, for instance, and the other might be the intellectual. What about your parents, partner, and your own kids? If you're an only child, what is your relationship with your parents like?

Families often have commonalities in their respective charts that illustrate the deep connections among them. The parents might have opposing signs, like Taurus/Scorpio, Gemini/Sagittarius, so there's a kind of balance. Then one child might have a moon in Sadge, and the other child has a Gemini sun. There's an infinite number of combinations, and some aren't as obvious as sun or moon signs. But for the purpose of this chapter, let's keep things simple.

Your Style as a Parent

Aries

Your parenting style isn't like anyone else's, that's for sure. Man or woman, you encourage independence in your children from a very young age. You're no control freak. Or, if you are, then it may be due to the sign of your moon. You may be one of those parents who keeps close tabs on your child's growth progress: *7 months, crawling; 9 months, utters first word; age 2, a puzzle prodigy!* Any rules you lay down are in the name of safety rather than an attempt to control your child's every move and decision.

Some Aries wing it as parents. They don't have a clue, really, about what they're doing, so they fine-tune their parenting style at every stage of their child's growth. But even for you, Aries, there are certain constants that probably won't change. In addition to the emphasis on independence, you have a finely honed sense of privacy and probably won't violate your child's unless you have a reasonable suspicion that you should. That's more likely to happen during the turbulent teen years. You give your child plenty of freedom to make his own choices. However, when you do offer guidance or advice, you may blurt it out, which could create some major tension if your child is an adult.

An *Aries mom* can be brash, funny, exciting, unpredictable. Kids enjoy her company because everything with her is an adventure. But she can be fiercely protective— that's the ram who symbolizes her sign—ready to defend her child's turf at the slightest provocation. She isn't nurturing in the traditional sense of the word, i.e., you won't find her slaving over a hot stove preparing the evening meals. She's more likely to have a pizza delivered. But when her child's in need, she's there in a flash.

When an *Aries dad* hangs out with the kids, there's an air of impatience, brashness, restlessness, a kind of *let's get this show on the road!* If he encourages his child to take risks—in sports, love, life—it's because he himself is so fearless. He's terrific at organizing activities, but they happen on the fly. *In ten minutes, we're going on a picnic,* he announces, and then everyone scrambles around grabbing stuff they need. He usually has great pride in and passion for his kids.

In 2012, with Uranus in your sign all year (until March 2019, actually), there may be sudden, unexpected events that impact your parenting style. If you've fallen into a personal rut (unlikely for an Aries, but it does happen now and then), then Uranus whips into your life, turns everything upside down, shakes out what is no longer needed or useful. Your temperament may be erratic, you may be more impatient than usual, your blood pressure could soar at the slightest provocation. Best advice? Sign up for yoga classes with your kids. Meditate with them. Hike with them. Engage them.

Taurus

Your parenting style reflects your stability, determination, and patience. You enjoy your children immensely and strive to nurture their talents, strengths, and gifts. You try to create a beautiful home environment, a place in which everyone delights, where your kids feel comfortable bringing their friends. HOME. In caps.

You probably enjoy music, art, books, movies, and politics, and these interests are reflected in your environment—and are passed on to your kids through a kind of osmosis. So don't be surprised when your son or daughter cranks up the music so loudly it threatens to shatter crystal or when the weekly allowance is blown at the local bookstore!

Since you're the most stubborn sign in the zodiac, that stubbornness certainly surfaces in your parenting. Your child says *yes*. You shake your head *no*. The child keeps saying yes, yes, his voice growing louder and louder until your patience snaps, and the legendary bull's rush seizes you. *No,* you shout, and slam your door. End of story, end of argument, end of struggle.

Since Venus rules your sign, though, your bull's rush usually passes quickly and peace and tranquillity are restored. But you still refuse to change your mind!

A *Taurus mom* is loyal and dedicated to her role as a mother. It won't be her *only* role, but she's likely to consider it her most important role. She's in the line for school drop-offs in the morning, in that same line for pickup in the afternoon. In between she's in court, defending someone like you or me, or she's writing the great American novel, or teaching English to recalcitrant seventh-graders. Or she's selling real estate or jewelry or scooping the next big political story.

The *Taurus dad* works hard and patiently at whatever he does. He finishes everything he starts—and that includes the projects his kids begin for their science classes! He, like his female counterpart, is usually health conscious and watches his diet, exercises regularly, and takes good care of himself. Part of this could be vanity, but whatever it is, his kids pick up on it and sometimes take up the same sports in which dad indulges.

In 2012, Uranus in Aries is transiting your solar twelfth house, that place in your chart that is most hidden and secretive. With Uranus here until 2019, your inner world is shaken up, elements of your unconscious surface abruptly and inexplicably. It's as if you're confronted with psychological archetypes in yourself that you haven't seen before. This kind of turmoil certainly will affect your family and kids—*if* you let it. The bottom line here is that Taurus rarely shows anyone the face of that inner world. The best way to navigate whatever stuff is surfacing is to deal with it and move on.

Gemini

Ideas and communication. That's what you're about, and it's evident in your parenting style. From the time your child is very young, you read to her, talk to her, encourage her to express herself verbally. You buy her puzzles, coloring books, picture books, anything that expands her knowledge and creativity. Your fascination with information and relationships is found in the way you encourage her to reach out to other people, to make friends, to invite them to her house. Don't be surprised, then, if by the time your child is a teen, she has several thousand friends on Facebook!

You're a voracious reader, and it's likely that your home has hundreds—if not thousands—of books. This love of reading is something you pass on to your child, and by the time she's preparing for college, her facility with language and ideas is a major plus. It's said that a typical Gemini is actually two people—the twins are the symbol for your sign—so you're comfortable with duality. This can be confusing to a young child, particularly if you vacillate about what's allowed and what isn't.

With Mercury ruling your sign, any connections between the Mercury in your chart and the sun, moon, rising, or Mercury in your child's chart portend strong communication.

A *Gemini mom* is the supreme multitasker. She can simultaneously pack school lunches, talk on the phone, and be writing a novel in her head. At times she may appear scattered to her kids, but then she suddenly comes out with a zinger of logic or insight that stops them in their tracks. Glances are exchanged, eyebrows shoot up. She's a fount of information and eagerly passes on what she knows to her kids—and their friends and the friends of their friends. If anything, when her kids are with their friends, she must learn to back off and give them space.

A *Gemini dad* is quick, witty, enigmatic. Just when his kids think they've got him figured out, he does or says something that makes him impossible to peg. His intellect is as finely honed as a Gemini woman's, but takes him in different directions. He might be an avid sports fan, for example, a master at chess, a general aviation pilot, or an animal lover. His interests and passions are passed on to his kids.

One thing is certain: a home with at least one Gemini parent in it is never boring!

In 2012, you have several fantastic things going for you astrologically that are sure to bolster your parenting style. First, Uranus in Aries is transiting your solar eleventh house, so you're going to be more involved with friends and groups that support your parenting style. These groups will be kid friendly, too, so it's not as if you have to find a sitter or drop the kids at someone else's place. These group associations may begin and end suddenly, but that's fine with you. They bring an excitement and unpredictability that suit you.

The second transit is fantastic—Jupiter moving

through your sign from June 11, 2012, to late June 2013. This transit enhances all the Gemini qualities of your parenting style—emphasis on communication, books, writing, travel. It will be a period your kids remember as pure fun and enjoyment.

Cancer

You're the nurturer of the zodiac, the one who needs roots, a home, a place or state of mind and spirit that you can call your own. You're a gentle, kind person who takes everything to heart—and this is certainly reflected in your parenting style. Through your example, your kids learn to respect all forms of life, to never hurt others, to treat them as he would like to be treated.

You can be overprotective, for sure, and before your child hits his teens, you'll have to come to grips with how to handle those feelings. Emotionally, you rarely reveal yourself. Like the crab that represents your sign, you tend to move sideways, skirting unpleasant issues, anxious to avoid confrontation, reluctant to discuss the heart of the matter. Your exceptional intuition keeps you in tune with your children, alerting you when they're in danger or happy. You forgive easily, but rarely forget. So if one of your kids hurts your feelings, you'll remember it thirty years from now.

A *Cancer mom* is the prototypical nurturer—always there for her kids, supportive of their wishes and dreams. Yes, if she cooks, you'll find her whipping up delectable dishes that include everyone's favorite foods, whatever they are. Her home is her palace—but it could be the cabin of a boat, a tent in the wilderness, an RV. No matter where she is, she tends to the creature comforts of her family. As a parent, she has rules, but they're emotionally based, just like everything else in her life, so they won't change unless the emotions behind them change first.

A *Cancer dad*, like his female counterpart, is kind,

affectionate, and nurturing, but only to a point. When he feels his personal space is being violated in any way, he backs off, scurries into his crab's shell, and retreats quickly. For a child, he's hard to figure out. Sometimes he's the hero of the child's latest adventure story; other times he's the wet blanket at the party. If he's into metaphysics and alternative healing, then chances are he's in deep, and his kids will pick up on this interest and explore on their own.

In 2012, the period from the beginning of the year to June 11 should be wonderful for you and your kids. You get involved with new groups, your friends become more integral to your life, and in some way, shape, or form you begin to realize your dreams. Your children and family are part of the process. The other transit to watch is Neptune's through Pisces, which begins on February 3 and continues for the next fourteen years. This one brings an emphasis on spirituality and intuitive development that you pass on to your kids. You and your family may travel internationally, but it won't be strictly for pleasure. You'll be on a spiritual quest of some kind. Stonehenge? An ashram in India? Crop circles?

Leo

You love being the center of attention, often surround yourself with admirers, and the world is your stage. But that's just the beginning of your story! You strive to succeed—to shine—at everything you do and to make an impact in every situation. Your personal magnetism draws admirers who are willing to help your cause, whatever it is. You prefer to hang with people whose beliefs are similar to your own, but can get along with just about everyone—as long as no one steals your thunder. Your kindness, generosity, and compassion are nearly legendary.

As a parent, you love unconditionally and fiercely. You tend to instill certain qualities into your children—optimism, loyalty, integrity, honor. When they're toddlers, you enjoy their company and watching them progress to each stage, from crib to crawling to kindergarten. Once they're off to school, particularly by the time they reach middle school and then high school, you may feel marginalized in some way. You really shouldn't. You've got enough interests and passions to fill your next five lives, and your ambitions keep propelling you forward. Generally, you delight in seeing your children fly off into the world, doing what they love.

The *Leo mom* is usually up front about everything—what she feels, why, and for how long. She's definitely disappointed when her kids aren't as forthright, but she gets over it! She likes being at the helm—at home, at work, while traveling—and can be a bit bossy at times. *You and you, do this and that.* Her kids quickly learn to either fall in line or stand up to her. Mom enjoys nice clothes and probably dresses with a flair and style all her own. She's clever at creating impressions and moods through the way she looks and acts (it's the actress in her), but her kids undoubtedly learn to see through it to the gem beneath.

The *Leo dad* is easy to get along with as long as you keep a couple of rules in mind. Never tell *him* what to do, and let him have center stage. If both of your parents are Leos, then the one thing you can count on in your household is plenty of drama! The Leo dad is fun, outgoing, and full of magic. He snaps his fingers and things happen. He has great leadership ability (and not just as a dad), and his energy and frankness endear him to children of any age.

In 2012, two transits will affect your parenting style. Uranus, the planet of sudden, unexpected change, is transiting fellow fire sign Aries, in your solar ninth house. This suggests that your belief system, your worldview, your spiritual beliefs are undergoing radical change. It will be an exciting, unpredictable time, and the whirlwind of events will sweep you and your kids and partner up into a vortex of unpredictable adventures.

The second transit, Jupiter's through Gemini, goes from June 11, 2012, to late June 2013, and emphasizes foreign travel, friends, mental stimulation. Suddenly everything in your life expands, you feel lucky, like you're in the right time and place, and this expansiveness is passed on to your kids.

Virgo

Your mind is lightning quick, just like Gemini's, and you're so mentally dexterous and agile that the competition can't keep pace with you. Due to your attention to detail, to the discerning turn of your intellect, you tend to delve more deeply into subjects than Gemini, and when you gather information it usually has a purpose. You pass this ability on to your children, and it serves you well as a parent, i.e., not much escapes your notice. Your kids will never be able to put anything over on you! Since you're Mercury ruled, like Gemini, you need sufficient outlets for all your mental energy.

You're an attentive parent who does all the expected things—for school, health, your child's happiness—but who may not play by the book. In other words, you probably won't raise your children the way you were raised. If you were brought up in a religious household, for instance, your child won't be. If your parents stressed school over fun, you may do the opposite. If your parents were inordinately strict, you won't be. It's not that you have the heart of a rebel (although you might!) but that your finely honed intellect connects all the dots, and you grasp what's needed for your children to evolve and to achieve their full potential.

The *Virgo mom* is vibrant, upbeat, conscientious, loving. Even though she never *tries* to project a particular image, others sense something different about her, perhaps her softness, her caring. Deep down, she can be a worry wart, fretting about the smallest details, the inconsistencies in life, in her kids, her family. It's part of her insecurity. When she's in that mode, she can be critical—of her kids, her husband, herself. But she can be cajoled out of that mood by lively discussions about ideas, books, travel, any kind of information that seizes her passions. She's generous with her kids and strives to enrich their world through her own wisdom.

The *Virgo dad* is as intellectually curious as his female counterpart. He's a hard worker, detail oriented, with a biting humor that is rarely malicious. He may take his role as dad a bit too seriously at times, but his kids quickly learn how to loosen him up, how to make him laugh. He's an attentive father, the kind who reads to his kids at night, who listens to their dramas and woes as teens, who applauds loudly when they graduate from college. Always with him—and with the Virgo mom—there is tremendous pride in his children, as if he can't quite believe his extreme good fortune.

In 2012, the first six months of the year will be magnificent for you as a parent, for your kids, your family generally. Jupiter will be transiting fellow earth sign Taurus, your solar ninth house. This transit promises international traveling, dealings with publishers and educators, perhaps even living abroad for a while. The living abroad may last longer than the transit because for a year—from June 11, 2012, to late June 2013—Jupiter will be moving through Gemini and your career area. This transit suggests that one possible manifestation is working abroad, and you'll take your loved ones with you.

Libra

You're one of the gentlest souls in the zodiac, usually soft spoken and treading lightly in all matters. You're also deeply romantic about your family and kids. They're your beacons. You love beauty in every shape and form, and when there's no obvious beauty, you find it in what you can imagine. You're an excellent strategist, a natural diplomat, and you often mitigate chaos and drama, dissension and disagreement. Sometimes you assume these roles to your own detriment, just to keep the peace.

As a parent, this tendency to keep the peace at your own expense could be thankless. So strive not to be a martyr, okay? Strive not to bend over backward to please ... well, everyone. Once you can do that, your natural artistic tendencies take over in your parenting. You nurture your children's passions and interests, their gifts and talents as they emerge. You're tuned in to who they are on a soul level and understand how to help them bring that soul into their conscious awareness. Your love of art, music, literature, and every other creative talent is passed on to your kids. Your grasp of the complexities of relationships is translated into language they speak. Facebook, Myspace, and every other social networking group become their community. In short, you usher your children into the finer beauties of the twenty-first century.

The *Libra mom* creates a domestic environment in which her children flourish. But she also has her career, friends, passions, and interests that get mixed up in this collective soup called life and which, in turn, affect her kids. She brings in music, art, gardens, books, and people. Lots of interesting people. She creates moods and atmospheres and invites her children to participate. The lessons they learn, the insights they carry away from these encounters influence them for life. There's no pinning down the Libra mom. Just when you think you've got her figured out, she surprises you. Boring? Never. Not a chance.

The *Libra dad* loves having a team—wife, kids, friends of kids, neighbors, even stray animals, it doesn't matter. Everyone and everything is part of this team. Membership is open. He's an excellent organizer, supportive of his children's endeavors and dreams. But his high ideals can be problematic once his kids are adults, making choices that don't measure up—in his mind—to those ideals. Like the Libra mom, he rarely loses his temper.

Between June 11, 2012, and late June 2013, Jupiter will be transiting fellow air sign Gemini, in your solar ninth house. This transit will lead to an expansion in your educational opportunities, worldview, even in foreign travel. Until October, Saturn will be in your sign. The combination of these two transits should have positive benefits for you as a parent, your family, and kids. Even if you run into restrictions and delays in your personal life or experience sudden events related to your daily work, you come through this period with a stronger grasp of what it means to be a parent.

Scorpio

You're intense, passionate, and strong willed. You often try to impose your will on others, a trait that may serve your children when they're young, but can prove to be problematic as they get older. Like Aries, you're fearless, but you possess an endurance that Aries lacks and can plow your way through virtually any obstacle, any challenge. This trait serves as an example to your children to never give up in their pursuit of what they want.

Your passions are such that you're never *indifferent*. You live in a world of either/or, approval or disapproval, agreement or disagreement, right or wrong. While this trait drives home the importance of values and purpose, it can be challenging for children whose lives are more nuanced. Your ability to dig deeply for the bottom-line answers indicates that you will usually know what's going on in your children's lives.

The *Scorpio mom* places a high value on honesty. It's the foundation of who she is. So it's no surprise that she expects honesty from her children. Even though she herself is secretive, she won't tolerate secrets from her child. She respects their privacy, certainly, but if she suspects something is going on that needs parental intervention, she investigates until she uncovers the truth. She is a loving, devoted mother who is very protective of her kids. At times she may be too protective and strive to shield them from the outside world.

The *Scorpio dad* is as intense as the Scorpio mom. Unless he has a moon or rising in an air or fire sign, he may be just as much of a control freak too. He often has a magnificent talent or interest that he pursues because he's passionate about it and not because he expects to make money at it. He's a nurturing parent, particularly when it comes to his children's talents and abilities and the educational training that helps them navigate life successfully.

In 2012, your role as a parent may shift in unexpected directions. Due to Uranus's transit through fire sign Aries, your work situation may be somewhat erratic at times—or, at the least, unpredictable. This may actually give you more time to spend with your kids, or you may decide to launch a home-based business or to enter a field that gives you more control over your time. With your ruler, Pluto, in compatible earth sign Capricorn until 2024, you're in the power seat when it comes to communication, Scorpio, so start talking to your kids about everything that interests you.

Sagittarius

You're a wild card. There's a part of you who is always looking for the larger picture, the broader perspective, another part who believes you're always right, and yet another part who focuses on the future and the larger family of humanity. You can be very logical, but there's also a mystical element in your psyche that enables you to glimpse the future.

You dislike having your freedom restricted in any way, so you probably don't have a roll call of rules and regulations for your children. You're a loving parent, but expect your kids to find their own way, their own path.

Yet when they make mistakes, you may offer advice that makes you sound like a know-it-all. Your versatility and natural optimism are hallmarks of your parenting style.

The *Sagittarius mom* thinks big. When she suggests a family outing, it isn't just a trip to the next town for a picnic. It's a trip across country or to some far-flung corner of the world, and who cares if it's beyond the family budget? She wears many hats and excels in everything she does as long as she doesn't feel confined, limited, penned in. Her independent spirit radiates from her every pore, and her kids quickly learn to honor it. She offers her children broad guidelines and her own wisdom, but doesn't force her opinions on them.

The *Sagittarius dad* has a broad, sweeping vision about life, love, and the universe. He talks about it freely with his kids, never holding back. He is loving and devoted to his children, but because he expects big things from them may not be satisfied with what they achieve. He enjoys foreign travel and, given his financial situation, exposes his children to foreign places whenever he can. This man is always moving and has dozens of projects going on simultaneously, and his children learn early on that goals are attained through action.

In 2012, Uranus will be moving through Aries and the children area of your chart (which also governs creativity, romance, and enjoyment). This transit will bring about sudden, unexpected events—exciting, unpredictable events—concerning your kids. You'll have to think more outside the box to keep pace with them, but with your vivid imagination and ability to see the broader picture, it'll be a piece of cake for you.

Capricorn

You're the worker bee of the zodiac, industrious, disciplined, efficient, focused. You dislike inertia in others, so it's likely that your children aren't couch potatoes! You probably get them involved in sports when they're young and nurture whatever athletic abilities they have. They learn their work ethic from you and develop common sense, a trait they witness constantly in you.

Even when you were a kid, you had a mature air about you, and as you get older, that maturity is a kind of calm presence, a rock-solid dependability that your children come to expect. Never mind that you're a worrier, that even when you've prepared long and hard and have all the bases covered, you're certain you've forgotten something. Your kids rarely see that side of you. You love them unconditionally—that's what they see.

The *Capricorn mom* always seems to know what she's doing, when, with whom, and what route she's going to take to get there. She appears to be self-confident, certain about who she is, tough as nails. But as her children come to know her as a person separate from her role as mother, they discover she's not tough at all. She simply runs her home and family life as though it's a business and she's the CEO. Even if she has a career—and many Capricorn women do—she's totally devoted to her kids. She might be a little rigid with rules and regulations, but if so, learns that such excessive control results in outright rebellion.

The *Capricorn dad* is as diligent a worker as the Capricorn mom. He's got work ethic written all over him. He prides himself on being well prepared for just about anything, including being a parent. He either has the answers or will find them—for himself, for his children, or their friends. He excels at problem-solving. He can be dictatorial and bossy, but if his kids call him on it, he backs off. For a while, anyway. He's as completely devoted to his kids as he is to his career goals. In fact, one mirrors the other.

In 2012, the period from January 1 to June 11 should be spectacular for you and your kids. Expansive Jupiter is transiting fellow earth sign Taurus then, and everything you and your kids engage in together turns to gold. The Midas touch, Capricorn. In addition, Uranus's transit through Aries and your solar fourth house brings surprising, unexpected events into your home life. A move, perhaps? The birth of another child? Once Jupiter enters Gemini on June 11, where it will be until late June 2013, your daily work schedule will expand and change, and it may be a bit tougher to accommodate your kids. Make time.

Aquarius

You're such an original thinker, a visionary, that of course you apply these talents to parenting. Your household is really atypical. You might live on a boat, in a commune, in the suburbs, in an RV, or hey, maybe even on the space station. Your family structure isn't business as usual, either. But you aren't interested in typical. Everything you do is *different* from the status quo. You think in unique ways, way outside the box, and rarely if ever trust what authority tells you to believe. This ability to think and perceive in new ways is passed on to your children.

Your interests are vastly varied, and any causes in which you get involved are discussed with and communicated to your children. They learn early in life that mom or dad's interests and causes don't have to become theirs, but deserve respect. There probably aren't many rules in your family. Individuality is honored, encouraged, and thrives.

The *Aquarius mom* is a complete paradox. She's a peace-loving rebel who moves against the tide of the status quo, yet conforms when it suits her. She has the patience of a saint—until she doesn't—and can be more stubborn than Taurus unless it suits her purpose to bend with the wind. If her children are as eccentric as she is, then they have learned the value of individuality and probably share mom's love of freedom as well. Mom allows her kids the freedom to make their own decisions, revels in their achievements, and never lets them down.

The *Aquarius dad* considers his family—partner, kids, animals and orphans of all sizes and shapes—to be his sanctuary. Even if he seems undemonstrative and emotionally remote at times, his love for his kids runs deep. He takes every opportunity to expose them to everything that interests him, from ancient sites like Stonehenge and the Nazca lines to books on what the future may look like in a century. If he's a movie buff, his children are exposed to movies at a young age. If he's a traveler, his kids will be well traveled. He's terrific at sharing his knowledge, expertise, and curiosity.

From June 11 to late June 2013, you're in for a treat as a parent. You'll be watching your children's lives expand in unprecedented ways. Whether they're toddlers or adults, you'll delight in what they're learning about themselves and their world. With Uranus transiting compatible fire sign Aries, your communication skills will be sharp, and your conscious mind will be innovative.

Pisces

Your wonderful imagination and remarkable intuition prove valuable in your parenting style. Your imagination enables you to enter the world of your children with ease and playful joy. Your intuition enables you to stay attuned to their emotions even if they don't discuss what they're feeling. Pisces individuals with highly developed gifts—psychics—may have to take a break now and then from parenting just to find their own centers. It's too easy for this type to be overwhelmed with what their kids are feeling.

At times you fluctuate between rigid left-brain logic and that softer intuitive certainty that you're doing the right thing. Try not to set down rules and restrictions when you're feeling like this. Moodiness and ambivalence can cause you to backtrack from your own rules. Guard against being a sucker for a sob story.

The *Pisces mom* often has a strong psychic connection to her children. If they have been together in past lives, chances are she has a grasp on which lives and how everyone's respective roles played out then. She's able to understand what they're feeling even when they're clueless. She is rarely dogmatic with her children, and any household rules she lays down are probably for the sake of safety—and her own peace of mind. Her love for her kids is bottomless. They're her greatest joy, and she just keeps on giving and giving.

The *Pisces dad* is a great listener. His self-containment, gentleness, quiet strength, and the full attention he gives his kids are enviable qualities that enable him to forge tight bonds with his offspring. He encourages and supports his children's artistic interests and may have artistic or musical talent himself. Like his female counterpart, he must learn to balance the demands of his inner life with his responsibilities in the outer world.

2012 should bring some surprises in how you parent and how you view your children. With Neptune in your sign from February 3 onward, your whole parenting approach may become more spiritual, creative, imaginative. Your own intuition is enhanced too during this fourteen-year transit, so you'll be in closer communication with your kids on an unspoken level, able to grasp their personal issues and concerns in a deeper way.

Kids of the Zodiac

Now that we've looked at adults and their parenting styles, let's explore the kids of the zodiac.

Aries

She's the kid who is off by herself, exploring fields and meadows for unusual bugs. Or she's the fearless teen who leaps into a rushing river to rescue a kitten stranded on a rock. Or on the family camping trip where the matches and lighter fluid have been left behind, she's the one who makes a fire by rubbing sticks together or using a magnifying glass to amplify the sunlight. Inventive, independent, entrepreneurial: welcome to the world of the Aries child. And whether she's a toddler or an adult, high drama and action swirl around her.

Taurus

He's the loner. Or he has a small group of friends with whom he hangs out. But whether it's his friends or his family, no one really knows him. Like an iceberg, nine tenths of his personality is hidden. He only shows what he wants you to know. Yes, these still waters run deep. So much goes on inside his head as he figures out where he belongs in the scheme of things that he wouldn't have a clue where to begin verbalizing any of it. So he nurtures his creative gifts, enjoys the sensual pleasures of physical existence, and moves forward at his own pace, patient, certain that the answers will come to him, from somewhere, when he needs them.

Gemini

If Taurus is the loner, she's the social butterfly, flitting from one person to another, one event to the next, and along the way she's passing on what she has learned, what she suspects, what she believes. She's impatient, quick, dexterous. Her life is propelled by a single burning question: *why?* Everything she does, every connection she makes, everyone she knows and loves serves to answer that question. Somehow. In some way. Forget trying to pigeonhole your Gemini child. It just won't happen. When she's young, provide her with an environment where she can learn and explore at her own pace. Nurture her self-confidence and her belief in herself. With those tools, she's well equipped for her journey out into the larger world.

Cancer

She's a tough one to figure out. She feels her way through life, but you may never know about it. She'll talk if she's in the mood, but otherwise nothing and no one will prod her into an explanation about her feelings. As a parent, you sort of have to divine your way through this kid's childhood and beyond. She needs roots. She needs to feel she's an integral part of the family and is appreciated. Much of her life as an adult is based on her childhood memories—the smells and sights and emotions she was feeling at a particular time. If her childhood is happy and secure, then she grows into a happy, secure adult.

Leo

The Leo child is like his own tribe. From the time he's very young, he has dozens of friends and they all hang out at his place. Even as he gets older, his friends are eager to spend time with him, and some of them are orphans and strays attracted by his innate generosity and compassion. Like fellow fire sign Aries, the Leo child is basically fearless. He accepts every dare and takes risks that would leave other kids gasping in awe. Most Leo kids enjoy the company of animals, and their homes tend to have a lot of pets.

Virgo

She's impatient, wants everything yesterday, and is graced with abundant energy. She has questions about everything and is so eager to learn that in the right environment, she explores until she drops from exhaustion. Like Cancer, she can be moody, but these swings usually occur when she doesn't understand something. Her restless mind gnaws away at the puzzle, dissecting it, scrutinizing the details, the minutiae, until she gets it. She has enormous compassion, a quality that is evident at a very young age, and her ability to connect with people is as easy for her as connecting disparate bits of information is for a Gemini. Even when young, Virgo kids show discernment. They may be picky about what they eat, read, or watch on TV.

Libra

The Libra child can be found listening to music in the comfort of his own room, connecting with friends on Facebook and MySpace, or hanging out with friends in some familiar and pretty spot. He isn't the type to play touch football (unless he's got a lot of fire or earth in his chart) or hunt for bugs under rocks or dissect frogs in the lab. As a youngster, the Libra child may have an imaginary playmate or one special friend in whom he confides. He's loyal to his friends, sometimes to a fault, so any friends he has as a youngster are probably going to be friends for life.

Scorpio

She's distinctive in some way—physically, mentally, intuitively. She has fixed opinions even as a youngster, as if she came into life with a particular agenda or belief system. She feels deeply, of course, one of the trademarks of this sign, and the intensity of her emotions may lead to sudden outbursts if her feelings are hurt or she doesn't get what she wants. She flourishes in an environment that is varied and rich, where she can explore her creative abilities. She won't always be forthright about what's going on inside of her, but if you simply come out and ask her, her response may surprise you. She's wiser than her years.

Sagittarius

This kid is Mr. Popularity, and it's evident from the time he's old enough to crawl and interact. He's vivacious and optimistic and makes other people feel good about themselves. It makes him a people magnet. He can be opinionated, though, and blunt. He doesn't think about what he's going to say before he says it. He just blurts it out, a tendency that can be disconcerting to people who aren't accustomed to it. But he needs the freedom to express himself and to know it's okay to defend what he believes. Rules and structure are a good idea as he's growing up. He probably has a fondness for animals, not surprising for a sign symbolized by a figure that is half human, half horse!

Capricorn

From the time she utters her first word, she's as comfortable being and conversing with adults as she is with her peers. Sometimes she has a seriousness about her that is usually evident in her eyes, in the way she watches and appraises you, sizing you up for who knows what reason. Other times, she can be as wild and playful as any other child. Even then, though, her organizational skills are evident, and she can be bossy, no question about it. She is infinitely patient, intent on achieving her goal, whatever it might be.

Aquarius

To this kid, all people truly are equal, so his friends span the racial and socio-economic spectrum. He's an extrovert, eager to know what makes other people tick, what motivates them, but he's also perfectly happy when he's by himself. His mind is as busy as a Gemini's, but in a much different way. Where a Gemini child collects trivia and information, the Aquarian child is immersed in the stuff of the universe. Although he enjoys people and gets involved in all sorts of groups, he's not a follower and will always defend not only his opinions, but his right to have those opinions.

Pisces

She doesn't need many rules. She's so sensitive to her environment and to the people who inhabit it that a cross look from mom or dad keeps her in line. She's a dreamer, this one, whose imagination soars through time and space with the ease of a bird through sunlight. If her intuitive gifts are allowed to develop, this child can become a genuine medium, clairvoyant, mystic, healer. Her strong creative drive manifests itself early.

CHAPTER 6

Your Finances in 2012

Beliefs

Money and relationships are probably the trickiest areas for most of us to navigate successfully. But if we create our realities from the inside out, then in these two areas it's vitally important that we understand our beliefs.

Let's take a closer look. Here are some commonly held negative beliefs about money and relationships. Do you hold any of these?

- Money is the root of all evil
- My relationships never turn out
- Money is nonspiritual
- True love is rare
- The rich have major problems in their lives
- Marriage is a joke
- Money corrupts
- I'm not worthy of (fill in the blank)
- If you have too much money, you have to worry about losing it

You get the idea here. Many of these beliefs we've adopted from family and peers and have held on to them because they're comfortable, we believe they're true, or because we don't even realize we believe them!

So if you're not satisfied with what you're earning, start monitoring how you think about money. Any time you find yourself thinking a negative thought about money, turn the thought around by thinking something more positive. Also, read *Money and the Law of Attraction* by Esther and Jerry Hicks and *You Can Heal Your Life* by Louise Hay.

Now let's take a look at how you can maximize your earning potential in 2012.

Jupiter

From chapter 2, we know that Jupiter represents luck, expansion, success, prosperity, growth, creativity, spiritual interests, higher education, and the law. It also governs publishing, overseas travel, and foreign countries and any of our dealings with them. But for the purpose of this chapter, we're going to focus on Jupiter's impact on our money for 2012.

This year, Jupiter transits two signs. From January 1 to June 11, it's moving through earth sign Taurus. From June 11, 2012, to June 25, 2013, it's moving through air sign Gemini. It will be retrograde in Gemini between October 14, 2012, and January 30, 2013. A Jupiter retrograde simply means that planet isn't functioning at full capacity.

Let's see how these two Jupiter transits this year impact your sun sign.

Jupiter in 2012 and Its Impact on Your Sun Sign

Aries

Jupiter's transit of Taurus, through your solar second house, began in early June 2011, and initially you may have been spending more money than usual. But as the transit stabilized, your income is likely to have expanded in some way. That trend will continue this year, until June 11.

Your second house doesn't just govern your income, but also your values, personal debt, giving and receiving, jewelry, possessions (particularly those that are valuable), reverses in finances, your earning and spending capacity. And with Jupiter in this house, in stable, dependable Taurus, you may be looking for long-term stable investments that will increase your profit and minimize your risk.

If you dislike your job, i.e., the way you earn your daily bread, then Jupiter should bring plenty of new options and opportunities for expansion. You may decide to return to school to update your skills and knowledge, may decide to go to college or graduate school, or may expand your earning possibilities to overseas markets. Since Jupiter governs publishing, law, and higher education, any of these areas are possibilities for increasing your earning capacity.

Once Jupiter enters Gemini for a year-long transit, you'll feel more comfortable because Gemini is compatible with your fire-sign sun. In fact, this transit should be terrific for you, expanding all the areas governed by the third house and Gemini: communication, your conscious mind, daily activities, siblings, short-distance travel. You may write that book you've had in your head for years, build a Web site, start a blog. More frequent travel could be part of your daily activities—car pools, a longer commute. However this transit manifests for you, Jupiter brings luck and expansion, and you, ever innovative, turn it into a potential cash cow.

Taurus

In early June of 2011, Jupiter entered your sign, Taurus, and suddenly life took on a whole new dimension. The trend of expansion and luck that started with that transit continues until June 11 of this year. Whenever Jupiter transits your sign, the ramifications are big—you're in the right place at the right time, luck is your new best friend, your options and opportunities broaden.

Sometimes when Jupiter initially enters your sign, it seems that more money is going out than is coming in. But eventually your net worth rises, you land the dream job, your investments begin to pay off. You tend to be conservative with money, but if there's something you really want, don't hesitate to buy it if you can pay cash for it. You want to avoid credit-card debt during this transit and the one coming up between June 11, 2011, and June 25, 2013. Conserve your resources, but don't be stingy and don't do it out of fear.

When Jupiter enters Gemini on June 11, you're in for another treat. It will be transiting your solar second house of money, so it's likely that your earning capacity will rise, your values will broaden, your opportunities for self-improvement will increase. Jupiter's transits are nearly always fortunate, but there's a risk with excess in some area. When you see a sharp increase in your income, follow your parents' advice—sock some of it away. But again, don't do it out of fear. Any action taken from a basis of fear is likely to attract circumstances that will cause real fear.

Gemini

During Jupiter's transit of Taurus between January 1 and June 11, your unconscious is easier for you to delve into. Dream work, meditation, yoga, or some other kind of mind/body activity benefits you. In fact, you may discover that your dreams hold important information that will help you with issues or concerns that you have. Ideas come to you through dreams and meditations. Consider a past-life regression with a qualified therapist. Everything you learn during this transit is creative fodder, Gemini, and is preparing the way for Jupiter's transit through your sign between June 11, 2012, and June 25, 2013.

Jupiter transits your sign just once every twelve years. So look back to 2000 for hints about what sorts of experiences you may have during this year-long transit. What were your finances like that year? Did you land a new job that paid more? Did you move into a better neighborhood, a larger house? Did you take unnecessary financial risks? All of these areas are possibilities this year.

One thing you definitely want to avoid during this transit is gambling or speculating with your money. Because Jupiter can be excessive, you may feel cocky, as if you can do no wrong. It's smarter to save and to invest in things that further your education, skills, and future.

Cancer

Since last June, Jupiter has been moving through Taurus and your solar eleventh house, a transit that continues until June 11 of this year. This brings an expansion to your social contacts, your wishes and dreams, and opportunities to promote and publicize your work or product or that of your company. Since this transit forms a beautiful angle to your sun sign, other areas of your life will benefit as well, and one of them is your finances.

You might decide, for example, to join an investment group that shares ideas about which stocks or bonds to buy. Or you and a group of friends may invest in rental property or even buy a place together, fix it up, and then sell it for a handsome profit. Any dealing with real estate and homes is a nonbrainer for you, Cancer. It's what you enjoy doing.

Between June 11, 2012, and June 25, 2013, Jupiter will transit Gemini, through your solar twelfth house. It makes it easier for you to delve into your own unconscious, to recall your dreams. If you don't meditate yet, then this transit presents the opportunity to do so. You may discover moneymaking ideas through meditations and dream recall. You may start a blog or build a Web site and find an innovative technique for making money in this way. Use this transit to find out who you are, Cancer. Self-knowledge can lead to a greater understanding about how the universe works, and such knowledge can lead to greater financial stability and more money.

Leo

Jupiter entered Taurus and your career area in June 2011 and won't leave it until June 11, 2012. That gives you six months this year to enjoy the professional expansion—and thus, the financial expansion—of this transit. The last time Jupiter touched this area of your chart was twelve years ago, so look back to 2000 for clues about how the last six months of this transit may unfold for you.

If you would like to change jobs or careers, then it could happen during this transit. Equally possible? Your responsibilities, job description, and salary increase substantially, you launch your own business, sell a book, work overseas. Regardless of the specifics, you will have plenty of opportunities to do what you do best, Leo—shine!

Between June 11, 2012, and June 25, 2013, Jupiter transits compatible air sign Gemini and your solar eleventh house. This transit not only stimulates your social life, but brings you into a whole new sphere of individuals who help you to attain your dreams, whatever they may be. Any groups you join may also prove to be helpful financially.

With Jupiter in Gemini, your communication skills—which aren't too shabby to begin with!—really sharpen. Your mind becomes a steel trap, and you're able to snap out facts, figures, statistics that astound even you. You learn to make money using your ability to communicate and connect with others.

Virgo

When Jupiter entered fellow earth sign Taurus last June, your income probably increased, and that trend will continue until June 11 of this year. It's possible that your work or a quest of some sort takes you overseas, and whatever you learn and experience changes your fundamental beliefs about money. You may suddenly realize, for example, that you're worthy of being rich. Or that your book is just as good as anything on the market and will find the right publisher. In other words, your inner world is shifting, becoming more certain, stronger. As that happens, your life in the outer world will change accordingly.

If you're a writer, this transit expands your publishing opportunities, could bring about significant foreign sales, and makes it easier, generally, to sell what you write. Regardless of what profession you're in, your business could expand to overseas markets. Other possibilities: you head off to college or graduate school, go to law school, or even move overseas.

Once Jupiter enters Gemini and the career area of your chart, you're in for an exciting time. The specifics of this transit vary for each of us, but here are some possibilities: you switch jobs/careers and land something with a larger salary; you work overseas; you sell your novel or screenplay. One way or another, the professional and financial payoff for you is excellent.

Libra

With Jupiter in Taurus until June 11, you and/or your partner may be accruing items like art and jewelry for investments, could delve more deeply into esoteric subjects like ghosts, past lives, communication with the dead, or may combine your resources in some way. Whatever it is, it pays off financially. Let's say that you and your partner have separate homes, then during this transit you may decide to sell one place and move in together. This transit should bring breaks with mortgages, loans, taxes, and insurance.

When Jupiter transits fellow air sign Gemini between June 11, 2012, and June 25, 2013, you have a wonderful opportunity to explore your worldview and spiritual beliefs and to divest yourself of any that are holding you back from achieving your financial goals. The exploration may come through opportunities for foreign travel, to write a book on whatever seizes your passions, or to even go to graduate school to further your skills.

Scorpio

With Jupiter transiting Taurus, your opposite sign, for six months this year, you and your partner may launch a business together, or you may find a business partner for a venture you've had in mind. By combining talents and resources, your income increases, your self-confidence benefits, and you discover that in order to live the way you want, it's important to do what you love.

Air signs aren't compatible with your water-sign sun. However, there's much to learn from this transit—namely, never hesitate to communicate what you believe and why. Don't hide your wisdom; share it with others. On a mundane level, this transit may increase your partner's income, and the two of you may find investments with large payoffs. Your joint finances benefit tremendously.

The trick with this transit is to share—not just money, but resources, time, energy. If you do that, if you go with Jupiter's flow, you'll benefit greatly from everything this planet has to offer.

Sagittarius

Since Jupiter started transiting Taurus in June 2011, your daily work schedule has been exploding like crazy. So much to do, so little time, but yes, you're having fun! Expect that trend to continue until June 11 of this year. If you work out of your home, then it's possible you add a room onto the house or expand your home to accommodate your office. If you work a regular job, then your schedule keeps growing by leaps and bounds until you feel as if you're all over the place. But it suits you. If you own your own business, then you may add more employees or expand your product/services to overseas markets.

Between June 11, 2012, and June 25, 2013, Jupiter transits Gemini, your opposite sign. This transit augurs well for any joint business venture—with your romantic partner or a business partner or both! By pooling talents and resources, anything done in partnership can pay off handsomely. If you're reading this and thinking that you don't have a partner—either romantic or business—don't fret about it. Chances are good that before this transit ends, you'll have both!

Capricorn

Since June 2011, you've been enjoying Jupiter's transit through fellow earth sign Taurus, in your solar fifth house. It is expanding all your creative ventures, your muse is undoubtedly in attendance 24/7, and some days the ideas flow so fast you forget them before you can find a pen or get to your computer to write them down. This trend continues until June 11. So enjoy it while it lasts, and have faith that your creativity is going to increase your bank account!

Jupiter's transit through Gemini and your solar sixth house lasts from June 11, 2012, to June 25, 2013. Buckle up for the wild ride, Capricorn. This transit should expand your daily work routine and schedule to the point where it's bursting at the proverbial seams. You'll have to be more organized than usual during this transit, but the potential benefits in terms of income can be great. With greater responsibility comes a salary boost. With a salary boost comes greater security for you. Even more important, though, is that with this expansion you can build stronger professional goals.

Aquarius

Jupiter has been transiting Taurus and your solar fourth house since June of 2011 and will be there until June 11 of this year. This transit should expand everything to do with your home, family, and the fundamentals of your life. A birth is a possibility. Or you may move into a larger home or expand the home where you currently live. One of your parents may move in with you. Since the fourth house also governs real estate, it's possible that you buy property as an investment.

Between June 11, 2012, and June 25, 2013, Jupiter transits fellow air sign Gemini in the creativity sector of your chart. It's your ticket, Aquarius. The more creative you are, the greater your earning capacity. You may get involved in a creative venture with one of your kids or a new romantic interest, and because it's done from a basis of pure joy, it has a positive effect on your finances.

Pisces

Since June 2011, Jupiter in Taurus, an earth sign compatible with your water-sign sun, has been transiting your solar third house, and it continues this year until June 11. During this period, your communication skills sharpen your conscious mind expands. You suddenly understand how to make money from, well, talking and writing. A blog, your Web site, magazine articles, a book: any of these venues is possible. The Taurus part of the equation helps to ground your imagination, to bring your ideas into the practical daily world.

From June 11, 2012, to June 25, 2013, Jupiter transits your solar fourth house and Gemini. This transit brings luck and expansion to your home life. In terms of finances, you may start working out of your home, doing something you love, and the money follows. Or perhaps you move to a different city or area where your opportunities for employment are better, where your family is happier, where conditions are more conducive to an increase in your income. Since Jupiter is coruler of your sun sign, its transits are nearly always significant for you in some way.

CHAPTER 7

The Structures in Our Lives

Saturn takes two and a half years to go through a sign, so its effects tend to unfold more slowly than those of the moon, which changes signs about every two and a half days. This planet governs the rules and parameters of physical life and represents responsibility, structure, discipline, limitations and delays, obedience, authority, the building of foundations. So by its transit we are confronted, challenged, or helped by Saturn, depending on the angle it makes to our sun signs.

With Saturn occupying two signs this year, the end of Libra and the beginning of Scorpio (which lasts until December 2014), we're all called upon this year to meet our obligations and responsibilities in two different areas. So let's take a closer look at how Saturn's transits in 2012 impact your sun sign.

Aries

Saturn has been opposite your sun sign since October 2009 and finally leaves Libra on October 5 of this year. During this transit, you're learning to structure your personal and professional partnerships and are deepening your understanding of team work and cooperative living. This last part may not be an easy lesson for a spirit as independent as yours, but learn you will. Chances are that your partner—business or romantic—may have met with some restrictions or delays during this transit that have in turn impacted you in some way.

The Saturn opposition to your sun can be a discouraging time—if you let it. You may feel drained physically, so it's important to have a regular exercise routine. It's also important to maintain contact with friends, family, and other people you love. Try not to resist things that are happening to you. Learn to go with the flow.

Once Saturn enters Scorpio, you feel a distinct relief. A weight has been lifted. During this transit, which lasts until December 2014, you'll learn how to accept other people's values, even when those values aren't in line with your own. It may be more difficult to obtain mortgages and loans during this transit, or sources of income you have depended on may dry up. So it's important that you become as self-sufficient as possible before this transit begins.

Taurus

During Saturn's transit through Libra and your solar sixth house, your daily work responsibility has undoubtedly increased. You may be working longer hours, too, but if you're doing something you love and are getting paid more for your efforts, then it certainly isn't a burden. Due to other demands on your time, you're probably learning how to maximize the time you have and are becoming more organized about your daily work schedule. If you're self-employed, then organization and good time use are vital tools.

Once Saturn enters Scorpio and your solar seventh house, you may be dealing with some of the same issues that Aries dealt with during Saturn's transit through Libra. If you allow this transit—an opposition to your sun—to discourage you, if you resist change, then the transit becomes much more difficult. The important lessons with this transit are about learning to cooperate with partners—business and romantic—and to allow relationships that no longer work to fall out of your experience.

Gemini

Saturn's transit through fellow air sign Libra should be quite productive for you, Gemini. Saturn is now forming a harmonious angle with your sun, strengthening your assets, enabling you to find the proper structures for your creative projects, relationships, your life! This transit may bring professional recognition of some kind and a solid boost in your career and creative output. During this transit, it's smart to establish and/or maintain an exercise routine. Although your health should be fine during this transit, you're building up stamina for times when you may have more stress in your life—like during the Saturn opposition to your sun. This transit also helps you to build solid relationships with your children and to find grounded venues of enjoyment.

Once Saturn enters Scorpio and your solar sixth house, your daily work schedule may have to be revamped. More responsibility will bring a greater need for organization and efficient use of your time. If you're self-employed, Saturn in Scorpio will prompt you to always look at the absolute bottom line—costs in terms of money, time, energy, and resources. Be sure to tend to your health during this transit too. Keep exercising and eating responsibly, and stay away from fad diets.

Cancer

As Saturn transits Libra and your solar fourth house, you're learning to balance responsibilities of home and career. This requires you to be more organized and use your time more efficiently. You may have to cubbyhole your life, with an emphasis on family on certain days and an emphasis on career/work on other days. You tend to go with the flow more than other signs, so it's important that you keep doing that. Any time you feel yourself resisting something that's happening, try to understand why and correct it. If you don't know why you feel resistance, then simply reach for a better thought and feeling.

Once Saturn enters fellow water sign Scorpio and forms a beneficial angle to your sun, you're a much happier camper. This transit helps you to solidify all creative projects. Instead of just writing screenplays, for instance, you begin selling what you write. You discover great depth in your own creativity, your relationship with your children, in romance, and in what you do for fun and enjoyment. Maintain an exercise program during this transit, so that when Saturn enters Sagittarius in late December 2014, your physical strength is at a peak.

Leo

Saturn in Libra forms a beneficial angle to your sun, so you're benefiting from this transit. Your communication skills find a proper venue for expression. A book? Blog? Web site? Radio or TV? Whatever it is, you dazzle with your language skills and win accolades from friends, family, peers. If you move during this transit, the place has to be exactly right for you—and your family. Preferably, it should be in the thick of things—theater, restaurants, bookstores. During this transit, you're enormously productive too and enjoy the work.

Once Saturn enters Scorpio and your fourth house, Saturn is opposed to your career area. This transit indicates that you'll have to learn how to reasonably balance your home and work responsibilities. You'll be aware of the absolute bottom line too, in just about everything—with your family, kids, parents, your family's budget. Your intuition should deepen appreciably, and it will be wise to follow any hunches you have.

Virgo

During Saturn's transit through Libra and your solar second house, your financial earnings may be restricted in some way. Or you find the proper structure for your finances through investments, for example, or a pension plan. You may feel that your values are somehow holding you back, preventing you from doing something or going somewhere. The truth is that you're the only one holding you back. During this transit, you're supposed to learn how to conserve your financial resources and to live within a budget.

When Saturn enters compatible water sign Scorpio on October 5, your relief will be palpable. During this transit, with Saturn forming a beneficial angle to your sun, you'll be in a very good position to bolster your communication skills, find a neighborhood that fits your specific criteria, return to school to enhance your skills. Your conscious mind will be able to take abstract ideas and turn them into practical tools. This transit lasts until December 2014.

Libra

Whenever Saturn conjuncts or opposes your sun sign, it's considered to be a major transit—challenging, but filled with potential. During this transit, you divest yourself of relationships and situations that no longer work or which aren't in your best interest. You may change jobs, get divorced or married, or have to provide support for one of your parents. There can be delays, or your freedom is restricted in some way, but the purpose is to slow down your life so that you tend to what is personal and immediate.

Sometimes Saturn conjunct your sun brings about external events that turn your life in a different direction. The more resistance you offer, the more difficult it is. So it's important to learn to go with the flow.

With Saturn's transit through Scorpio and your solar second house from October 5, 2012, to late December 2014, you learn how to conserve your financial resources, how to budget, how to save. If there's a decrease in your earnings during this transit, try not to fret about it. Your intuition should increase. It's the small voice whispering in the back of your mind to go here, do that, try this. Follow its guidance.

Scorpio

During Saturn's transit through Libra and your solar twelfth house, you're being asked to funnel your discoveries about your own psyche and unconscious into some sort of structure. This transit would be a great time to go through therapy, to take up yoga or some other mind/body discipline, and to start meditating, if you don't already. The twelfth house governs not only the personal unconscious, but past lives, institutions, and everything that is hidden. So with Saturn here, you may run into people you have known in previous lives, will have greater access to your dreams and information that comes to you through meditation, and may have contact with institutions like hospitals and nursing homes, even prisons. This doesn't mean *you* will be institutionalized, but that someone you know may be.

Once Saturn enters your sign, you may feel that your freedom of movement is restricted in some way. It could be due to increased responsibility in some area of your life—career, family, work, no telling. The last time Saturn conjuncted your sun was about twenty-nine to thirty years ago. If you're old enough, look back to that time and remember what was going on in your life. Big changes? How? In what areas? One thing you'll have to do is divest yourself of relationships and situations that aren't in your best interest. You may change jobs, move, get married or divorced. Regardless of the specifics, offer no resistance to events. Go with the flow.

Sagittarius

Saturn's transit through Libra forms a beneficial angle to your sun. It brings structure and solidity to your friendships and wishes and dreams. It actually should be easier to attain your dreams during this transit, particularly if you have laid the groundwork and met your obligations and responsibilities to others. If you don't attain your dreams during this transit, then before it ends you'll have a clearer grasp of what you need to clear out of your life to make room for the attainment of these dreams. Saturn's transit through Scorpio and your solar twelfth house should give you the opportunity to do that.

Saturn transits Scorpio from October 5, 2012, to late December 2014. During this period, you benefit from therapy, meditation, yoga, or any other mind/body discipline. Your dreams can be a source of information and insights. Since the twelfth house represents institutions—prisons, hospitals, nursing homes—it's possible that you have more contact than usual with these places. Basically, this transit enables you to clear your life of what no longer works—relationships, situations, belief systems.

Capricorn

Saturn's transit through Libra and your career area is a major transit that could solidify your professional life and bring recognition from peers and bosses. You may assume more responsibility during this period and work longer hours, and there could be some delays or restrictions on your freedom to come and go as you please. Hard work has never bothered you, especially if you're compensated fairly for it. If you're self-employed, then this transit enables you to solidify your business, client base and income.

During Saturn's transit through compatible water sign

Scorpio and your solar eleventh house, you'll be more in your element. Your friendships and any groups to which you belong will be helpful in achieving your dreams and goals. It's important that you learn how to work with groups and to grasp what group dynamics are in a work situation.

Aquarius

During Saturn's transit through fellow air sign Libra and your solar ninth house, you benefit in a major way. This transit solidifies your worldview and spiritual beliefs and enables you to find the right structure for expressing these beliefs. The ninth house also governs higher education, overseas travel, and foreign cultures, countries, and people, so any foreign travel you do will be structured in some way to fit your goals or needs. If you're in a business that sells products overseas, this transit helps to create a good foundation in overseas markets.

Saturn's transit through Scorpio and your solar tenth house brings increased responsibility in your career, longer hours, perhaps recognition by peers and bosses. It could bring about a promotion, or you may decide to launch your own business. If it's the latter, you're going to love the freedom even if it means a lot of hard work and long hours.

Pisces

During Saturn's transit through Libra and your solar eighth house, your access to funds that have been available previously may be restricted or denied you. If you apply for a mortgage or loan, for example, it may be difficult obtaining it. Your partner's income may take a hit. With Saturn here, you're urged to conserve your resources—money, time, energy. This transit helps you to channel your enormous imagination and intuitive ability.

During Saturn's transit through fellow water sign Scorpio and your solar ninth house, you'll benefit from a positive angle that Saturn makes to your sun. This transit should enable you to explore your worldview and spiritual beliefs in a structured way. You may, for instance, travel overseas to various sacred sites on some sort of spiritual quest. Or you may take courses or workshops in metaphysical areas to explore your intuition or alternative healing methods. This transit lasts from October 5, 2012, to late December 2014.

Saturn in Your Birth Chart

Wherever Saturn appears in your birth chart indicates an area where you will learn lessons in this lifetime. It also indicates life issues you may have brought in from previous lives. Saturn's lessons can be harsh, but it teaches us through experience what we need in order to grow and evolve and what our souls intend to accomplish in this life. It shows us our limitations, teaches us the rules of the game. Without it, our lives would be chaos. Individuals with well-aspected Saturns in their birth charts—the angles other planets make to it—have a practical outlook. With a poorly aspect Saturn, growth may be restricted or limited in some way, and the person's outlook could be rigid.

The sign that Saturn occupies shows how we handle obstacles in our lives, deal with authority, and cope with serious issues. The house placement in your natal chart indicates the area of your life that's affected. If you have Saturn in your tenth house, for example, then your career ambition is one of the driving forces in your life, and you'll work tirelessly to succeed. If your Saturn is in Leo, you may need to learn that it isn't all about just *you* and your career.

Every twenty-eight to thirty years, we experience a Saturn return, when transiting Saturn returns to the place it occupied at our birth. The first return, around the age of twenty-nine, brings major life transitions—we get married or divorced, start a family, move, begin a career. The second return, between the ages of fifty-eight and sixty, is considered to be the harvest. We experience major events—retirement, our kids have left home, we downsize, move, inherit money.

Whenever a Saturn transit hits a natal planet, that period should be navigated carefully, with understanding of what's required of you. Saturn takes about twenty-nine years to circle the zodiac. It entered Libra in late October 2009, retrograded from January 13 to May 29, 2010, then entered Libra again on July 22, 2010, and will be there until October 5, 2012. Then it enters Scorpio for a run of about two and a half years.

Natal Saturn in Aries

Your impetuosity and rashness need to be tempered somewhat, so that you think before you act. You consistently encounter circumstances that force you to develop patience and initiative. If you push against these circumstances, then setbacks occur. With Saturn, you can't take shortcuts. This position of Saturn urges you to develop resourcefulness and discipline and to complete what you start. Once you learn these lessons, you're capable of innovative and unique creations.

The downside with this placement is that you're prone to defensiveness and a kind of self-centered attitude that puts people off. Tact and diplomacy will take you farther and, in the end, may be one of the lessons you're here to learn.

Natal Saturn in Taurus

One of your lessons in this lifetime is to develop persistence and resoluteness, an unshakeable belief in yourself and your talents. This belief helps you to win material security and comfort through hard work, discipline, and perseverance. You may not be the fastest-moving person in the world, but you hang in there long after the competition has bitten the dust.

It behooves you to learn how to handle money and your finances. You tend to be frugal even when you don't have to be, but this frugality may become one of your hobbies. You might, for example, hit garage sales, flea markets, any spot where secondhand goods are sold, and could develop a business around it. On the other hand, if this frugality turns to miserliness, you may want to rethink your attitudes and beliefs about money. The downside is a preoccupation with materialism.

Natal Saturn in Gemini

Since Saturn corules air sign Aquarius and is exalted in air sign Libra, it's pretty comfortable in air sign Gemini. It brings discipline and structure to your mental process and suggests that part of what you're here to learn is how to think through problems logically, working them out in detail so that your solutions are practical. Saturn here may restrict a free flowing expression of ideas, but once you've learned to channel your ideas in a pragmatic way, perhaps through writing or some sort of group activity, you reap the benefits. In other words, it's not enough to have a great idea. How can the idea be put into practice to benefit not only you, but others?

Communication is important to you, but it has to be organized, structured in some way, honest, and dependable. That may be one of the lessons you're here to learn. Downside? If you don't do the grunt work this placement demands, your obstacles multiply.

Natal Saturn in Cancer

This placement may restrict your intuitive gifts and your emotions. Or it could provide the proper structure for expressing both. It depends on how you use your conscious desires and intent to create your life. It depends, too, on your deepest beliefs. Do you believe we have free will or that life is somehow scripted, destined? Are events random, or do they rise from some hidden quantum order? While your crablike tenacity helps you to navigate successfully through obstacles, Saturn here urges you to confront obstacles head on, to reveal what's in your heart, and to channel your intuitive talents in a practical, focused way.

Your home and family are important to you. But strive not to impose so many restrictions in this area that the people who are closest to you—and you yourself—feel suffocated.

Natal Saturn in Leo

This placement is all about power and recognition. The desire for both, however, takes many forms. At one extreme, it results in a need to control your environment and everyone inside of it and a hungry ambition that blinds you to everything else. At the other extreme, this placement results in structures that help you to channel your ambition in a constructive, directed way. This placement also suggests that your ego and need for recognition can be your worst enemies, so be aware of that tendency and do whatever you can to mitigate it.

For Boomers born with this configuration, there can be multiple setbacks that prompt you to work harder, put in longer hours, meet all your obligations—and then some. Eventually, though, if you learn patience and resilience, you succeed. You achieve your goals. Cooperative endeavors are beneficial with this placement, i.e., anything in the professional arena in which you have partners, where you're a team player, where your voice is just one among many.

Natal Saturn in Virgo

The tendency with this placement is that you're such a perfectionist you get bogged down in details. You walk into someone else's house, for example, and immediately notice streaks on the cabinets that scream for a dose of Pledge. Or you enter your son's apartment and are overwhelmed by the disorder and chaos. But if you can direct this tendency toward your work and career, you can handle anything, manifest anything, and perform a service that helps many people understand their roles in this lifetime. It's simply a matter of separating the essential from the inconsequential.

Your intuition is highly developed, just waiting for you to pay attention, to connect all the dots. Find humor in everything you do. Take breaks from work. Treat yourself to a trip to Paris or some other far-flung corner of the globe. Learn to revel in your experiences.

Natal Saturn in Libra

Your lesson this time around is to learn the value of co-operation. The success of any partnership, personal or business, involves the ability to compromise. What can you live with to keep the peace? How much can you surrender without giving away your personal power? Your values? Karma is part and parcel of your most intimate relationships, and the sooner you recognize that, the better off you are. The question, though, is how do you recognize which relationships are karmic and which ones are just the luck (or misfortune) of the draw? Well, bottom line, it's about what you feel when in the presence of another person. It comes down to resonance.

The dark side of this placement is a tendency to surrender too much in the hope that you can keep the peace. The real key here is the ability to forgive and forget and move on.

Natal Saturn in Scorpio

In your work, you're as much of a perfectionist as Saturn in Virgo. But in everything else, you're pure Scorpio— after the bottom line, the absolute truth, the real deal. You're secretive in the way you handle stress and difficulties of any kind and must learn how to deal with this stuff in a calm, centered manner. Allow your intuition to guide you. It's an infallible tool. Your persistence, resilience, and determination are among your greatest assets.

That said, there's a proclivity here for incredible discipline in achieving your goals, but you may need help, and help won't be forthcoming unless you ask for it. *Can* you ask for it? Is a request for help even in your lexicon? Check out the sign of your moon. If it's in a water or earth sign, chances are good that you realize you are part of a collective of like-minded individuals. Start there. You won't be disappointed.

Natal Saturn in Sagittarius

Your pursuit of philosophy and/or religious and spiritual beliefs is one of the primary driving forces in your life. You may have a desire to be recognized as an authority in one of the above areas or in higher education, publishing, politics, or the law. You probably have a strict moral code that guides you, but which could stifle creative thinking. Any kind of rigid approach to problem-solving complicates your challenges and problems. It's best to loosen up, to allow yourself the freedom to explore your ideals free of political or religious restraints.

You're happiest if you can structure your life by incorporating your ideals into your daily life in a practical way. Your professional reputation is vitally important to you, but try not to obsess about every little detail, every little word. You're after the big picture. The darker side of this placement is self-righteousness.

Natal Saturn in Capricorn

Saturn rules this sign, so it's very happy here and functions at optimum capacity. Your ambitions are powerful, and from the time you're old enough to understand what a career is, you are pursuing your own. Your talents are varied, and you may be able to integrate all of them in some unique way to achieve what you desire. Your goals are specific; your discipline is astounding.

The usual description about this placement is that the person may appear cold, detached, remote. But I've found this isn't necessarily true. My daughter and her friends, all of them born in 1989 when Saturn was in the early degrees of Capricorn, are among the most joyful group of people I've ever known. But they're also incredibly focused in their pursuit of educational goals, which certainly fits this placement.

Natal Saturn in Aquarius

Saturn, as the coruler of Aquarius, is pretty comfortable here. Your visionary qualities are channeled and expressed in practical ways that benefit others. Your intellect is organized, focused, objective, and capable of innovative discoveries and solutions. With this placement, there's usually mathematical and scientific ability and the ability to conceptualize. The challenge is to integrate your abilities into your daily life and to ground them. You benefit from regular physical exercise that serves to remind you there's more to life than the mind! Yoga, tai chi, or any other mind/body discipline would be a good place to start.

The downside of this placement can be a lack of feeling, intellectual pride, and impersonal relationships.

Natal Saturn in Pisces

The consensus about this placement is that it's difficult. But any challenges can be overcome by channeling your intuitive ability through a structure that Saturn provides. Instead of letting your memories of the past trap you, use memories of past triumphs as a springboard to achieve what you desire. Your psychic ability is the doorway to spiritual and creative development and to higher spiritual truths.

There can be an inordinate amount of worrying that accompanies this placement, so be sure you always allow yourself solitude, a refuge where you can kick back and relax. It helps to practice yoga, meditate, nurture yourself first.

CHAPTER 8

Health and Fitness Tips for the Paradigm Shift

When paradigms shift, it's not just belief systems that are impacted. Our minds, spirits, and physical bodies are also affected. The slowest-moving outer planets exert the most influence over our lives, so let's take a look at the areas of the body these planets rule for hints about how we can take better care of ourselves in 2012.

Saturn

This planet rules bones, teeth, joints, knees, and spine. So during Saturn transits, these are the areas in your body that are most likely to be affected. With Saturn in Libra until October 5, 2011, your lower back, kidneys, ovaries, and sugar levels—all governed by Libra—could be impacted too. Between October 5 and late December, Saturn transits Scorpio, which rules the endocrine system, menstruation, sex organs, and blood, so these areas could be affected too.

Uranus

This planet rules ankles, nervous ailments, miscarriages, reflexes, and sprains. With Uranus in Aries all year, other areas that could be affected are: adrenals, head, insomnia, retinas, scalp.

Neptune

With Neptune in Pisces, the sign that it rules, from February 3, 2012, for the next fourteen years, areas of the body that can be affected are: feet, glandular swellings, eyes, addictions, parathyroid, pituitary, hard to diagnose diseases.

Pluto

Pluto will be in Capricorn until 2024. Possible trouble areas include: enzyme levels, reproductive organs, hemorrhoids. Capricorn rules pretty much the same areas that Saturn does: bones, joints, knees and kneecaps, gout, rheumatism, sprains.

So when you know that one of these outer planets will be forming an angle to one of your natal planets—your sun, moon, and rising in particular—then you can take extra care with the parts of your body that may be more vulnerable. If Saturn is forming a difficult angle to your sun sign, for example, then it would be smart to take yoga regularly to keep your spine and joints flexible.

Your General Health

If you were an alien watching the evening news and the drug commercials that sponsor it, you might get the impression that Americans are a sickly lot in search of the quickest fix. While drugs certainly have their place, more and more Americans are seeking alternative treatments for whatever ails them. From acupuncture to yoga and homeopathy, from vitamin regimens to nutritional programs, we're seeking control over our own health and bodies.

Health and fitness is more than just eating right and getting sufficient exercise. It's also about our emotions, our inner worlds, our belief systems. How happy are you in your job? Your closest partnerships? Your friendships? Are you generally happy with the money you earn? What would you change about your life? Do you believe you have free will or that everything is destined? Is your mood generally upbeat? Do you feel you have choices? Do you feel empowered? By asking yourself these kinds of questions, you can glean a sense of your emotional state at any given time. The state of your emotions may tell you a great deal about the state of your health.

Louise Hay, author of *You Can Heal Your Life* and founder of Hay House Publishing, is a living testament to the impact of emotions on health. As a young woman, she was diagnosed with vaginal cancer. The doctors wanted to operate, but Hay bought herself time—three months—by telling them she didn't have the money. She then took control of her treatment.

As a battered child who had been raped at the age of five, it wasn't surprising to her that the cancer had shown up where it had. She knew that cancer was "a disease of deep resentment that has been held for a long period of time until it literally eats away at the body." She felt that if she could change the mental pattern that

114

had created the cancer, if she could release the patterns of resentment, then she could cure herself.

She set out a program for her treatment—and forgiveness was at the top of her list. She also knew she had to "love and approve" of herself more. In addition, she found a good therapist, a nutritionist, a foot reflexologist, had colonics three times a week, exercised. Her treatment is spelled out in her book. The end result? Within six months, the doctors pronounced her free of cancer.

In her book, there's an invaluable list: next to every ailment and disease is the probable emotional cause and the new thought pattern that will lead to healing. Her techniques may not be for everyone, but when dealing with health and fitness issues, remember that medical science doesn't have all the answers, and you, in fact, may be your own best healer.

The Physical You

These descriptions fit both sun and rising signs. For a more complete look at the physical you, of course, your entire natal chart should be taken into account, with a particularly close look at the sign of your moon—the root of your emotions, the cradle of your inner world.

Aries

Rules: head and face

What You Look Like

Physically these people tend to have ruddy complexions, narrow chins, and arched eyebrows. Sometimes they have a scar or mole on the head or face. Aries men often have profuse body hair, and in both men and women the hair is sometimes tinged with red.

Health and Fitness Tips

Aries rules the head and face, so these areas are often the most vulnerable physically. Headaches, dizziness, and skin eruptions can be common. If you're an athletic Aries, then do more of whatever it is that you enjoy. Competitive sports? Great, go for it. Long-distance runner? Run farther. Gym? Double your time and your workout. Yoga once a week? Do it three times a week. One way or another, you need to burn off your excessive energy, so that it doesn't turn inward and short-circuit your body!

As a cardinal fire sign, you're an active person who gravitates toward daring, risky sports—mountain climbing, rappelling, bungee jumping, trekking through high mountainous regions, leaping out of airplanes. It's probably a great idea to have good health insurance or to have a Louise Hay attitude toward your health—*I'm attracting only magnificent experiences into my life.*

For maximum benefit, you probably should try to eliminate red meat from your diet. Chicken and fish are fine, but a vegan diet would be best. Herbs like mustard, eyebright, and bay are beneficial for you. Any antioxidant is helpful—particularly vitamins C, E, A or Lutein for your eyes, zinc, Co-Q10, Black Cohosh if you're a female in menopause, or Saw Palmetto if you're a man older than fifty. If you pull a muscle or throw your back out of whack, look for a good acupuncturist and avoid painkillers.

Taurus

Rules: neck, throat, cervical vertebrae

What You Look Like

In a Taurus, the neck is usually thick and sturdy and rises from broad, often muscular shoulders that seem to bear the weight of the world. They tend to be attractive individuals with broad foreheads and expressive faces. Yet their faces can be as inscrutable as fortune cookies when they are hiding something or feel threatened in some way. They usually look more youthful than other people their age, the result of good genes and a daily regimen of exercise.

Health and Fitness Tips

Thanks to the sensuality of your sign, you may be a gourmet cook and enjoy rich foods. But because your metabolism may be somewhat slow, you benefit from daily exercise and moderation in your diet. In fact, moderation in all things is probably a good rule to follow.

As a fixed earth sign, you benefit from any outdoor activity, and the more physical it is, the better it is for you. Hiking, skiing, windsurfing, biking are all excellent pursuits. You also benefit from any mind/body discipline like tai chi or yoga. The latter is especially good since it keeps you flexible, and that flexibility spills over into your attitudes and beliefs and the way you deal with situations and people. You probably enjoy puttering in a garden, but because you have such an artistic side, you don't just putter. You remake the garden into a work of art—fountains, bold colors, mysterious paths that twist through greenery and flowers. Once you add wind chimes and bird feeders, nature's music adds the finishing touches.

If your job entails long hours of sitting in front of a computer, your neck and shoulders may be more tense than usual. You would benefit through regular massage and hot tub soaks.

If you're the silent type of Taurus, then chances are you don't discuss your emotions. This tendency can cause health challenges if you keep anger or resentment bottled up inside you. Best to have an outlet—through exercise, for example, or through some sort of creative endeavor. Art, music, photography, writing: any of those would help. Better yet, learn to open up to at least one or two people!

Gemini

Rules: hands, arms, lungs, nervous system

What You Look Like

Geminis generally radiate a lot of nervous energy. It keeps them slender and wiry, and they're always on the move—if not physically, then mentally. They often have twinkling eyes, clear-cut features, a nose that turns up slightly at the end. Some of them have thick hair. They talk and move fast, many are ambidextrous and usually have excellent coordination.

Health and Fitness Tips

You benefit from periodic breaks in your established routine. Whether it's a trip to some exotic port or a trip to the grocery, it's a breath of fresh air, a way to hit the pause button on your busy mind. Regular physical exercise helps to bleed off some of your energy and keeps your already youthful body supple and in shape.

As a mutable air sign, you need intellectual stimulation and a constant array of experiences and information to keep your curiosity piqued. Otherwise it's too easy for all that nervous energy to turn inward and affect your health. The kind of work you do is important in the overall scheme of your health. You do best in nonroutine kind of work with flexible hours or, preferably, in a profession where you make your own hours! Any job in communication, travel, public relations, would suit you. When you're passionate about what you do, you're happier. If you're happy, your immune system remains healthy.

With your natural dexterity and coordination, you

would do well at yoga. If you don't take classes yet, sign up for some. Not only will it keep you flexible, but you'll benefit mentally. Meditation would also be an excellent practice for you. Anything to calm your busy head!

Since your respiratory and nervous systems are your most vulnerable areas, your diet should include plenty of fish, fresh fruits, and vegetables. If you live in a place where you can garden, then plant some of these items for optimum freshness. Vitamin C, zinc, the B vitamins, and vitamins E and A are also beneficial for you. With your energy always in fast-forward, it's smart to get at least seven and preferably eight hours of sleep a night. If you're the type of Gemini with a high metabolism, then you benefit from eating several small meals throughout the day rather than just the usual three.

Cancer

Rules: breasts, stomach, digestive system

What You Look Like

Cancers are recognizable because of their round faces. Their bodies are sometimes round, too, though not necessarily overweight. Those who don't have roundness as part of their physical appearance may have some other distinguishing trait—liquid, soulful eyes, a lovely-shaped mouth, generally expressive features. They're moody individuals, and their moods are often reflected on their faces and in the way they walk and carry themselves.

Health and Fitness Tips

As a cardinal water sign, you benefit from proximity to water. If you can live or work close to a body of water, you'll notice a marked difference in your energy and intuition and how you feel and think. Even a vacation close to the water is healing. This seems to hold true not only for Cancer sun signs, but for moon and rising signs in Cancer too. The body of water can be anything—a lake, river, ocean, salt marsh, even a pond!

Not surprisingly, you benefit from any kind of water sport, even a day at the beach or a picnic by the river. The point is that water speaks to you. It feels like your natural element. You might want to read *The Secret of Water* or any of the other books by Masaru Emoto. You will never think of water in the same way again and will be more conscious of how human emotions affect water—and thus our bodies, since we consist of nearly 70 percent water.

Emotionally, you may cling to past injuries and hurts more than other signs or may still be dragging around issues from childhood or even from a past life. Unresolved emotional stuff can lodge in your body and create problems. So it's important that you rid yourself of past resentments and anger. Use hypnosis to dislodge these feelings. Forgive and forget. Have a past-life regression. Read Louise Hay's book *You Can Heal Your Life.*

If you have a moon, rising, or another planet in an earth sign, then consider regular workouts at a gym.

Leo

Rules: heart, back, spinal cord

What You Look Like

From Jacqueline Kennedy to Madonna to Presidents Obama and Clinton, the typical Leo looks regal. Hair that is thick or in some way distinguished, compelling eyes, a smile that can light up the dark side of the moon: these are the Leo hallmarks. Male or female, they project dignity and intelligence and move with a certain elegance. In a crowded room, the Leo is usually the one surrounded by people!

Health and Fitness Tips

Leo rules the heart. So you benefit from a low-fat diet, exercise, work that you love, and relationships in which you are recognized as the unique person that you are. Yes, those last two things count in the overall picture of your health!

Let's talk about your work. Acting, of course, is what you're known for. And performance. And politics. And, well, anything where you can show off your abundant talents. So if right now you're locked into a humdrum job, are the low person on the bureaucratic totem pole, and don't receive the attention you feel you deserve, then your pride and ambition are suffering. That, in turn, creates resentment that could be eating you alive. Turn the situation around by finding a career or an outlet where your talents shine and you're appreciated and recognized. You're a natural leader whose flamboyant style and magnetism attract the supporters who can help you.

You have a temper, but once you blow, that's it. Unlike Cancer, you don't hold on to grudges or harbor resentments or anger from childhood. You tend to be forward looking in your outlook, and your natural optimism is healthy for your heart and immune system. Anything you can do to maintain your cheerful disposition is a plus. When you feel yourself getting down, rent comedies, find books that make you laugh out loud, blog about your feelings.

Virgo

Rules: intestines, abdomen, female reproductive system

What You Look Like

Their physiques are usually slender and distinctive in some way—beautifully sculpted fingers and hands, for instance, nice legs, gorgeous teeth. They're physically attractive as a rule, which they enhance through their fastidious attention to detail. Their eyes may be unusual in some way, and their features tend to be sharp, clearly defined. They're fastidious about personal hygiene.

Health and Fitness Tips

If you're the type of Virgo who worries and frets a lot, then the first place it's likely to show up is in your digestive tract. You might have colic as an infant, stomach upsets as a teenager, ulcers as an adult. The best way to mitigate this tendency, of course, is to learn how NOT to worry and to simply go with the flow.

You do best on a diet that includes plenty of fresh fruits and vegetables, fish, and chicken. Try to stay away from fried or heavily spiced foods. Red meat might be difficult to digest. If you live in a place where fresh fruits and vegetables are difficult to find during the winter, then supplement your diet with the appropriate vitamins and minerals. If you're a fussy eater—and some Virgos are—then the vitamin and mineral supplements are even more important.

You benefit from hot baths, massages, anything that allows you to relax into the moment. Yoga, running, swimming, gym workouts, any of these exercise regimens benefit you. Some Virgos, particularly double Virgos— with a moon or rising in that sign—have an acute sense of smell. If you're one of those, then be sure to treat yourself to scented soaps and lotions, fragrant candles and incense, and any other scent that soothes your soul.

Virgo is typically associated with service, and you may find that whenever you do a good deed for someone, when you volunteer your time or expertise, you feel better about yourself and life in general. The more you can do to trigger these feelings, the healthier you'll be. You have a tendency toward self-criticism that's part and parcel of your need for perfection, and whenever you find yourself shifting into that critical frame of mind, stop it in its tracks. Reach for a more uplifting thought. This will help you to maintain your health.

Libra

Rules: lower back, kidney, diaphragm

What You Look Like

Even in a crowd of beautiful people, they stand out in some way. As a Venus-ruled sign, they have distinctive features—beautiful eyes, gorgeous skin, well-formed bodies, expressive mouths. They're often slender, good-looking. They enjoy beauty—in their partners, their surroundings, their aesthetic tastes. So it isn't surprising that they often dress beautifully and have homes that are boldly colored and uniquely decorated.

Health and Fitness Tips

If your love life is terrific, then your health probably is too. You're happiest when you're in a relationship, preferably a committed, lifetime relationship. When things between you and your partner are on an even keel, your energy is greater, your immune system works without a hitch, you sleep more soundly, and you're more apt to have a healthier lifestyle.

You prefer working in an environment that's aesthetically pleasing, where there's a minimum of drama with congenial people. If your work situation doesn't fit that description, then it could affect your health—and for the same reasons as a love life that is lacking. Emotions. Your lower back, kidneys, and diaphragm are vulnerable areas for you, and unvented emotions could manifest in those areas first. If it isn't possible to change jobs or careers right now, then find an artistic outlet for your creative expression. Music, photography, art, writing, dance, any area that allows you to flex your creativity.

You benefit from yoga, walking, swimming, and any kind of exercise that strengthens your lower back muscles. Meditation is also beneficial, particularly when it's combined with an awareness of breathing.

The healthiest diet for you should consist of foods with varied tastes, plenty of fresh fruits and vegetables, organic if possible, and a minimum of meats. Anything that benefits your kidneys is good. Drink at least eight glasses of water a day, so that your kidneys are continually flushed out.

Scorpio

Rules: sexual organs, elimination

What You Look Like

The body types vary, but the eyes ... well, the eyes are nearly always compelling, intense, piercing. They rarely reveal what they're feeling and are masters at disguising their expressions. Their masks are carefully honed through years of hiding their emotions. Many Scorpios have thick eyebrows, sharp noses, seductive mouths. Their voices are often husky and low.

Health and Fitness Tips

As a fixed water sign, you probably benefit by a proximity to water every bit as much as Cancer does. Lake, ocean, river, pond, salt marsh: take your pick. If none of these is available, then put a fountain in your backyard or somewhere in your house and create a meditation area. It's important that you have a quiet center where you can decompress at the end of the day, particularly if you have a busy family life and a lot of demands on your time.

You tend to keep a lot of emotion locked inside, and if the emotions are negative—resentment, anger—they fester and affect your health. So try to find someone you can talk to freely about your emotions—a partner, friend, family member. Or pour these feelings into a creative outlet. One way or another, get them out.

Scorpio rules the sexual and elimination organs, so these areas could be where ill health hits first. Be sure that you eat plenty of roughage in your diet and enjoy what you eat while you're eating it. Stay away from the usual culprits—fried or heavily processed foods. You do best with plenty of fresh food, but may want to consider eliminating red meats. Consider colonics treatments for cleaning out the bowels.

For your overall health, it's important to enjoy sex with a partner whom you trust. Avoid using sex as a leverage for power in a relationship.

Sagittarius

Rules: hips, thighs, liver

What You Look Like

They tend to come in two types—tall and broad through the shoulders or shorter and heavier. The second description comes in part from Jupiter, which rules the sign and causes them to indulge their appetites. They look athletic and have high foreheads that get higher in men as they age and their hair recedes. They move quickly, but not necessarily gracefully.

Health and Fitness Tips

As a mutable fire sign, you can't tolerate any kind of restriction or limitation on your freedom. You must be able to get up and go whenever you want. If you work in a job that demands you punch a time clock, where your hours are strictly regulated, or are in a relationship where you feel constricted, then you probably aren't happy. For a naturally buoyant and happy person like you, that could spell health challenges. Sadge rules the hips, the sacral region of the spine, the coccygeal vertebrae, the femur, the ileum, the iliac arteries, and the sciatic nerves, so any of these areas could be impacted health-wise.

You benefit from any kind of athletic activity. From competitive sports to an exercise regimen you create, your body craves regular activity. You also benefit from yoga, which keeps your spine and hips flexible.

If you're prone to putting on weight—and even if you're not!—strive to minimize sweets and carbs in your diet. The usual recommendations—abundant fresh vegetables and fruits—also apply. If you're the type who eats on the run, then you may be eating fast or heavily processed foods and should try to keep that at a minimum or eliminate it altogether. Even though your digestive system is hardy enough to tolerate just about anything, the fast foods and processed foods add carbs and calories.

Antioxidants are beneficial, of course, and these include vitamins C, A, and E. Minerals like zinc should be included in your diet and also a glucosamine supplement for joints.

Capricorn

Rules: knees, skin, bones

What You Look Like

As a cardinal earth sign, these individuals understand the benefits of exercise, and their bodies show it. While they generally aren't muscular—some are, but not as a rule—they look to be in shape. Their bodies are often angular and slender, and their faces, regardless of their age, have a maturity about them.

Health and Fitness Tips

Since you seem to have been born with an innate sense of where you're going—or want to go—it's likely that you take care of yourself. You know the routine as well as anyone—eat right, stay fit, exercise, get enough rest. But there are other components to living long and prospering (to paraphrase Spock!), and that's your emotions.

You, like Scorpio, are secretive, although your motives are different. For you, it's a privacy factor more than anything else. You keep your emotions to yourself and may not express what you feel when you feel it. This can create blockages in your body, notably in your joints or knees. It's vital that you learn to vent your emotions, to rid yourself of anger before it has a chance to move inward.

You're focused, ambitious, and patient in the attainment of your goals. But your work—and your satisfaction with it—is a primary component in your health. If you feel you've reached a dead end in your career, if you're frustrated more often than you're happy with what you do, then it's time to revamp and get out of Dodge. By taking clear, definite steps toward something else, you feel you're more in control of your destiny and mitigate the possibility of health challenges.

Since your knees are vulnerable, running is probably not the best form of exercise for you, unless you do it only once or twice a week and engage in some other form of exercise the rest of the time. For a cardio workout that isn't as tough on your knees, try a rowing machine. For general flexibility, there's nothing like yoga!

Aquarius

Rules: ankles, shins, circulatory system

What You Look Like

Tall and slender or short and round, their body types are as different and varied as they are. But many have deeply set eyes and classic profiles. Many of them move as quickly as Geminis; others move like molasses. Most aren't particularly coordinated, but some are. So, bottom line, it's tough to spot these individuals in a crowd. But as soon as you listen to them for five minutes, they're easier to peg. They talk eloquently about their ideas and ideals, and you'll recognize them by their discussions of alternative foods, alternative fuels, alternative lifestyles, alternative everything.

Health and Fitness Tips

Let's start with the effect of Uranus ruling your sign. It sometimes can set your nerves on edge—too many sounds, too much chaos around you, loud noises deep into the night, the backfiring of cars, the incessant drone of traffic, even a crowd at the local mall. You're sensitive to all of that. It's part of what makes it important for you to have a private space to which you can withdraw—a quiet back yard filled with plants, a room inside your house with an altar for your Wiccan practice filled with scents from candles or incense that soothe your frazzled nerves. Or perhaps a book on tape can shut it all out. But shut it out you must to protect your health.

Because you live so much inside your own head, exercise is definitely beneficial for you. It doesn't have to be anything complicated—yoga done in the privacy of your own home, long walks, regular bike rides. But do *something* to ground your body, to get your blood moving, to silence the buzz inside your head. It will all benefit your health.

Nutrition? Well, for an Aquarian, this can go any number of different ways. You enjoy different types of food, so that's a place to start—with what you *enjoy*. The foods are likely to be unusual—organically grown, for instance, prepared in unusual ways, or purchased from a local co-op. If you live in the city, then perhaps you purchase food from a grocery store you've been frequenting for years. The idea here is that *you* know what's best for your body, what you can tolerate, what you need. Even though Aquarians aren't generally as in touch with their bodies as earth signs, they have an intuitive sense about what works for them. In the end, that's all that matters.

Pisces

Rules: the feet, is associated with the lymphatic system

What You Look Like

Common wisdom in astrology says there are two types of Pisces—the whale and the dolphin. And this goes for the sun, moon, or rising in Pisces. The whale is, well, large, but also tuned into everything and everyone on the planet. The dolphin type is slender, sleek, quick, joyful, graceful. But both body types usually have extraordinary eyes that are not only soulful, but seem to be able to peer through time.

Health and Fitness Tips

Let's start with emotions. Let's start with the fact that you're a psychic sponge, able to absorb other people's moods and thoughts with the ease of magnet attracting every other piece of metal around it. Yes, let's start there. It's why you should associate only with optimistic, upbeat people. The negative types steal your energy, wreck your immune system, and leave you in a tearful mess at the end of the rainbow with nothing to show for your journey.

Like your fellow water signs Cancer and Scorpio, you probably benefit from proximity to water. Whether you live near water, work near it, vacation near it, water refreshes your soul, spirit, intuition, and your immune system. Read Masaru Emoto's books on how water responds to emotions and intent. You'll never think about water in the same way again. You'll never think about your sun sign in the same way again, either.

You benefit from any kind of exercise, but try something that speaks to your soul. Swimming. Rowing, but in an actual boat, on an actual river instead of in a gym. Even a hot tub where you kick your legs is beneficial. Pay attention to the water you drink. Is your tap water filled with fluorides? Then avoid it and look for distilled water. Drink at least eight glasses a day. Indulge yourself in massages, foot reflexology, periodic dips in the ocean. Any ocean.

Meditate. Find the calm center of your storm.

CHAPTER 9

Aspects

Throughout this material, we've talked about beneficial or challenging angles that a transiting planet makes to your sun sign or that transiting planets make to each other. These angles are called *aspects*. Think of them as a symbolic network of arteries and veins that transport the blood of astrology. In a natal chart, these angles connect our inner and outer worlds, accentuate certain traits and play down others. Each aspect represents a certain type of energy, so there really aren't any good or bad aspects because energy is neutral. It's what we do with the energy that counts. It comes back to free will. When transiting planets make angles to each other, energy is also exchanged.

For instance, every year there is at least one very lucky day when the transiting sun and transiting Jupiter form a beneficial angle to each other—a conjunction (same sign and degree), a sextile (60 degrees apart), or a trine (120 degrees apart). The lucky day in 2012 falls on May 13, when the sun and Jupiter are exactly conjunct. This means that the sun's life energy and Jupiter's expansive energy combine and create, well, some magic for all of us! It's especially good for Taurus and other earth signs, but since we all have Taurus somewhere in our charts, everyone benefits.

If you look back to the presidential election in November 2008, Saturn in Virgo and Uranus in Pisces formed an exact opposition to each other. They were 180 degrees apart, an aspect that is like a tug-of-war. In this case, the tug-of-war was between the candidate that represented the old paradigm, the established order—Saturn—and the candidate who symbolized sweeping change—Uranus.

Aspects are most powerful as they are approaching exactness. So even though a conjunction, for example, is 00 degrees of separation or a square is technically 90 degrees of separation, many astrologers use *orbs* that can be as wide as five or ten degrees. Some astrologers use small orbs, but others assign larger orbs for the sun and moon and smaller orbs for other planets. The closer the orb, the more powerful the combination. If you're sensitive to transits, then, you may be feeling lucky for several days before May 13!

In terms of a natal chart, any transiting planet that is approaching an aspect with one of your natal planets is also most powerful on its approach. The traditional aspects have been used since the second century A.D. They are the conjunction, sextile, square, trine, and opposition. These aspects are considered to be the major or hard angles and are also the most powerful. There are other minor aspects that astrologers use, but for the purpose of this chapter, we'll only talk about the traditional aspects.

At the end of this chapter is a natal chart. We'll be referring to it as we go through the aspects.

Conjunction, major hard aspect, 0 degrees

This aspect is easy to identify—clusters of planets within a few degrees of each other, usually but not always in the same sign and house. But it's a complex aspect because energies combine, fuse, merge. Think of it as power, intensity. So if you have conjunctions in your natal chart, the astrologer who reads for you should address what it means and how you can use it to maximize your potential.

Let's look at the young woman's chart. With her Saturn—♄—and Neptune—♆—conjunct in her tenth house of career, there's already a tension and power in her chart. Saturn builds structures and boundaries and seeks to hold back, restrict. It's about rules and responsibilities. Neptune urges us to allow boundaries to dissolve, to release the ego, to reach for higher ideals. So this woman will confront these dualities in her career—her tenth house.

With Uranus—♅—thrown into the mix, these experiences and dualities will come at her out of the blue, suddenly and without warning. Her career will be unusual, strange, filled with idiosyncratic people and defined by strange experiences—the Uranus influence. Uranus shakes up the status quo and when it's conjunct Saturn—even widely, by 7 degrees in this case—she will feel conflicted at times about which path to follow, which choices to make.

In this same chart, notice the close conjunction between the moon—☽—and Mars—♂—in the sixth house. One degree of separation. One possible repercussion is that her emotions are especially intense, even volatile at times, when it comes to her daily work routine and the maintenance of her health. Her health stuff may occur in fits and starts—one week she'll run two miles a day, the next week she's a couch potato, and the next week she meditates and practices yoga. It's the same way with her work. Erratic, moved by the spirit and passion of the moment. But because Mars is in Virgo, she's diligent, a hard worker at whatever she takes on.

Since Mars is within a degree of the seventh-house cusp, this passion she has spills over into her personal and business partnerships.

Sextile, major soft aspect, 60 degrees

Again, look at the young woman's chart. An example of a sextile occurs between her sun—☉—at 8 degrees Virgo in her sixth house and her Jupiter—♃—at 5 degrees Cancer in her fourth house . The orb, according to the aspect grid, is 2 degrees and 41 minutes. Close enough to have significant impact.

A sextile is a point of ease. It represents a free-flowing energy between the planets involved. No tension. The sextile is a kind of buffer, a shield against turmoil, indecision, instability. But if there are too many sextiles, then the person may be too passive!

In the young woman's chart, her Pluto in Scorpio in the eighth house—12♀♏49—is closely sextile her Neptune in the tenth, within 5 degrees of her Saturn in the tenth, within a 6-degree orb of her Virgo Mars in the sixth, and within 5 degrees of her Virgo moon in the sixth. That's a whole lot of energy stacked in her favor and suggests that whatever she does on a daily basis with her work somehow feeds into the larger picture of her career. During her college years, she was able to manifest jobs out of thin air while in school and during the summers.

When she was in high school, for instance, she and her parents vacationed in windsurfing spots in the Caribbean and South America because her dad is a windsurfer. So she learned to windsurf and became so proficient at it that she was able to teach windsurfing at her college, through the sailing club, to any students who were interested. The college paid her ten bucks an hour. Gas money! Food money!

From the time she was old enough to walk, she enjoyed horseback riding and loved working with horses, being around them. She lived near an equestrian community, so becoming a barn rat was not a tough thing to do. During the summer of her freshman year, with her parents breathing down her back about getting a job, she manifested a job teaching riding at an equestrian summer camp.

These examples are precisely the kinds of experiences that accompany the sextiles in her chart. That Pluto in Scorpio, a sign that planet rules, gives her enormous power and ability to hone in on what she needs and wants and make it happen.

Square, major hard aspect, 90 degrees

Friction, angst, *oh my God, the sky is falling*: that's how squares feel in a natal chart. The sky, of course, is never falling, but the friction and angst are quite real and act as triggers for action, forward thrust. They force us to develop, evolve, and reach aggressively for our desires.

How's this play out in real life? Look at the young woman's chart. She has three squares to her natal Mercury in Libra, in her seventh house of partnerships, all of them from that cluster of planets in her tenth house of career. Her natal Mercury—05♀︎♎︎33—is square to those tenth house planets from between 2 to 4 degrees. Ouch. The need to achieve something professionally is very strong. But it's not just about achieving. She wants to make her mark on the world, to leave something behind, some sort of legacy, something unique that bears *her stamp*. Because Mercury rules communication and this young woman enjoys writing and is good at it, that could be one of her signatures.

Mercury is also square her Jupiter in Cancer in the fourth house, suggesting that she may try to take on too much—in her writing, her life, her partnerships. Hit the pause button, breathe, ask for guidance through imagination, visualization, your family (fourth house), and dreams.

Squares spur us to action.

Trines, major soft aspect, 120 degrees

This aspect works like a sextile, linking energies in a harmonious way. It's associated with general ease and good fortune. Again, though, if there are too many in the chart, passivity may result.

Look at the chart again. The young woman's 8-degree Virgo sun in her sixth house is closely trine to both Neptune and Saturn in Capricorn. The Saturn/Sun trine enables the young woman to set realistic goals and to attain them. The Neptune/Sun trine gives her deep compassion, psychic and artistic ability. She's able to attract the right opportunities for her career. The trine to Uranus is a bit wider—7 degrees—but is still significant. It suggests that her profession is or will be unusual and that her freedom is important to her. It's doubtful this young woman will be found in an office, confined to a 9 to 5 job. Whatever she does is likely to be unique.

Opposition, major hard aspect, 180 degrees

This aspect feels like a persistent itch that you can't reach and usually involves polarities—Taurus/Scorpio, for example, or Aries/Libra. It brings about change through conflict and sometimes represents traits we project onto others because we haven't fully integrated them into ourselves.

In the woman's chart, her natal Jupiter in Cancer is opposed to all three planets in her tenth house. Jupiter expands everything it touches, so with Saturn, the woman's professional success comes about through persistence and dedication and by working with her beliefs in a constructive, positive way. With her Jupiter opposed to Uranus, the freedom to call her own shots, make her own schedule, to do her own thing, is paramount. In a chart that lacks direction and focus, this aspect can lead to involvement with revolutionary groups or religious cults. In a strong chart like this one, however, the Uranus/Jupiter opposition can indicate involvement in humanitarian efforts. The Neptune/Jupiter opposition can indicate utopian ideals, getting suckered by a sob story or trusting smooth talkers with a devious agenda. But it can also lead to great spiritual awareness and enhanced psychic ability.

Some other minor aspects that astrologers use are:

- the semi-square, 45 degrees. It creates irritation and friction between the planets involved.
- the septile, 51 degrees. Indicative of harmony and union in a nontraditional way. Can suggest spiritual power.
- the quincunx or inconjunct, 150 degrees separation. Indicates a need for adjustment in attitude and beliefs.

FEMALE

Aug 31, 1989
08:10:00 PM EDT
FEMALE
Fort Lauderdale,FL
ZONE: +04:00
080W08'37"
26N07'19"

Geocentric
Tropical
Koch Houses

Thursday, Aug 31, 1989
The 243rd day of the year
08:10:00 PM EDT +04:00
LMT: 18:49:26
UT: 00:10:00
UT-LMT: 05:20:34
ST: 17h30m00s
RAMC: 202°30'
Local Apparent Time 18:49:17
Equation of Time: 00m08s
Planetary Hour: Moon (☽)
1st Hour of Jupiter-Night
Sunrise (aprox.): 07:04 EDT
Sunset (aprox.): 19:37 EDT
Moon in 1st Quarter
☉)☽ Angle: 008°36'
☽'s Motion: +12°06'19"

Pl	Geo Lon
☉	17°☍08' 39"
☽	08°♍32' 54"
☿	05°♎32' 33"
♀	16°♎30' 00"
♂	18°♍02' 35"
♃	05°♋52' 10"
♄	07°♑23' 16"
♅	01°♑22' 23"
♆	09°♑43' 09"
♇	12°♏48' 47"
☊	25° ♈49' 51"
⚷	23° ♋07' 47"
⚸	19°♓38' 46"
⊗	25°♓39' 46"
⚹	21°♓50' 03"
⚶	11°♋03' 08"
⚳	14° ♋26' 28"
⚴	02° ♎12' 32"
⚵	00° ♏24' 36"

Adjusted Calculation Dates
0h: Aug 29 12h: Feb 27

CHAPTER 10

The Astrological Neighborhood

Whether you're just learning astrology or are a seasoned pro or somewhere in between, the Internet is a wonderful tool for studying astrology. You can Google anything—a planet, an aspect, some obscure detail about astrology—and some Web site or blog undoubtedly has the information you're looking for.

Astrology sites offer a vast spectrum of services, from free natal charts, daily transits, and monthly horoscopes to political and world predictions—it's all at your fingertips. Here are some of the best sites:

www.astro.com: Enter your birth data and obtain a free natal chart. This site is also chocked full of information about astrology. Great for the beginner, the intermediary, and the advanced astrologer. Something for everyone here. There are also some terrific articles by well-known astrologers.

www.astrologyzone.com: Susan Miller's site is a favorite for neophytes and pros alike. Every month she writes around three thousand words per sign about what you can expect in the upcoming month. Her predictions are eerily accurate!

www.moonvalleyastrologer.com: Celeste Teal is *the* expert on eclipses, a specialized area of astrology that few have researched the way she has. Her two books on eclipses are seminal works.

www.astrocollege.com: Lois Rodden's site is extraordinary. This woman spent most of her life collecting birth data and then created a piece of software that is invaluable in research. This site also rates and sells astrology software. Lois has passed on, but her work survives.

http://astrofuturetrends.com: Author and astrologer Anthony Louis does just what the site says. He predicts future trends, covers political stuff, and provides an overall view of astrology.

www.starlightnews.com: Click on Nancy's blog. Here you'll find the latest predictions and insights about world affairs. Nancy's predictions about politics have been right on. Before the 2004 election, she made some predictions about tight senatorial races that were totally accurate. She also called the presidential race in 2008. We've been following her closely ever since.

www.astro-yoga.com: This site combines astrology and yoga. We created it and this system of yoga.

www.tjmacgregor.com: Here you'll find monthly astrological predictions for writers.

www.ofscarabs.blogspot.com: About synchronicities—what they are, how they show up in our lives, what they might mean, and hundreds of stories.

Software

Computers have transformed everything about astrology. In the days before, you had to figure all this stuff by hand, through complicated mathematical formulas that left you gasping.

Our first piece of software was a really simple program we found at some computer store for ten bucks. It erected a chart in about sixty seconds. There it was—rising, moon, sun, planets, the houses—everything set up on the computer screen as if by magic. In the late 1990s, we bought our first really terrific astrology software from Matrix for about $300. In the years since, http://www.astrologysoftware.com has supplied us with endless data and information and revolutionized the study of astrology.

But it's not just enough to have a great piece of software. When your computer crashes, when you receive updates that screw up, when windows updates to a new system, you call the Matrix help line and their people walk you through it until everything works. The employees on their help lines aren't outsourced. You won't reach India. You'll talk to someone in Michigan who is not only an astrologer, but a computer geek who knows how to fix your problem. If by some fluke they can't fix your problem, they'll credit you for one of their other terrific programs.

The only complaint we have about Matrix is that to activate the software, you have to call or contact them through the Internet to receive a special code. If your computer crashes, if you buy a new PC or laptop . . . well, it's annoying. When you pay this much for software, you shouldn't have to obtain a special access code.

Another great piece of software is SolarFire. Astrologers are as dedicated to this program as they are to Matrix's software. Check out http://www.alabe.com for current prices. While the two programs offer similar features and capabilities, preferences seem to be individual. Both Matrix's Winstar and astrolabe's SolarFire offer many alternative features—like reports for natal, transit, and progressed interpretations.

Kepler's astrology program—http://www.astrosoftware.com—is beautiful in its rendition of charts, interpretations, and just about anything any astrologer could use or need. We like it for its ease, its beauty. But it's not a Winstar or SolarFire.

If your exploration of astrology takes you deeper, there are other software programs that take you there. Bernadette Brady is the undisputed mistress of fixed stars. Her software program, Starlight, is remarkable not only for its accuracy, but for its presentation. You will never think of fixed stars in the same way once you play with this program. What won't make sense in a natal-chart interpretation suddenly snaps into clarity when you use Brady's software. Be sure to download a print to file version for the software—through a PDF file—so that you can maximize usage. Their Web site: http://www.zyntara.com.

Lois Rodden's AstroDatabank is the software that Lois Rodden developed. It contains over thirty thousand birth records, "carefully documented and coded for accuracy with the popular Rodden Rating system. AstroDatabank includes intriguing biographies, revealing personality traits, important life events, and significant relationships." For the curious, the researcher, the neophyte and pro alike.

Both Winstar and SolarFire produce computerized report software. These reports are handy for when a friend of a friend is in a fix and you don't have the time to interpret transits and progressions for the person's birth chart. Winstar also produces software on the tarot and numerology.

Day Watch, another Winstar program, is forecasting software that is invaluable for astrologers. From their site: "Certainly it creates personalized astrological calendars, a great tool for professional astrologers and those who have an understanding of astrological terms, symbols, and technique. But Day Watch also contains a full range of onscreen and printable interpretations of events that even someone with absolutely no astrological training can read, understand, and immediately put to use in their daily lives."

At the beginning of every month, we bring up our personalized calendars that tell us what is happening daily in our natal charts and also lists which planets are changing signs in that month, on what date, and which planets are turning retrograde or direct. Each month includes an ephemeris and lunar charts for the new and full moon. The program also offers various types of reports.

Getting a Reading

So now you're ready for an astrological reading. But where do you start? Which astrologer should you use?

The best way to find an astrologer is through soeone who has gotten a reading and recommends the individual. If you don't know anyone who has had an astrological reading, then the next best course is to head over to the nearest bookstore and look through the astrology books. Browse through titles that interest you. Note the author's style. If the author uses a lot of astro jargon or seems to write in a depressing or heavy-handed way, move on. Once you find an author whose book you like, check to see if he or she has a Web site and get in touch with the person.

Rates for a reading vary from one astrologer to another and usually depend on what you want. Would you like just an interpretation of your natal chart? Would you like a forecast for the next six months or a year? Do you want a compatibility chart for you and your partner? Some astrologers prefer to do phone readings and record the reading. Others prefer to work through e-mail. If the astrologer you've chosen lives close to you, all the better. Have the reading done in person.

What to Expect During a Reading

Every astrological reading begins with your natal chart, so an accurate birth time is essential. It should come from your birth certificate or a parent's memory. An approximate time means the entire reading won't be as accurate.

This reading differs from a daily horoscope you find in a newspaper or on a Web site because it's tailored to your specific chart rather than just to your sun sign. If you're getting a reading only on your birth chart, then the astrologer interprets the entire chart, not just pieces of it. The astrologer looks at the signs and house placements of the various planets and the angles the planets make to each other.

Think of a natal chart as a holographic depiction of who you are. It's an organic blueprint, where the parts fit together in certain ways. In a reading, the signs of your sun, moon, and rising are where most astrologers begin. The sun represents your total personality, the moon symbolizes your inner world, and your rising sign is the doorway to your chart—the portal through which all your experiences enter. So an astrologer would look at the mix of these planets and then look at how they meld or oppose, facilitate or challenge other planets in your chart.

In addition to planets and aspects, astrologers also look at some other things in natal charts: the Nodes of the moon, part of fortune, various asteroids, Chiron, Vertex, and Sabian symbols. The Nodes are discussed in the next chapter, so let's go through the other parts of the list.

Part of fortune ⊗ **:** This is the most commonly used Arabic part, of which there are dozens. Its placement by sign and house designates where your "pot of gold" lies. It's your luck factor.

Asteroids: There are probably hundreds of asteroids, but astrologers use only a handful of them. Thanks to the work of astrologer Demeter George, four asteroids are the most commonly used: Vesta, Ceres, Athena, and Juno. Here are their general meanings:

Vesta ⚶**:** This asteroid's position in a natal chart describes where we are dedicated and how we can use our energies to bring about the greatest change in the larger world.

Ceres ⚳**:** How were we nurtured and how do we nurture others? That's what Ceres shows us, according to the sign and house position.

Pallas Athena ⚴: How do you fight for what you want? How do you pursue what you desire? Pallas, the warrior queen, describes the battles we choose to fight.

Juno ⚵: The asteroid of marriage. It generally describes the romantic/marriage partner we need and get.

Chiron ⚷: Known as the wounded healer, this planetoid describes where we are wounded and how healing this wound, which often stems from early childhood, can lead to greater wisdom and the healing of others.

Vertex: It's a point that describes agreements we made prior to being born into this life, a point of destiny. Since we have free will, we can choose not to keep these appointments, but it's probably a good idea if we do. Often the sign of our Vertex is the sign of someone to whom we're close—parent, partner, child, friend, mentor.

Sabian Symbols: Back in the early part of the twentieth century, astrologer Marc Edmund Jones spent hours with a clairvoyant, Elsie Wheeler, who gave him psychic impressions of each of the 360 degrees of the zodiac. The impressions are usually couched in metaphors, but over the years have proven to be eerily accurate. To test it, go to one of the sites listed in this chapter and get a free birth chart. Then go to www.cafeastrology.com, search for Sabian symbols, and look up the degree of your sun sign.

There are other points and asteroids that astrologers use, but when you're just starting out in your interpretation of your own chart—or of someone else's—keep the chart as clean as possible. Stick to the planets. Once you've got those meanings down, start adding other elements to the chart.

Your Soul's Agenda

The Soul

There are various ways to look for spiritual aspects in a chart. Some astrologers use Neptune and the angles it makes to other planets. Others use the moon and its aspects. We use the North and South Nodes of the moon.

The Nodes aren't planets. They're points formed by the moon's orbit around Earth that intersect with the Earth's path around the sun. They're always separated by 180 degrees, so they form an axis of energy. If your North Node falls in Gemini, then your South Node falls in Sagittarius, the sign that is six away from Gemini. If you haven't done so already, turn to the appendix, locate the time span that includes your birth date, and find out the sign of your North Node. Then look at the table below to find your South Node.

The South Node represents our comfort zone, the accumulation of characteristics, attitudes, and talents that we bring into this life from other lives or—if you don't believe in reincarnation—that are laid down early in childhood. We retreat to our South Node when we're hurt, feel sick or threatened, or perhaps when we're in a new relationship and aren't sure yet where things are going. We also retreat here when we feel unsure of ourselves. The South Node is the psychological equivalent of comfort food.

The North Node symbolizes the direction we should move in this life to fulfill our talents and potential and to evolve spiritually. It represents the soul's agenda this time around, the qualities, traits, and experiences our higher selves felt that we need to evolve spiritually and to reach our potential.

LUNAR NODES

If your north node is in	*your south node is in*
Aries	Libra
Taurus	Scorpio
Gemini	Sagittarius
Cancer	Capricorn
Leo	Aquarius
Virgo	Pisces

The sign of your North Node describes the types of experiences you should strive for in this life. It can also describe the psychological bent, potential, and talents that you should try to develop, to reach for, in order to attain your soul's agenda and to achieve your creative and spiritual potential. The sign of the South Node describes all of the above, but from previous lives. It's "been there, done that, and still feel comfortable here."

The house placement of your South Node describes the area that is your comfort zone. The house placement of your North Node describes the area where your greatest potential and talent can be achieved and the way in which you can evolve spiritually.

Take a look at the natal chart at the end of chapter 9. The woman's South Node in Leo—☋12♌32—falls in her fourth house of the home, her domestic environment. Her North Node in Aquarius—☊12♒32—falls in her tenth house of career. These signs suggest that to evolve spiritually, to achieve her full potential, she should strive to create a career that helps others. Aquarius is the sign of the humanitarian, who often works with groups to achieve a common goal.

She feels most comfortable when she's in the spotlight, or when she's involved in some drama involving her family and personal environment. She's such a warm, caring person that she's a people magnet (South Node in Leo). The house placement of her South Node suggests that she feels most comfortable in her personal environment. But the path to her spiritual evolution and to her achievement lies in the public arena.

Nodes Through the Signs

Aries North Node

Your soul craves independence. But your comfort zone lies in the embrace of others. You're at ease in most relationships, within groups, and seek balance in everything you do. Sometimes your need for balance is so great that you bend over backward to accommodate others and end up compromising your own values. That's your comfort zone—Libra South Node—speaking.

It's your South Node, too, that constantly sends you off in search of the perfect partner, the elusive soul mate. But you probably won't find the ideal partner until you know who *you* are and what you believe separate from your parents, family, authority figures, and anyone else who seeks to define you. That's where your Aries North Node comes in, where you must reach for your independence and freedom.

This node is about *you*—your independence rather than your codependence, about following your impulses, passions, and hunches rather than pressing the pause button on all that and doing something to please someone else. You're here this time to develop independence in thought, action, words, deeds. You're here to define your values according to who *you* are rather than through group consensus. Don't hesitate to take risks. Live like the *Star Trek* motto, boldly going where no man (or woman!) has gone before. Spiritually, you must sprout your wings and fly.

Easier said than done because it begins with solitude, a state of being that is foreign to you. As you begin to carve time for yourself, your Libra South Node may throw a major tantrum and urge you to get out and about, to hurry to that party, that get-together, that crowd of friends and strangers so that you can work the room. Resist those temptations, regardless of the comfort they promise. Ignore the criticisms of others—a difficult challenge because Libra South Node can't abide disapproval. The moment it detects disapproval, it causes you to run around apologizing to everyone, making excuses, laughing, oh, you were just kidding, really, and how about if we all get together tomorrow night for another party?

While your Libra South Node seeks to smooth things over with family, friends, coworkers, and everyone else who disapproves, your Aries North Node coaxes you to continue following impulses and forging your own path. It urges you to be spontaneous, to take off at a moment's notice with just a backpack and your ATM card and head for parts unknown. It demands that you become an individual separate from the collective called family, relationships, the community. It pushes you beyond consensus reality to test the limits of your soul. Once you're able to do that, you can successfully draw on your Libra South Node for harmony and balance.

Examples: Ram Dass, Jay Leno, Neil Armstrong.

Taurus North Node

Your soul seeks stability. With this fixed earth-sign node, your mission this time around is to define your values and realize your potential through everything the physical universe has to offer. It's a magnificent banquet of sensual delights, glittering beauty, unimagined riches. Your playground is physical reality, and you're supposed to build something meaningful and lasting while you're here. You're supposed to do it patiently, with resilience to any obstacles in your way, and whatever you tackle isn't done until it's done!

But your Scorpio South Node resists. It demands that you merge with whatever you're doing, that you become the project, the relationship, the ideal, and that you control it. It urges you to work privately, in secrecy, never letting on what your real agenda is. Your South Node investigates, researches, digs for answers and truth, and does it with a kind of terrible impatience and intensity. Your North Node asks that you take some things on faith and trust, that you let your soul speak, and allow events to unfold naturally, organically.

The Scorpio South Node suggests that in past lives, you've dealt with crisis, calamity, excessive sexuality, suspicion, deceit, profound transformation. This time around, one of your callings is to find the calm center of the storm. While everything is collapsing around you, while people you care for are losing their minds and swept up in high drama, you are as still and centered as Buddha.

To achieve this requires enormous practice and patience. Start meditating. Have a physical exercise routine that grounds you completely in physical reality. Yoga, running, swimming, tai chi, biking, the gym: do anything that heightens your awareness of your physical body. And be selfish. Yes, that last part sounds strange because we're taught from a young age to practice the opposite. But for the Taurus North Node, selfishness is self-empowerment. It means you put your own needs and desires first. You're a survivor. Once you do that, you won't feel the need to manipulate and control others.

The sensuality part of the Taurus North Node can be

troublesome because all too often you're working from the raw sexuality of your Scorpio South Node. Try to balance your sensuality. Instead of leaping into sexual relationships, ease yourself into sensual relationships. Experiment, follow your passions in areas other than sex. Otherwise, the seductiveness of the Scorpio North Node takes you into the really dark places—excessive sex, drugs, eating, spending, booze. Kurt Cobain, heroin addict and suicide, is the dark example of this nodal axis. Jacques Cousteau, underwater explorer, and J. R. R. Tolkien, author and creator of the Hobbit world, are more evolved examples. They built legacies and worlds and touched the lives of millions.

Other examples: Greg Allman, Lucille Ball, Pearl Buck, Harry Houdini

Gemini North Node

Your soul seeks diversity and wants to tell everyone about the journey. It is as if you're searching for a unified theory of the universe. Why, why, why? Your insatiable curiosity urges you to gather information to answer these burning questions and then to disseminate what you learn in any way you can, through many venues simultaneously. That's why you're here this time around. As one of the two signs symbolized by two of something, you multitask with ease.

Your Sagittarius South Node practically guarantees that you have a worldview or belief system that serves as a solid foundation in your life. It enables you to take in other people's belief systems and to compare and contrast them with your own. But when you're deep inside this comfort zone, you may think *your* belief system is the only truth. You may become intolerant of other people's spiritual and political beliefs and become a self-righteous stick in the mud.

It's likely that someone in your immediate circle of family and friends holds a belief system radically opposed to yours—parent, friend, partner, sibling, other relative, neighbor, coworker. This opposition probably leads to heated discussions and arguments. You're intent on convincing the other person that you're right, but this only creates further dissension. Instead, look at this person as your teacher. What can you learn from him or her? Listen with an open mind—and *really* listen. Also listen to what your soul whispers in the silence of your own mind and body. All too often, you're so intent on what you're going to say next that you're deaf to what the other person is saying and dismiss the whispers of your soul as nonsense.

Once you're aware of this pattern within yourself, you can catch yourself before it happens. Here are some guidelines to help you along:

Maintain your curiosity. It's one of your most valuable resources. When someone says something that pushes your buttons, ask yourself why you feel the way you do. Resistance is usually a clue to something within yourself that you should explore and strive to understand.

Always believe in yourself. Yes, this can be challenging for a Gemini North Node person. The twins that symbolize Gemini indicate a duality in your personality. One twin urges you to reach for the seemingly impossible and the other twin is laughing into her hands, snickering, *Yeah, right.* The best way to reconcile this duality is to develop a firm certainty about your talents that gets you through both good times and bad.

Examples: Susan Sarandon, Deepak Chopra, Bill Clinton

Cancer North Node

Your soul searches endlessly for someone or something to nurture—a person, a cause, a mission. You're here to navigate the world of your emotions and intuition, to learn to nurture others as you have nurtured yourself in past lives. You need to discover what makes you feel emotionally secure and to establish that security in your life in order to achieve your potential.

Your Capricorn South Node brings clear goals and ambitions. But because work, goals, and ambition are your comfort zone, you may feel you have to control everything and everyone within your environment. You have a heightened sense of responsibility too, believing that you must assume all the responsibility—at work, at home, with your family. Your desire to achieve and be recognized for those achievements suggests that you work extremely hard. But since these traits come from your South Node, you may not make significant progress until you're living from a centered, emotionally secure place.

If you can stay in tune with your emotions, they will act as an infallible guide. When a negative emotion surfaces, don't just shove it aside, but don't obsess about it, either. Take note of it—then release it and let it flow out of you. In the same way, you should release your need for control too. Control of others is an illusion fostered by your South Node. The only person you can control is yourself—your own thoughts, actions, choices, your home and personal environments. You can't control what others think, and do, and believe.

The Cancer/Capricorn axis is about how we live our private and public lives. Home and family versus career and profession, right brain versus left brain, the inner world versus the outer world. The Cancer North Node urges you to open your heart, to listen to the whispers of your intuition, to lower your defenses. As a cardinal water sign, this node also urges you to explore the unknown.

Examples: Elisabeth Kübler Ross, Erma Bombeck, Daphne du Maurier

Leo North Node

Your soul craves recognition, so baby, let the good times roll! You're here this time around to explore all forms of creative expression. You're supposed to learn what you love, what you truly desire, to have fun and be happy and how to manifest all of it. Along the way, you're also supposed to learn how to give and receive unconditional love. Sounds like a Disney movie, right?

Thanks to your Aquarius South Node, you're tolerant of people who are different from you, understand group dynamics, believe that we're all created equal. Your comfort zone is the world of ideas, the mind, the intellect. In fact, you may be more comfortable with ideas than you are with people or more comfortable putting the group before the individual, friends before partner and family. But your Leo North Node urges you to reach beyond ideas, beyond the group, to plunder the depths of your creativity and express yourself as an individual.

To navigate your Leo North Node successfully, here are some essentials:

- Nurture your creativity on a daily basis—not just whenever the spirit moves you. Once you learn to do this out of sheer enjoyment, your heart opens wide, and you start to realize that it's okay to be recognized for your achievements. It's okay to stand out from the group, to step out into the limelight and announce who you are.
- Ignore peer pressure. Whether this is difficult or easy depends on your age, of course, and the type of work you do.
- Create your life consciously. This requires awareness of your internal patterns. If you dislike some of the patterns you find, then reshape them or break them altogether.
- Don't depend on others to make you happy. Whenever you find yourself doing this, break the habit by

making a conscious decision to create your own joy. Then go do exactly that.

The beauty of the Leo North Node is about *you*—as an individual separate from any collective, any tribe. Love yourself first so that you're whole enough to love others.

Virgo North Node

Details, perfection: that's what your soul hopes to find this time around. You're the Swiss watchmaker, immersed in the details of creating the best watch in the world. All those intricate levers, the beveled glass face, the tiny little hands. Somehow you bring all these parts together and do it with utter perfection. Now apply the watchmaker analogy to your life. Somehow you're supposed to bring all these disparate bits and pieces together, analyze your experiences, and then manifest your beliefs and ideals in a practical way. The heart of your journey is self-perfection.

Your Pisces South Node offers some of the tools you need—a deep compassion, magnificent imagination, excellent intuition and healing ability. But when your inner critic is screaming, and you retreat into your Pisces South Node out of fear, then it's easy to become trapped in a victim consciousness. You know the routine—you're not good enough, not quite up to the task, there are others more qualified . . . and so on. First, silence the inner critic and resolve not to quit. Once you do that, the rest becomes easier.

When you feel that coiled serpent of fear in the pit of your stomach, tackle it. When you feel unable to make a decision, take a few deep breaths and try to explore your resistance. Don't obsess about the fear or tear it apart, scrutinizing every bit of it. Just acknowledge it and try to move through it.

Share your knowledge and skills with others, without

thought of compensation, but do so only because you want to, not because you feel obligated. By performing a service out of compassion rather than obligation, you mitigate the risk of victim consciousness.

Remain in the moment. Or, as Ram Dass said, *Be here now.* By being fully rooted in the moment, fear can't choke you. Read Eckhart Tolle's *The Power of Now.* By doing this, you also mitigate self-criticism. Any time you find yourself falling into this frame of mind, tell yourself that you're perfect as you are. *Love and approve of yourself.*

Your Virgo North Node urges you to navigate your daily life with reason, logic, and attention to detail. Once you're able to do this, you can draw on the South Node's power of imagination and intuition and can manifest virtually anything you desire.

Examples: Harrison Ford, Michael J. Fox, Kurt Vonnegut Jr.

Libra North Node

Your soul seeks balance: that's what this lifetime is about. Specifically, you're here to learn how to balance your needs with those of your partner, kids, friends, parents, and just about everyone else. You do it by walking in the other person's shoes.

Your comfort zone, of course, is the exact opposite of everything in the first paragraph. When you're afraid or uncertain, hurt or not feeling well, you retreat into an independent, *I can do it myself* frame of mind. You become selfish, intolerant of people who are different from you, and aren't open to any kind of compromise.

This *me first* attitude can be tough to overcome. But a good first step is to put others first. Yes, balk all you want, but it's the perfect place to start. Try it in small increments at first. Perhaps your partner needs the car at the same time that you're scheduled to have lunch with someone. Instead of insisting that you should get the car, make other arrangements. Or once a week or once a month, put someone else before yourself—let someone else go before you in the grocery store line, at the theater, the gas station. When you start doing this on a regular basis, then you're moving along the path of your North Node.

The Aries South Node prompts you to act decisively, impulsively, rashly because you assume you know what's going on, that you've got the right information and the right answers, and it inadvertently hurts someone. Better to pace yourself, ask questions, interact with people around you, and gather the information you need. Use tact and diplomacy rather than the blunt force of words and actions.

Once you're able to embrace the art of relating to others, then you can successfully draw on the independence and fearlessness of your Aries South Node.

Examples: Madonna, Frédéric Chopin, Anaïs Nin

Scorpio North Node

Your soul cries out for personal power. You're here to learn about using that personal power and magnetism in a positive, constructive way. Through intense experiences, you learn to purge your life of the nonessential or of whatever is stagnant in any area—relationships, jobs, careers, belief systems, habits. Then you can draw on your Taurus South Node to build what is durable, lasting.

You've got plenty of help on this journey. Your South Node gives you ample physical energy, practicality, and a stubborn determination that can see you through anything. Your Taurus South Node urges you to collect things—old books, stamps, art, jewelry—and it whispers, *I want to be surrounded by comfort and beauty.* But when you become obsessively attached to these possessions, to comfort and beauty for their own sake, you may attract a situation that teaches you possessions are just stuff we own.

Your work ethic is stellar, nose to the ground, immersed in whatever you're doing, for as long as it takes. But you make some things harder than they need to be. That's when you know you're being resistant to change. Yet change is part of what you're here to learn.

When change knocks at your door, invite it in for coffee and a chat. If you can't learn to do that, then circumstances will force change and it will be something profoundly transformative and probably not pleasant. Again, take small steps. Once a week, do something you've never done before. If you're terrified of heights, then the step could be something as dramatic as skydiving or as small as walking to the end of a high diving board.

Empower others by supporting their creative endeavors, spiritual values, raises and promotions, or anything else that is important to them. Use your exceptional intuition to gain insight into others—who are they in the privacy of their own hearts? What are their dreams, motives, and hopes? Use your intuition as often as you can. It's like a muscle. The more you use it, the stronger it becomes.

When you feel fear that threatens to send you scampering back to your comfort zone—to the nearest mall to shop for anything, to the comfort of rich foods, booze, drugs, the entire physical spectrum of sensual delights—stop. Breathe. Then investigate. What are you afraid of? Has it happened yet? Or are you afraid of something that *may* happen? Once you become aware of the pattern, you can break it, and when you break it, you're truly advancing along the path of your Scorpio North Node.

Examples: Tiger Woods, Edgar Allan Poe, Francis Ford Coppola

Sagittarius North Node

Your soul is seeking truth—specifically, your personal truth. It may sound like a major undertaking, but you can achieve it by using your intuitive ability to grasp the big picture rather than collecting endless, disconnected facts. The emphasis for you in this lifetime is on right brain, intuition, and imagination rather than logic and reason.

Your comfort zone—the Gemini South Node—is about information, facts, and figures. You can talk to anyone about anything, have terrific communication skills, and are one of the most social creatures in the zodiac. But when you feel threatened and afraid, you retreat into the darker aspects of your South Node—you talk when you should be listening, second-guess what people are thinking and feeling, make up facts, change rules in the middle of the game.

To use your North Node energy successfully, learn to trust yourself. To trust that inner voice of your intuition rather than the voices of everyone you consult before you make a decision. Strive to be more spontaneous. By allowing yourself freedom to take off at a moment's notice for an exotic port, to call in sick to work so you can attend your kid's play at school, to run off and get married in Vegas—well, it's part and parcel of the Sadge North Node. Honor it! Spontaneity is the manifestation of your intuition.

Strive to be more patient. Yeah, your Gemini South Node won't want to hear about it, but patience leads you to realize there are no quick fixes, and what's the big rush about, anyway?

Your North Node urges you to explore the unknown, to delve into spiritual, political, and metaphysical issues that people around you may not want to discuss. Just resist the temptation for self-righteousness and go about your business. This journey doesn't belong to anyone else. It's *yours*.

Examples: Drew Barrymore, Colin Powell, Zelda Fitzgerald, Angelina Jolie

Capricorn North Node

This time around, your soul seeks to control its own destiny. That's it in a nutshell, that's why you're here this time around. Already, your Cancer South Node is sobbing in a corner for that orphan on the news tonight, for the starving animals roaming the ruins of the latest disaster, for the most recent genocide somewhere. She doesn't want to hear about your ambitions, about you taking charge, about you controlling your destiny. So she pouts, she plunges you into a depression, and here *you* now sit, worrying yourself into a frenzy about stuff that hasn't even happened yet.

Let's back up. Your Cancer South Node offers plenty of tools for your journey—intuition and compassion, a sense of personal history, deep emotions that are your gauge to what's really going on in your life. Your South Node knows how to comfort anyone and anything in need that's hurting, that needs a shelter for the night—or for a year. This includes strays—cats, dogs, birds, whatever finds its way to your doorstep. The problem arises when you nurture and heal at the expense of your own needs or when you nurture others without first nurturing yourself. That's when your South Node becomes an impediment to achieving your potential. That's when you become like Rapunzel, trapped in her tower.

Your Capricorn North Node urges you to reach for everything you want and to achieve your potential through careful planning, strategizing, and hard work. But your Cancer South Node keeps hurling up images of your past mistakes, the issues you dealt with in childhood, how your mom or dad or family might object to what you're doing. You stop in your tracks, suddenly paralyzed and filled with doubt.

So your first order of business is to release the past.

The present is your point of power. The present is the place from which you write the script of your life. Honor the past, certainly, but recognize that your childhood, your parents, the bully in the sixth grade have no say over your life now.

Your second order of business—and imagine this as a Power Point presentation—is to stay tuned in to your feelings. But don't use your emotions to manipulate or control others. When you feel negative, don't dwell on it. Let the negativity wash through you, put one foot in front of the other, and move forward again.

Third point? Always express what you feel, when you feel it. Don't keep it all bottled up inside, as your South Node would like. Let it all out. Not only will you feel better, you'll be advancing on the path of your North Node.

By the way, you are in illustrious company! Examples: Indira Gandhi, Robert Redford, Oprah Winfrey

Aquarius North Node

Your soul searches for the collective experience, so this time around, you're here to learn about the importance of groups. Whether it's your family group, your community, a social circle, a political or spiritual movement, or some massive humanitarian effort that impacts the family of man, you're supposed to learn you can't always be the center of attention.

Your Leo South Node won't be happy about this development. It basks in applause and recognition. Yet your South Node also confers a terrific personality, great warmth and magnetism, and such radiant joy for life that if you can direct those qualities toward something larger than yourself, you will succeed at everything you do.

Your ego is well developed, thanks in large part to your Leo South Node. But ego alone won't do the job this time around. You're called upon to reach beyond the self, to extend yourself into the larger world, into the family of man, where you can make a tremendous difference, an integral component in a paradigm shift. You may do this through any number of creative venues, through your career, through volunteering, through your family life or the way you earn your living. But there are some definite steps you can take toward embracing your North Node, and foremost among them is to minimize drama.

Your South Node, see, is all about drama—in temperament, relationships, activities. In every single phase and area of your life there may be drama that your South Node stirs up, stokes. So strip away the drama, and what do you have? Someone with great talents and potential who can achieve that potential through shifting focus from self to the group, the tribe, the community, whatever it is.

Use your Leo South Node to cultivate and nurture your creative passions. If you can pour your emotions into a creative outlet, especially one that brings insights and pleasures to a larger group, you're well on your journey into your North Node.

Examples: Leonard Cohen, F. Scott Fitzgerald

Pisces North Node

Your soul wants to sink into the depths of imagination and intuition to discover the larger spiritual and creative picture that governs your life. This lifetime is about unearthing everything that is hidden in your life—power you have disowned, secrets that are kept in family vaults, in genealogy books, in the deepest reservoirs of your DNA. Your life is about bringing all this stuff into the light of day.

Your Virgo South Node brings a lot to the table for this journey—a discriminating intellect, a penchant for details, a remarkable ability to connect the dots in any situation, event, crisis, relationship. You name it, the Virgo South Node grasps how all the connections are made. Your South Node is terrific in any situation where rapid solutions are needed, where connections must be made at the speed of light, and where everything—all the information and details—are *correct*.

But, *correct* aside, this is the life where you go with the flow, avoid self-criticism, trust the universe to deliver what you need and desire, and develop your spiritual beliefs. All of this can be done through your daily work, but in terms of the big picture, the larger canvas of possibilities, the forest as opposed to the trees. Maybe you blog about your experiences. Maybe you set up a Web site that sells a particular product or service that helps others to reach their highest potential. The bottom line about the Pisces North Node is, ultimately, unknown and unknowable, too mystical to penetrate unless it's your conscious path, and too complex to decipher unless your intuitive skills are remarkably developed.

But remember this. When your Virgo South Node slaps its ruler across your desk in ninth grade and demands that you memorize how to conjugate the verb "to be" in Latin, Spanish, French, and German, it's your Pisces North Node that hurls your arm upward, knocking that ruler away, and says, "Chill. I'm on my own path to enlightenment."

Examples: Matt Damon, Naomi Campbell, Isadora Duncan

CHAPTER 12

By the Numbers

Even though this is an astrology book, we use numbers in some of the daily predictions because we're attempting to remain true to what Sydney Omarr did. The legendary astrologer was also a numerologist and combined the two forms in his work. So let's take a closer look at how the numbers work.

If you're familiar with numerology, you probably know your life path number, which is derived from your birth date. That number represents who you were at birth and the traits that you'll carry throughout your life. There are numerous books and Web sites that provide details on what the numbers mean regarding your life path.

But in the daily predictions, what does it mean when it's a number 9 day, and how did it get to be that number? In the dailies, you'll usually find these numbers on the days when the moon is transiting from one sign to another. The system is simple: add the numbers related to the astrological sign (1 for Aries, 2 for Taurus, etc.), the year, the month, and the day.

For example, to find what number June 14, 2011, is for a Libra, you would start with 7, the number for Libra, add 4 (the number you get when you add 2011 together), plus 6 for June, plus 5 (1+4) for the day. That would be 7+4+6+5 (sign + year + month+ day) = 22= 4.

So June 14, 2011, is a number 4 day for a Libra. It would be a 5-day for a Scorpio, the sign following Libra. So on that number 4 day, Libra might be advised that her organizational skills are highlighted, that she should stay focused, get organized, be methodical and thorough. She's building a creative future. Tear down the old in order to rebuild. Keep your goals in mind, follow your ideas.

Briefly, here are the meanings of the numbers, which are included in more detail in the dailies themselves.

1. Taking the lead, getting a fresh start, a new beginning
2. Cooperation, partnership, a new relationship, sensitivity
3. Harmony, beauty, pleasures of life, warm, receptive
4. Getting organized, hard work, being methodical, rebuilding, fulfilling your obligations
5. Freedom of thought and action, change, variety, thinking outside the box
6. A service day, being diplomatic, generous, tolerant, sympathetic
7. Mystery, secrets, investigations, research, detecting deception, exploration of the unknown, of the spiritual realms
8. Your power day, financial success, unexpected money, a windfall
9. Finishing a project, looking beyond the immediate, setting your goals, reflection, expansion.

Simple, right?

CHAPTER 13

Love and Timing in 2012 for Leo

In 2012, the stars stack up in favor of love and romance for you, Leo. If you know the favorable dates ahead of time, then you're better equipped to take advantage of them. So timing is where we look first.

If you're already in love, the dates can be useful for you too. You'll have a clearer idea when to romance the one you love, when to travel together, start a family, move, or make major changes in your living situation.

Venus, Mars, and Mercury are the inner, fast-moving planets, so their impacts tend to be more fleeting. Venus, for instance, stays in a sign for about three weeks, unless it's moving retrograde, then the transit can last several months. The transit of Venus through your sign goes from September 6 to October 3. But Venus in Gemini, where it turns retrograde this year, extends from April 3 to June 27.

Mercury, unless retrograde, zips through a sign in just under three weeks. Mars, unless retrograde, takes about forty-five days to move through a sign. Compare this to the snail of the zodiac—Pluto, which entered Capricorn in 2009 and won't leave until 2024.

Venus rules love and romance, Mars governs sexuality, Mercury rules communication. Beneficial angles among these three planets or from these planets to your sun sign usually indicate a winning combination for relationships. We'll include new and full moons in the love and romance equation too, since the moon rules our emotions and intuitive selves. New moons generally usher in new opportunities, and full moons bring insights, news, and a touch of craziness!

For the Single Leo

Lights! Drama! Action!

As one of the warmest and most passionate signs in the zodiac, you're forever on the lookout for romance, and the more theatrical and dramatic it is, the happier you are. You're one of those people who believe in love and romance, and it's tough for you to ever become cynical about it. You fit the adage: *If not for love, then what?*

The best dates for connecting with a potential partner on a deeply intuitive level occur when Venus is in your sign or that of another fire sign. Between February 8 and March 5, Venus in Aries transits your solar ninth house, so the initial attraction between you and someone else occurs because of your respective worldviews or spiritual beliefs.

Also circle September 6 to October 3, when Venus is in your sign. This period is one of the most romantic all year for you, Leo. Your head and heart are in complete agreement. Any relationship that begins during this period will have a dramatic, theatrical quality to it—flowers, moonlight walks, poetry, long conversations deep into the night.

The next set of dates to remember? December 15 to January 9, 2013, when Venus is in Sagittarius and your solar fifth house. This transit marks one of the most romantic times for you all year. You may not be interested so much in commitment as you are in having fun and enjoying yourself.

The best dates for meeting someone with whom you connect intellectually are when Mercury is in your sign. Those dates: June 25 to July 14, then August 8 to 31.

In between those two periods, Mercury is retrograde. While it's direct in your sign, though, you're at the top of your game, with your communication skills sharp and witty. Good backup dates? Look to Mercury transiting fellow fire sign Aries between March 2 and 12 and April 16 and May 9. In between, Mercury is retrograde. Another good period falls between December 10 and 31, when Mercury transits fellow fire sign Sagittarius. These transits fit your nature well and fire up your mind.

The period between October 6 and November 16 should stoke your sex life for sure. Mars will be moving through fellow fire sign Sagittarius in the romance area of your chart. Any relationship that starts during this transit may not last forever, but there should be enough drama and excitement so that you thoroughly enjoy yourself.

From June 11 to June 25, 2013, Jupiter transits compatible air sign Gemini in your solar eleventh house. This beautiful bonus expands your social contacts and makes it possible to meet a romantic partner through friends or through any groups to which you belong. People see you as an energetic individual, joyful, and filled with curiosity about the world around you and the people who inhabit that world. Any relationship that begins during this transit is likely to be exciting, happy, and fun. So open up your social calendar, and don't hesitate to strike up conversations with strangers.

While Jupiter transits earth sign Taurus between January 1 and June 22, romantic possibilities open up with coworkers, even bosses. This trend is especially strong when Venus travels with Jupiter between March 5 and April 3.

Although we're going to talk more about Uranus in Aries in chapter 15, let's look at this transit in terms of love and romance. Until March 2019, Uranus in fellow fire sign Aries will form a beneficial angle to your sun. It will bring excitement and unpredictability, idiosyncratic people, and radical, liberating change to your worldview and belief system. You may travel abroad more frequently, move overseas, go to college and/or graduate school. But throughout all of these exciting changes, you will be attracted romantically to a different kind of individual. If you're in a committed relationship already, then Uranus in Aries brings renewed excitement to the relationship.

This year, Uranus and Venus connect between February 8 and March 5, so anyone you meet during this period is going to appeal to you on a wildly visceral level. You may not have a clue why you're attracted to this person, but attracted you will be.

A Venus retrograde isn't as eventful as Mercury retrogrades are. This year's, in Gemini, occurs between May 15 and June 27. It can heighten tensions with a partner, mostly through misunderstanding.

Mercury (communication) turns retrograde three times a year, so be sure to note those dates and ramifications in the Big Picture section for Leo. A relationship that begins under any of those retrograde periods will be messed up in the communication department. Those dates:

March 12–April 4, in Aries
July 14–August 8, in Leo
November 6–26, in Sagittarius

For the Committed Leo

The dates listed above for the single Leo also apply to the committed Leo, but for different reasons. When Venus transits Sagittarius and your solar fifth house, for instance, you may want to plan something special for yourself and the one you love. Show your appreciation for your partner in some way—flowers, a romantic dinner, a weekend getaway, or all of the above!

Venus transits Sagittarius between December 15 and January 9, 2013, so that should be an especially good time for you and your partner. The holidays will be memorable, and you and your partner will not only enjoy each other's company, but may decide to work together on a creative project. Another good time frame is when Venus transits compatible air sign Libra and your solar third house between October 28 and November 21. The communication between you and your partner should be particularly strong. You may be searching for the right neighborhood in anticipation of a move.

During the above time period, Venus is traveling with Saturn in Libra, and the combination brings a seriousness to the relationship. This could be when you take your relationship to the next level—you move in together, get engaged or married, decide to start a family.

If you're doing any of the above, avoid the Mercury retrogrades mentioned earlier.

So let's look for some dates this year that favor marriage and which dates you might want to avoid:

- When Venus is in your sign between September 6 and October 3
- On or after the new moon in your sign on August 17
- On or after the full moon in your sign on February 7
- On or after a new or full moon in your partner's sign
- Avoid eclipse dates
- Any time between June 25 and July 14 and August 8 and 31, when Mercury is moving direct in your sign

For All Leos

Keep in mind that any relationships which begin this year will be impacted by Uranus in Aries, which is forming a beneficial angle to your sun. Earlier in the chapter we talked about the kind of impact this can have on your relationships. Thanks to Saturn in Libra until October 5, all your relationships this year will be more structured and more serious.

Other Considerations

Strange events and feelings are triggered by eclipses. There are three this year that fall in Gemini in your solar eleventh house. The solar eclipse on May 20 is one of them. This brings about new opportunities to communicate in some way—through writing, a blog, teaching, public speaking. It forms a beneficial angle to your sun.

The lunar eclipse on June 4, in Sagittarius and your solar fifth house, stirs emotions concerning your love life. It should be positive.

The lunar eclipse in Gemini on November 28 brings up emotions concerning your social life. Any news you hear should be positive.

CHAPTER 14

Career Timing in 2012 for Leo

Leos are dramatic individuals, so it's not surprising that many of you end up in professions where you can express that dramatic flair—in the arts, on stage, in the movies, in prominent business positions, in organizations where you can lead. This year, lucky you, expansive Jupiter spends six months in your career area. In addition, Uranus is transiting fellow fire sign Aries, forming a beneficial angle to your sun throughout this year—and until 2019. In short, 2012 promises to be an exciting year professionally, with many changes and opportunities.

Some possibilities: you get a substantial raise and promotion; you find a job that pays more and is more in alignment with your values and ideals; you start your own business; you attract unusual individuals who are helpful to you professionally. Or, while Jupiter transits your career area between January 1 and June 11, you may move your company overseas, be transferred overseas, or travel abroad more frequently for business.

However the specifics unfold for you, one thing is for sure: in the professional arena nothing will be predictable, and all of it will be exciting and expansive in a way it hasn't been for a long time.

In 2012, when paradigms are shifting, take stock early on. Are you happy in your job? Is your career satisfying? What kind of work would you do if you had the opportunity? Would you like to go to graduate school to study something else? Is there a talent or interest you have that you would like to develop more fully? Does your job just pay your bills, or is it a focal point in your life?

Once you answer these questions, you can start putting the energies of 2012 to work for you. So let's take a closer look at how you can create a professional life that you love. If you already have that, then let's see how you can improve what is nearly perfect.

Why 2012?

Most metaphysical teachers talk about the importance of being fully present, fully grounded in the moment. In *The Power of Now*, *The Law of Attraction,* and *Seth Speaks,* the message is the same: our point of power is the present. We may cling to the past and yearn for the future, but neither will bring us the power we have in this moment, in this breath, in this present action.

So before this year is already behind you, make a list of your professional goals and dreams. If you haven't attained all of them, what's holding you back? Chances are that the only thing holding you back is . . . well, *you*. Perhaps you think you might fail at something new. Maybe you think you lack the proper education or skills. In other words, your insecurity could be your obstacle to attaining your goals.

As a fixed fire sign, you don't change your opinions and beliefs easily. But in a year when paradigms are shifting, when the larger world is in flux, it's to your advantage to work consciously with your beliefs and change the ones that may be holding you back.

Dates to Watch For

January 1 to June 11: Jupiter's transit through Taurus and your career area. Expansion, expansion. Jupiter has been transiting this area since June 2011, so you're accustomed to the energy. But you've got another six months this year to enjoy this transit, so make the best of it.

During this transit, be sure to circle the period from March 5 to April 3, when Venus travels with Jupiter through Taurus in your career area. Any time these two planets travel together, magic happens. This would be the time to schedule a pitch, for example, or ask for a raise, start your business, gather support for an idea or project.

Another nice period professionally occurs between September 6 and October 3, when Venus transits your sign. This is one of the best periods all year to push your professional agenda forward. Other people will be receptive to you and your ideas, and you shouldn't encounter road blocks. But if you do, practice nonresistance and watch the blocks evaporate.

Another period to anticipate is from December 15 to January 9, 2013, when Venus transits fellow fire sign Sagittarius in your solar fifth house. This transit heightens your creativity, so reserve it for brainstorming with colleagues, experimenting with new approaches, and implementing new ideas.

What the Moons Say

New moons generally mean new opportunities. Full moons are usually equated with news, insights, and a tad of craziness tossed in just to keep things interesting!

The April 21 new moon in Taurus and your career area is one for which to anticipate and plan. It should usher in new professional opportunities that are in alignment with your ideals. Thanks to a beneficial angle from Neptune, there's a spiritual and creative quality to this new moon that may urge you to take a more spiritual approach to what you do.

The new moon in your sign on August 17, with both Saturn and Mars forming beneficial angles to it, suggests that any new opportunity that surfaces deserves your serious consideration. It may involve working in some capacity with groups of people and suggests a lot of activity around this date.

The new moon in fellow fire sign Aries on March 22 should be a beauty for you. Mercury and Uranus form tight conjunctions to the new moon, suggesting new opportunities that come out of the blue to travel abroad or to expand your client base overseas.

Because your friends are generally very important to you, the solar eclipse on May 20 is a date to anticipate. This eclipse occurs in your eleventh house of friends and groups and should trigger new opportunities to meet people. Some of these individuals may be helpful to you professionally. So keep your social calendar open around the time of this eclipse.

The new moon in Libra on October 15 could also be quite positive. Libra is an air sign compatible with your fire-sign sun, so it looks as if you may have new opportunities for communication. Perhaps you start a blog or build a Web site for your company or for your own business. Or you start a newsletter. Or do some public speaking.

What the Planetary Transits Reveal

There are a number of important transits in 2012 that are favorable for professional matters. We've talked about some of them already, but let's broaden our scope.

Once Jupiter enters Gemini and your solar eleventh

house on June 11, you're in for a very nice treat. The expansion that took place professionally during the last year with Jupiter's transit through your career area now pays off in other ways, as your dreams and wishes expand, taking you, perhaps, in new unimagined directions. Your social venue also expands, and helpful people enter your life. This transit lasts until June 25, 2013.

From March 2 to 12 and April 16 to May 9, Mercury transits Aries and your solar ninth house. This could be the period where your client base expands to overseas markets, where you travel abroad for business, or when you have increased contact with people overseas.

Between June 25 and July 14, Mercury transits your sign, heightening your communication abilities.

The period from October 6 to November 16 favors grasping and exploring the larger picture of your creative goals. Mercury will be in fellow fire sign Sagittarius then, so one thing on your agenda is having fun!

Saturn's Movements

Until October 5, Saturn is in Libra in your solar third house, strengthening all your communication abilities. There may be a seriousness in your tone now, and you find the proper structure for your self-expression. Overall, this transit is beneficial for you (and has been since October 2009).

Once Saturn enters Scorpio on October 5—for a run of two and a half years—your comfort level may not be quite as high. Scorpio is a water sign, and just on the most basic levels, water and fire don't mix! That said, you'll be able to delve into the most fundamental compartments of your own psyche to grasp, rifle around, and correct attitudes and habits that hamper your progress. There may be some delays and restrictions related to your domestic life, which in turn impacts your professional life.

Parting Thoughts About Career Matters

Whenever you feel discouraged about your career or anything else this year, get out and do something you enjoy. Leos enjoy people, theater, movies, books and bookstores, parties, shopping, travel ... well, you get the idea. Do what you love. Do what makes your heart sing.

The more you do what you enjoy, the better you feel. The better you feel, the more likely it is that you'll attract experiences, people, and situations that increase that feeling. The law of attraction.

CHAPTER 15

Navigating Uranus in Aries in 2012

Even though we talked about Uranus in Aries in the last chapter, as it relates to your career, let's take a general look here at its impact on your life generally.

Uranus's transit through Aries until early March 2019 will be forming a beneficial angle to your sun. This transit will bring a lot of excitement and positive change into your life. Your personal freedom will be very important to you. It's possible that certain relationships and situations will fall out of your experience, especially those that restrict your freedom in some way or that don't allow you genuine self-expression.

One repercussion of Uranus's trine to your sun is that it may be difficult for other people to pin you down, to define you. That's fine with you, but it may be confusing for the people around you—family, partners, friends. Your belief system may undergo radical change too, but it's all positive for you. You may take up the study of astrology, start developing your intuition, go to grad school, college, or law school.

In any area where your life is stuck in a rut or routine, Uranus is going to shake things up and sweep things clean, and when the dust settles, you'll be amazed that you have arrived in a better place.

During these seven years, your need for greater and more genuine self-expression can manifest itself in different ways. You might, for example, give away all your clothes and completely revamp your wardrobe. You might decide to get body piercings, tattoos. You might question your sexuality. You might just take off with a backpack and your ATM card and hit the road. One way or another, the genuine you will be uncovered.

During tumultuous times, meaningful coincidences—synchronicities—tend to proliferate. So pay attention to these nudges from the universe. Decipher the messages, and know that every time you experience one of these, you're on the right track or are being warned that a particular path isn't in your best interest.

What's particularly notable about the Uranus transit is that from June 11, 2012, to June 25, 2013, it fits in nicely with Jupiter's transit through Gemini. The two planets form harmonious angles to each other. The unpredictability and chaos Uranus brings allow Jupiter to expand the possibilities of new experiences, relationships, and situations. Until October 5, Saturn in Libra is moving in opposition to Uranus. If we look at Saturn as representing the established way of doing things and Uranus as the new way, there can be some significant tug-of-wars. Just let the new win!

Here are some possibilities that may unfold with this Uranus transit. The abrupt changes can be troubling, but the end result seven years from now will be beneficial to you.

Possibilities

1. You land a dream job
2. You change jobs
3. Your income plunges
4. Your income soars
5. Relationships break apart
6. New, more exciting relationships enter your experience
7. You take more risks

8. The risks pay off
9. The people around you are confused by your behavior
10. You start your own business
11. Loss of a loved one
12. Child leaves home
13. Child returns home
14. You find a gap in the market that your product or services fill
15. You change careers
16. Your creativity flourishes
17. Unusual psychic or spiritual experiences
18. Your marital status changes
19. You inherit money, win the lottery, or earn more than you dreamed possible
20. Your belief system undergoes radical change
21. A tremendous thrust toward personal freedom
22. You go to college or graduate school or seek additional training
23. You start meditating
24. You encounter people from past lives

These possibilities are just that—merely possibilities. To really grasp how the transit will affect you, get out your natal chart. Look at the house where Aries is found in your chart. Look for any planets you have in Aries. These areas—plus your sun—are the ones that will be impacted more strongly by Uranus's transit through Aries.

Turn to the natal chart at the end of chapter 9. This woman is a Capricorn with a tenth-house sun, has a Leo moon in the fifth house, and has Aries rising at 19 degrees and 54 minutes—19♈54. The rising is the cusp of her first house, which governs the self. So Uranus has been in her twelfth house since it was at 17 degrees and 16 minutes of Pisces—17♓16—the cusp of her twelfth house.

During this period, with Uranus stirring up all the hidden stuff in her unconscious, she got married and divorced, landed a great job in an assisted living facility as the wellness director (she's an RN), was nearly forced to resign by an abusive boss, fought it, held onto her job, and got a raise. All three of her sons left home during this transit—to jobs and college. She moved twice.

As of this writing, in 2010, she is now accustomed to this Uranian energy and is planning to branch out as a consultant in her field, helping other men and women to navigate the labyrinth of health care and options for their aging parents and grandparents. In other words, she sees a gap in the health-care market and is figuring out ways she might fill that gap. That's the innovation part of the equation.

Once Uranus enters Aries in March 2011, it will be on its approach to her rising—an important, major life transit. The rising, as the portal to our charts, is where our experiences enter into our lives. The closer Uranus gets to her ascendant, the more unpredictable, exciting, and high energy her life will become. The conjunction is exact in March 2016, but she may start feeling it as early as the summer of 2012, when Uranus reaches 8 degrees Aries (eleven degrees from her rising) before it turns retrograde. It turns direct again in early December 2012 and gets to within 7 degrees of her ascendant by July 2013, before it retrogrades again. By July 2014, Uranus gets to within 3 degrees of her rising before it retrogrades once more. In late May 2015, it hits her rising.

What all this means is that each year as Uranus inches closer to that exact hit on her rising sign, she feels a progressively stronger urge to break free of any restrictions that are holding her back. The closer it gets to her rising, the closer it also gets to forming beautiful angles—trines—to her South Node in Leo (fourth house)—☋12♌32, and her natal moon and Pluto in Leo in the fifth house—☽21♌48 and ♇22♌54. So while she's feeling this tremendous urge for freedom, Uranus is making it easier for her to bring about major changes in her emotional, inner life (moon). A new relationship could enter the picture, and it will be one wild, wonderful ride, different from anything she has experienced before. She might move.

With Pluto thrown into the mix, she has a marvelous opportunity to understand her innermost being—the unconscious beliefs and attitudes that have resulted in negative situations or relationships in the past. The trine to Pluto from Uranus gives her enormous personal power. One of her sons (fifth house) may get married. She might do or create something so innovative that she is recognized for it by peers. The trine to her South Node and sextile to her North Node in Aquarius in the eleventh house—☊12≈32—suggests that people she has known in the past (this life or others) may surface. She will have an opportunity to attain her dreams.

These possibilities are due to the transit of just one planet, Aries. So when you look at your natal chart to see where Uranus's impact will be felt most strongly, look beyond your sun sign. Look at other planets and points too.

Notice, for instance, that in this same chart the woman has Jupiter in Taurus in her first house—♃10♉59. This means that during the first six months of 2012—as well as the last six months of 2011—this woman enjoys a Jupiter return. This is when Jupiter returns to the place it was when you were born, which happens every twelve years. It marks the beginning of a new cycle. So even while Uranus is upsetting the apple cart, she's benefiting tremendously from her Jupiter return during the first six months of 2012. New opportunities will surface in her personal life, she may have opportunities to travel internationally, she might get married.

In addition, see her Capricorn sun up there in the tenth house—☉13♑ 03? Pluto in Capricorn is now transiting her tenth house—her career area—creating profound change in her professional path. In March 2014, Pluto will conjunct her sun, so as it approaches, the changes will become more intense. She'll feel a greater urge to alter her path and will gain insight into her own motives and psyche.

So when you look at your own chart, study how the other transiting planets are affecting your natal blueprint. You probably will find there's a balance. If one area of your life is chaotic, there will be other areas where life is truly exciting and prosperous.

Dates to Watch For

March 22: On or around this new moon in Aries, life is going to feel quite chaotic. Uranus will be close to this moon, suggesting sudden, unexpected events that catch you by surprise. You may have a chance to travel abroad, go to college or graduate school, or even move overseas. But you'll need to stay alert to seize these opportunities as they appear.

May 20: Solar eclipse in Gemini in your solar eleventh house. This one attracts new communication opportunities within groups and with friends. In fact, there may be a lot of new people entering your life around this time—interesting, exciting people. The eclipse stimulates your social life.

June 4: Lunar eclipse in fellow fire sign Sagittarius in your solar fifth house. News about a relationship or a creative project comes your way, and the news looks positive!

One possible trouble period this year may occur between **November 16 and December 25,** when Mars joins Pluto in Capricorn, in your solar sixth house. The Pluto transit is going to profoundly change your daily work between now and 2024, when it finally moves into Aquarius. But whenever Mars joins Pluto, there can be power struggles with authority, with coworkers and employees, and your ambition ramps up. Try to use the energy constructively by applying it to your work.

Between **February 8 and March 5,** Venus and Uranus are traveling together in Aries, a surefire combination that revs up your love life—perhaps with someone from another country or with an individual who works in higher education, the law, or publishing. Then, between **September 6 and October 3,** Venus transits your sign and forms a beneficial angle to Jupiter, so this period should be very pleasant. Think: romantic interludes, muse up close and personal.

Venus is retrograde in Gemini between **May 15 and June 27,** a period when there may be some bumps in the road regarding romance, friends, and attaining your dreams.

CHAPTER 16

Leo and Mars in 2012

Mars. Probably no other planet in our solar system has fueled so much speculation and imaginative books and movies. Just walk into the science fiction section of your local bookstore, and take a look at the cover art for the latest books. Chances are you'll find one or several that feature Mars.

Our fascination with the red planet probably began with the publication of H. G. Wells's *War of the Worlds* in 1898. The novel's story idea is simple: Mars is dying and the Martians flee their world and invade Earth, planning to take over the planet and all its resources. Their first attack on London with advanced weaponry seems to ensure their victory, but they're eventually defeated by germs—Earth germs.

Edgar Rice Burroughs had a thing or two to say about Mars too. In 1911, he wrote *A Princess of Mars,* the first of eleven novels about the red planet. The protagonist was John Carter, a confederate Civil War veteran who is transported to Mars. Over the course of the series, Carter settles into life on his adopted planet—he gets married, involved in Martian politics, and fights the good fight.

In 1951, Ray Bradbury's *Martian Chronicles* twisted the idea of Martian as invader in a new way. Human settlers arrive on Mars, and the Martians are killed by the bacteria that the humans bring with them. But these

Martians capture our hearts because they are beautiful people of an ancient civilization.

Robert Heinlein, with his 1961 publication of *Stranger in a Strange Land*, brought another curve into the Martian theme. His story centers on a human born on Mars, the only survivor of the first manned space mission to the planet. The protagonist, Valentine Michael Smith, is raised and educated by Martians, then is returned to Earth as a young man, with the sensibilities of a human, the perspective of an alien, and incredible psychic powers.

In terms of TV, there was *My Favorite Martian*, and in film a host of many forgettable movies. An exception was *Total Recall,* based on a Philip K. Dick short story. In the film, Arnold Schwarzenegger plays a man haunted by suppressed memories—specifically, journeys to Mars. The story has all the complex hallmarks of Philip K. Dick—paranoia, duplicity, deep and powerful secrets, and plenty of corrupt bad guys. The ending takes place on Mars, when atmospheric gases and water are freed from deep within the planet's rocks.

But what do we actually know about the red planet? We know that it bears some similarities to Earth and may have been habitable at one time in the past—and may be in the future. Its surface has been dramatically changed by volcanism, impacts by asteroids and meteors and other celestial bodies, violent movements in its crust, and great cyclonic dust storms that frequently swallow the entire planet. Its polar ice caps grow and recede, like ours, with the change of seasons. Near the poles, the layered soil indicates that the planet's climate has changed more than once. Its ancient volcanoes, once powered from the heat of the Martian core, rise against the starkness with a kind of fierce purity. The largest volcano, Olympus Mons, is seventeen miles high and may be the largest in the solar system. There's also a titanic canyon about the size of the distance between New York and L.A.

Due to several unmanned missions to Mars, our

knowledge about the planet is growing. Thanks to the Mars Odyssey spacecraft, launched in 2001, it's now believed that billions of years ago Mars was inundated by the largest floods in the solar system. No one knows where all that water went, but the Mars Odyssey detected substantial quantities of water mixed into the soil about three feet down, near the Martian south pole.

On August 12, 2005, the Mars Reconnaissance Orbiter was launched, and it entered the orbit of Mars on March 10, 2006. After five months of a technique called aerobraking—a three-step procedure that cuts in half the fuel needed to achieve a lower, more circular orbit—the orbiter started its scientific tests. These lasted until November 2008. Since then, NASA has released thousands of high-resolution photos of the Mars surface that have broadened our knowledge about the fourth planet from the sun. The photos may answer the basic questions about whether Mars had water, if it was once inhabited and if so, was it destroyed by a catastrophe? Can it sustain human life in the future?

Images of recent impact craters on Mars have revealed subsurface ice midway between the planet's north pole and equator. A geologist with the U.S. Geological Survey claims he has found evidence of an extensive cave system among ancient volcanoes at Mars's equator. He believes the depressions visible in the high-resolution photos are consistent with lava flows on Earth that produce caves. Some of these depressions are more than 60 miles long and 150 feet across. If the geologist is right, then caves may provide early colonists with protection from the harsh environment and lethal cosmic rays.

On a clear night at certain times of the year, you can walk outside after dark and glimpse Mars in the sky, a speck of rose-tinted light between 56,000,000 and 399,000,000 kilometers from Earth. Its diameter is a little more than half that of Earth, the length of a Martian day is 24.6 Earth hours, a Martian year is 1.88 Earth years, and gravity on the surface is about a third of Earth's. Ninety-five percent of the atmosphere consists of carbon dioxide; it's toxic. It has two moons, but both are so small that they may not be moons but just rock formations that have gotten trapped in the planet's gravitational pull. They are named after the two squires who served Ares, the Greek god of war: Phobos, which means "fear," and Deimos—"panic."

Mars in Astrology

To the ancient Greeks, he was Ares, a savage god who was little more than a bloodthirsty SOB. In the *Iliad,* Zeus says it like he sees it, that he finds Ares, his son, completely odious because he enjoyed nothing but "strife, war, and battles." On Olympus, he was intensely disliked for his blind violence and brutality.

This theme is beautifully illustrated in the movie *Gladiator.* Times are brutal, and brute strength is held in such high esteem that the populace turns out to watch men kill each other in the stadium. Not surprisingly, Aries Russell Crowe won an Oscar for his performance. Now skip ahead a couple thousand years. In *The Running Man,* one of the novellas that Stephen King wrote as Richard Bachman, this same theme is repeated, but now the protagonist (played by Arnold Schwarzenegger in the film) is running for his life on national TV and surviving by his wits and brute strength. Same theme, different century.

But aggression, survival, and war are only one side of Mars. The Greek side. On the Roman side, he was called by the name we know him—Mars. He was first and foremost the god of agriculture—the protector of cattle, the preserver of corn—and was associated with the woodpecker, the horse, and the wolf. As the husband of Rhea Silvia, a vestal virgin, he fathered Romulus and Remus, who were suckled by a wolf.

The connection between Mars and sex probably

came about as a result of Ares's affair with the goddess Aphrodite. She was married to a cripple, Hephaestus, and compared to him Ares was handsome, dashing, courageous—all the things the Olympians looked for in a mate. Ares, of course, took advantage of the situation, and their lustful encounters on the "marriage couch" became well known to the other gods when Hephaestus ensnared the adulterous couple in an invisible net.

In 2012, Mars makes it through six signs and spends less than a week in a seventh. Let's take a look at what these transits mean for you, Leo.

Important Dates

January 1 to July 3: Mars in Virgo, your solar second house of finances. This transit stimulates everything connected to your money—how you earn it, spend it, what you think about it. You may be working longer hours or doing twice the work to earn your daily bread, Leo. But you don't mind hard work if you're doing something enjoyable. If, however, your job is just a job, i.e., you find little pleasure in it, then this transit may feel like drudgery to you.

With Mars in Virgo, you're urged to stay on top of your finances, to be efficient and precise in what you buy.

July 3 to August 23: Mars in Libra, transiting your solar third house. You'll like this transit. Libra, an air sign, is compatible with your fire-sign sun and helps to bring balance to your busy life. During this transit, your daily life is likely to be quite hectic—but in a good way!—and your conscious mind will be chewing away at all sorts of things. The emphasis will be on communication, so perhaps you start a blog, put up a Web site, start a newsletter. You may have more contact with siblings and other relatives during this transit too.

August 23 to October 6: Mars in Scorpio in your solar

fourth house. This transit may feel pretty intense, Leo. Unless you have a lot of water-sign planets in your natal chart, you may feel overwhelmed during this time frame. There could be a lot of activity at home—people coming and going, moving in or out, conflicts, confrontations, *stuff* that requires your attention. However, your sex life during this period should be amazing, and if you and your partner can agree on the big details, the smaller details will take care of themselves.

October 6 to November 16: Mars in Sagittarius, your fifth house of romance and creativity. With this transit, your focus is on your own enjoyment. Any relationship that begins during this period is apt to be passionate, exciting, and fun. You and your partner may travel overseas together; if it's something you both enjoy, you may work on a creative project together, or you could even move in together. A lot of your energy is poured into your creativity—a novel you're writing, the refurbishment of your home, or something else about which you're passionate. Mars forms a beneficial angle to your sun when it's in Sagittarius, so you're in good shape during this transit.

November 16 to December 25: Mars in Capricorn, your solar sixth house. This one really accelerates activity with your work routine. You may suddenly have more work than you bargained for, may have increased responsibilities, may be doing not only your job but someone else's too.

Capricorn is symbolized by the goat, an animal that can climb virtually anything, but moving only at its own pace. It can't be rushed or hurried—unless that's what it wants. So to make the most of this transit, move as the goat moves. Know where you're going, and know your end point. Have a plan B. Be focused in your work goals.

December 25 to February 2, 2013: Mars in Aquarius in your solar seventh house. This one brings your focus to personal and business partnerships. If you've been looking for a business partner, this transit could attract the person you need. If you're involved in a relationship already, you and your partner may take things to the next level. You move in together, get engaged or married, or start a family. However it unfolds, it's a time of high energy and cutting-edge ideas.

CHAPTER 17

The Big Picture for Leo in 2012

Welcome to 2012, Leo. This year is marked by leadership, independence, and an entrepreneurial spirit. It's the year for fresh starts, new beginnings, new experiences and people. Let's take a closer look.

Pluto, the snail of the zodiac, starts off the year in Capricorn in your solar sixth house, where it has consistently been since November 2008. You're accustomed to its energy now. Its transit, which lasts until 2024, is bringing profound and permanent change globally, evident in the economic challenges that now face the U.S. Most institutions are in the throes of great change—the healthcare industry, the petroleum and insurance industries, mortgages/lending, housing, aviation, even the Internet. You name it, and Pluto's fingerprint can be found.

On a personal level, this planet's transit through your daily work area has been altering your work schedule and bringing profound and permanent change. You're more aware of your own needs and motives now, particularly as they pertain to your career ambitions. You may be discovering that your attitudes and beliefs about your work are changing. If you change jobs during this long transit, it's likely that you'll find work that is much different from what you were doing when this transit began.

Neptune entered Pisces and your solar eighth house on April 4, 2011. But by early August 2011, it had slipped back into Aquarius. On February 3, 2012, it enters Pisces again and won't move on until January 2026. This transit forms a challenging angle to your sun, so its initial impact can create confusion. For hints about what this may mean for you, look back to that period in 2011 when Neptune was in Pisces.

Neptune symbolizes our higher ideals, escapism, fiction, spirituality, and our blind spots. It seeks to dissolve boundaries between us and others. One possible repercussion of this transit is prolonged religious wars, which proliferated during Uranus's transit in Pisces from early 2003. On a personal level, though, Neptune's transit through your solar eighth house suggests that you may try to integrate your spiritual beliefs more readily into other areas of your life. There may be some confusion concerning a partner's finances, about wills, inheritances, taxes. It's a wonderful placement for the study and investigation of psychic phenomena and for intuitive development. You could embark on some sort of spiritual quest that takes you to sacred sites overseas. You may meet people you have known in past lives.

Uranus entered Aries and your solar ninth house in March 2011. This transit probably has already attracted new and unusual people into your life and will continue to do so. It may be altering the landscape of your belief system and spiritual views in new, unprecedented ways. You may have opportunities to travel abroad that occur suddenly and without warning. By all means, take advantage of these opportunities. They will broaden your worldview and could lead to unexpected new relationships and opportunities.

Since Uranus is forming a beneficial angle to your sun until 2019, your life is apt to be more exciting and unpredictable. Your need for greater freedom will cause you to get rid of any relationships or situations that are restrictive. You are urged to reach for and embrace the new, the innovative, the different.

Saturn begins the year in Libra in your solar third house. It has been there since the summer of 2010 and will be there until October 2012. This transit brings greater structure to your creative endeavors, your relationship with your kids, and everything you do for fun and pleasure. Instead of taking a vacation just to get away, for example, you might travel for research or on a spiritual quest with a group of like-minded individuals.

Once Saturn enters water sign Scorpio on October 5, the transit won't have the same level of comfort. It will be in your solar fourth house of the home, so you may discover certain elements in your domestic life that are restricting your freedom in some way. A parent may need additional help and support. An adult child could move home. However the specifics unfold for you, you will have to make better and more efficient use of your time.

One of your best periods this year falls between June 11, 2012, and June 25, 2013, when Jupiter transits compatible air sign Gemini and your solar eleventh house. This transit should expand your social venues—you join new groups, make new friends, link up with individuals who share your passions and interests. You may do more public speaking or become involved in publicity and promotion for your company's products or your own services. If you're self-employed, you could see a marked expansion to overseas markets.

Between January 1 and June 11, Jupiter transits earth sign Taurus and your career area. This transit has been going on since June of 2011, so you already should have seen professional expansion. That trend will continue. You may find that your career options broaden or that you launch your own business, and it takes off beyond your wildest dreams.

From January 1 to June 11, Jupiter transits compatible earth sign Taurus, a wonderful aspect that expands your circle of friends and your wishes and dreams and opens doors to new opportunities in many different areas of your life. You should be acquainted with Jupiter's energies by now. It's been in Taurus since June of 2011 and should continue to bring luck and expansion into your life.

They say that timing is everything, so with that in mind let's look at some specific areas in your life in 2012.

Romance/Creativity

The most romantic and creative time for you all year falls between December 15 and January 9, 2013, when Venus transits Sagittarius and your solar fifth house. If you're not involved before this transit begins, you probably will be before the transit ends. And if you're not, it won't matter because you're having too much fun. Your creativity soars during this transit, too, with your muse up close and personal. This would be an excellent period to travel with a partner.

Another good period: September 6 to October 3, when Venus is moving direct in your sign. Things really seem to flow your way then in many areas, but particularly with romance and creative ventures. The best time for serious involvement and deepening commitment in an existing relationship occurs when Venus transits Aquarius, your seventh house of partnerships, which occurs between January 1 and 14. You and your partner may decide to move in together, get engaged, or get married. Just be sure that you don't do any of this under a Mercury retrograde. Take a look under the appropriate section below to find out when Mercury will be retrograde this year.

Other good backup dates: October 6 to November 16, when Mars transits fellow fire sign Sagittarius. This stirs up a lot of activity with a partner.

Career

Usually, you should look for Venus and Jupiter transits to your career area. This year, lucky you, Jupiter in Taurus transits your career area from January 1 to June 11. Venus transits it between March 5 and April 3. So this second period, when the two planets are traveling together, is the time to circle. Use this period for pitching ideas, socializing with peers and bosses, asking for a raise, applying for a promotion, or for launching your own business. Use this period for pushing your professional agenda forward. You'll find all the support you want or need.

Another nice period is when Mercury joins Jupiter in Taurus, between May 9 and 24. Your communication skills are especially strong then, and you have just the right amount of stubbornness to take things to the finish line.

Between November 16 and December 25, Mars in Capricorn links up with Pluto, and both planets form a beneficial angle to your career area. The energies of this powerful duo should be used carefully. You can achieve a great deal professionally, but you don't want to alienate people with an overbearing attitude.

Best Times For

Buying or selling a home: November 21 to December 15, when Venus is in Scorpio and your solar fourth house; October 5 to 29, when Mercury transits the same sign and house.

Family reunions: Any of the dates above or when Venus is in your sign between September 6 and October 3.

Financial matters: The period from October 3 to 28, when Venus transits Virgo and your solar second house.

Signing contracts: When Mercury is moving direct!

Mercury Retrogrades

Every year, Mercury—the planet of communication and travel—turns retrograde three times. During this period, it's wise not to sign contracts (unless you don't mind renegotiating when Mercury is moving direct), to check and recheck travel plans (or, better yet, don't travel), and to communicate as succinctly as possible. Refrain from buying any large-ticket items or electronics during this time too. Often, computers and appliances go on the fritz, cars act up, data is lost . . . you get the idea. Be sure to back up all files before the dates below:

March 12–April 4: Mercury retrograde in Aries, your ninth house—higher mind, overseas journeys, worldview.

July 14–August 8: Mercury retrograde in your sign.

November 6–26: Mercury retrograde in Sagittarius, your solar fifth house of love and romance and creativity.

Eclipses

Solar eclipses tend to trigger external events that bring about change according to the sign and house in which they fall. Lunar eclipses trigger inner, emotional events according to the sign and house in which they fall. Any eclipse marks both beginnings and endings. The solar and lunar eclipse in a pair falls in opposite signs. If you're interested in detailed information on eclipses, take a look at Celeste Teal's excellent and definitive book, *Eclipses: Predicting World Events & Personal Transformation.*

If you were born under or around the time of an eclipse, it's to your advantage to take a look at your birth chart to find out exactly where the eclipses will impact you.

Most years feature four eclipses—two solar and two lunar, with the set separated by about two weeks. In November and December 2011, there were solar and lunar eclipses, so this year the first eclipses fall during May and June.

May 20: Solar eclipse at 0 degrees Gemini. This one should bring in new opportunities to meet people, join groups, and reach for and attain your dreams.

June 4: Lunar eclipse in Sagittarius, your solar fifth house. This should be a positive eclipse for your love life!

November 13: Solar eclipse in Scorpio in your solar fourth house. New opportunities surface in your domestic life.

November 28: Lunar eclipse, Gemini. Jupiter forms a five-degree conjunction to the eclipse degree, suggesting that news you receive around this time will be cause for celebration!

Luckiest Day of the Year

Every year there's one day when Jupiter and the sun meet up, and luck, serendipity, and expansion are the hallmarks. This year that day falls on May 13, with a conjunction in Taurus.

CHAPTER 18

Eighteen Months of Day-by-Day Predictions: July 2011 to December 2012

Moon sign times are calculated for Eastern Standard Time and Eastern Daylight Time. Please adjust for your local time zone.

JULY 2011

Friday, July 1 (Moon in Cancer)   Today's new moon in Cancer brings new opportunities to work behind the scenes, to delve into your own psyche, and to nurture yourself and others. Jupiter forms a beneficial angle to this new moon, suggesting that the work you'll be doing involves professional matters and issues. Expansion will be part of the new-moon package.

Saturday, July 2 (Moon into Leo, 5:44 p.m.)   Mercury enters your sign today and will be there until July 28. This transit brings the gift of gab, making it possible for you to sell anything to anyone. You're able to express yourself clearly, passionately, and with great conviction. So figure out how you would like to use this wonderful energy to communicate, and then get busy doing it!

Sunday, July 3 (Moon in Leo)   Whether you're traveling this weekend or staying close to home, you're in rare form. The moon and Mercury are both in your sign, and Uranus is in fellow fire sign Aries, so you've got plenty of passion and enthusiasm in your court. Specifically, you're on center stage, Leo. And the applause is loud.

Monday, July 4 (Moon into Virgo, 9:16 p.m.) Happy Independence Day! Venus enters Cancer and your twelfth house, where it will be until July 28. During this period, a secret love affair is possible. If you're involved already, then you and your partner may be lying low together, perhaps celebrating the long weekend at a romantic getaway. Intuitively, you're right on target.

Tuesday, July 5 (Moon in Virgo)   Back to work? If so, your focus seems to be centered on money—what you earn and spend, how to earn and save more, and how to make money in a way that's in line with your values. Tall order? Not for you, Leo. You have it all figured out by the end of the day!

Wednesday, July 6 (Moon into Libra, 11:54 p.m.) The moon enters compatible air sign Libra, a nice location for you. It ramps up your social skills, urges you to touch base with friends and acquaintances, and may have you updating your blog or Facebook profile. Groups and relationships are more important to you today, and there's an artistic streak running through everything you do.

Thursday, July 7 (Moon in Libra)   Relatives and neighbors figure into the day's events. You and a brother or sister may be planning a family reunion this summer and are trying to figure out where and when. Iron out the details; be sure to jot the dates on your calendar. With your busy schedule, it's easy to forget what is happening when.

Friday, July 8 (Moon in Libra)   Take in an art exhibit, an art film, or even a photography exhibit. Go to the opera, a concert, or a book fair. You get the idea. The Libra moon brings on a hunger for beauty and art, and you may decide to spiff up your home, community, or neighborhood.

Saturday, July 9 (Moon into Scorpio, 2:32 a.m.) Uranus turns retrograde in Aries, your ninth house, and won't turn direct again until December 10. This movement urges you to look within concerning your spiritual beliefs, your educational goals, and your worldview generally. With Uranus in Aries, moving retrograde or direct, you attract unusual people and experiences that help you clarify your views and beliefs.

Sunday, July 10 (Moon in Scorpio) With the moon entering your solar fourth house, your emotions intensify, particularly where family, parents, and home are concerned. You may not know what to do with such intense and powerful emotions, except to stand your ground on an issue and then retreat into a shell until the moon is in a sign friendlier to your fire sign—like tomorrow's moon.

Monday, July 11 (Moon into Sagittarius, 3:47 a.m.) This fellow fire-sign moon makes it easier to grasp the larger picture and implications of a relationship, a creative project, or even where your kids are concerned. But the Sadge moon also urges you to do something you enjoy, something that reminds you that life is also about having fun, being creative, and finding work that you love.

Tuesday, July 12 (Moon in Sagittarius) Romance and creative projects are your focus today. You're a bit more flexible emotionally, which can be a major boost in a relationship or while working on a project. If you have a romantic partner, consider working together on something that you both enjoy. With the big picture at your fingertips, there's no better time.

Wednesday, July 13 (Moon into Capricorn, 10:14 a.m.)
Here comes that earth energy again—you know, that sign that seems to stifle your enthusiasm. Well, change your attitude about the Capricorn moon. Instead of resisting its call for focused work, for establishing goals, embrace the energy, run with it.

Thursday, July 14 (Moon in Capricorn)   Your daily work routine becomes more streamlined, with not a moment wasted. You're able to delegate well, and you may do a lot of that today. Your desk is piled high with calls to return and projects to complete, and your in-box is filled. Get busy, Leo.

Friday, July 15 (Moon into Aquarius, 4:30 p.m.)
The full moon in Capricorn illuminates a work or health issue. There could be news about either of these areas. Jupiter is still transiting your career sector and expanding your options, so the news could be connected to résumés you sent out or to interviews you've had.

Saturday, July 16 (Moon in Aquarius)   The moon entered your opposite sign. Your ideas today are wildly imaginative, totally outside the box. With your flair for theatrics and drama, and with Mercury still in your sign, you can certainly communicate the ideas and the feelings you have about them. Start preparing now for the new moon in your sign on July 30. This one comes along just once a year and sets the tone for the next twelve months. What kinds of experiences and relationships would you like to manifest in your life?

Sunday, July 17 (Moon in Aquarius)   Uranus forms a beneficial angle to this moon, indicating that you respond emotionally in unusual ways today. Your intuition is strong and accurate, so don't hesitate to listen to that small voice in your head that urges you to do this or that. You won't need to check these feelings against fact. In some instances, there may not even be time for a fact check.

Monday, July 18 (Moon into Pisces, 1:13 a.m.)   Unless you have a lot of water or earth signs in your natal chart, you may not like the Pisces moon any more than you do the Capricorn moon. That said, allow this lunar energy to trigger your imagination and your compassion. Let your heart speak today.

Tuesday, July 19 (Moon in Pisces)   Today your imagination is the bird that takes flight as soon as you open your eyes. Everything seems to pass by in a dream. If you need a vacation from reality, Leo, the Pisces moon delivers it. If you have to make decisions, function well enough to get stuff done, and meet your responsibilities, best to wait until tomorrow, when the moon enters fellow fire sign Aries.

Wednesday, July 20 (Moon into Aries, 12:26 a.m.) Breathe, Leo. You love this moon, remember? Today you may be shuffling your schedule around in anticipation of an overseas trip. Or if you're on the road already, you may discover that your path is not necessarily the path that others follow. Ordinarily this might bother you. Today it doesn't. You know you're right. Onward.

Thursday, July 21 (Moon in Aries)   With Mercury still in your sign and both the moon and Uranus in Aries, your mind moves at the speed of light. And it may not know when to shut off. If you've got a regular exercise routine already, increase the time you spend doing that routine. If you don't have a routine yet, start one. The exercise will make it more likely that you won't have trouble turning your head off tonight when you're ready to go to sleep.

Friday, July 22 (Moon into Taurus, 12:59 p.m.)   This afternoon, the moon joins Jupiter in your career sector. Even though these two will travel together throughout the weekend, you can still take advantage of the expansive energy by planning ahead. What would you like to get done in your life next week? What pressing issues or challenges would you like to tackle? Or what would you like to enjoy? To experience?

Saturday, July 23 (Moon in Taurus)   Stubborn? You bet. Taurus, like Leo, is a fixed sign. You don't change your mind easily, and when you do, it's only because another person has convinced you your opinion is wrong or because you have done your homework. Today, though, you'll stick to what your gut tells you.

Sunday, July 24 (Moon in Taurus)   The Taurus moon enjoys aesthetic, artistic surroundings. As a result, you may be putting some surface touches on your personal environment. Freshly cut flowers in the kitchen, pastel paint on hallway walls, a new piece of art, new music pouring from your speakers—you get the idea. You're setting the mood for something grand, Leo. A new romantic interest, perhaps?

Monday, July 25 (Moon into Gemini, 12:35 a.m.) This moon forms a harmonious angle with Saturn in Libra, Uranus and Mercury in Aries, and your sun in Leo. The result? You have a silver tongue. You are the absolute life of any social gathering, and you're able to find exactly the right venues for your creative expressions. Is that good enough? No? Okay, specifically, you say what you think and feel and don't hold back. Yes, this may put off a business or romantic partner. But that person's reaction doesn't faze you in the least.

Tuesday, July 26 (Moon in Gemini)   The Gemini moon loves information—gathering it, absorbing it, disseminating it. The information is likely to be general, but that reflects your varied interests. And your interests grab the attention of someone intrigued by you. You may even know this person, perhaps as a friend. And now the friendship is redefined. As a romance?

Wednesday, July 27 (Moon into Cancer, 9:12 p.m.)
The month is going to end on a power day, with the moon in your sign, always a nice way to end or begin a month. But for today, it's in that troublesome air sign that makes you nostalgic, brings an undercurrent of feelings you may not understand, and asks only that you reflect on who and what you are. How are you unique, Leo? Define that, and you have the answer to many of your concerns.

Thursday, July 28 (Moon in Cancer)   Two transits occur today. Mercury enters Virgo and Venus enters your sign. The Venus transit lasts until August 21 and marks one of the most romantic and creative periods for you all year. So if you're single, get out into the world, be seen, accept social invitations, or sign up for an online dating service. If you're involved already, you and your partner may deepen your commitment to each other. Creatively, regardless of what field you work in, you're on a roll.

Friday, July 29 (Moon in Cancer)   The Mercury transit that began yesterday takes you to September 25. Between August 2 and August 26, Mercury will be retrograde in Virgo, in the financial sector of your chart. This retrograde could delay receiving money that's owed you, or you may be revisiting a promotion or raise that was denied earlier. Remember to back up computers on August 1!

Saturday, July 30 (Moon into Leo, 2:16 a.m.)   Here it is! The new moon in your sign, which comes along just once a year and sets the tone for the next twelve months. Venus forms a close and beneficial angle with this moon, suggesting a smooth unfolding of events, that you and your work are warmly received by others, and that a raise or financial boost of some kind is definitely a possibility.

Sunday, July 31 (Moon in Leo)   Party time! Today you may feel like surrounding yourself with friends and family. So send out your e-mails; make your calls. Whip up a menu; fire up the grill. Enjoy!

AUGUST 2011

Monday, August 1 (Moon into Virgo, 4:42 a.m.) The month begins with some self-doubt, perhaps about your abilities. So, before this kind of doubt takes root, vanquish it! Refuse to go that route. Meditate for a few minutes, and turn your thoughts in a more positive, upbeat direction. Mercury turns retrograde tomorrow, so be sure to back up all your files, finalize travel plans, and sign contracts.

Tuesday, August 2 (Moon in Virgo) Mercury turns retrograde today and remains that way until August 26. By now, you know the drill on this one, Leo. But in case you need a refresher, read over the section on Mercury retrogrades in the Big Picture section. You may feel very picky today about people within your environment. It will be easy to criticize and look for things that are wrong with them. Resist this impulse.

Wednesday, August 3 (Moon into Libra, 6:05 a.m.) Mars enters Cancer and your twelfth house. From now until September 18, there will be a lot of activity behind the scenes. You may be delving into your own psyche—through meditation, therapy, dream recall. If a relationship begins during this transit, it probably will have a deeply intuitive component to it.

Thursday, August 4 (Moon in Libra) You wake up this morning with a more optimistic view on life. Thank the Libra moon. It brings a softer, more artistic perspective into your life and helps to lighten any load you feel you're carrying. It asks that you do appreciate what you have and that you show this appreciation toward loved ones.

Friday, August 5 (Moon into Scorpio, 7:57 a.m.) Ah, sweet revenge, right? Wrong. If you've been slighted, if your feelings have been hurt, if a relationship has just ended, you may be tempted to strike back at the other person, to extract your revenge. These kinds of feelings are sometimes part of the Scorpio moon. So, if you find yourself feeling like that, do nothing. Say nothing. Reach for better feelings, more joyous thoughts.

Saturday, August 6 (Moon in Scorpio) Intense feelings are also part of the Scorpio moon, and they don't have to be negative. The more deeply you feel something, the more aware you are of your humanity. The more deeply you feel, the greater your desires, imaginings, and hopes. Today, share your feelings with someone close to you.

Sunday, August 7 (Moon into Sagittarius, 11:21 a.m.) Finally. A fire-sign moon! And it's a day to play and enjoy yourself. Pretend that you're a five-year-old. Everything you see and hear, touch and feel, is a wonder, awesome, a thing of great beauty. By looking at the world in this way for today and tomorrow, you're preparing yourself for that moon in Capricorn on Tuesday and attracting more into your life that you can appreciate.

Monday, August 8 (Moon in Sagittarius) Keep up your optimistic outlook. You may be surrounded by people who don't share it or who denigrate your worldview or belief system in some way. Don't worry about them. You can't change their beliefs. It's not your job to do so. Work on yourself. Don't push back against the naysayers.

Tuesday, August 9 (Moon into Capricorn, 4:38 p.m.) Order is imposed on your life this afternoon. It comes in the form of the Capricorn moon. The effect of this lunar transit may not be subtle, either. One moment you're drowning in disorganization. The next moment, something happens that forces you to find something, perhaps a piece of information buried somewhere on your desk. And then the purge begins. By tomorrow, you'll be organized enough to find exactly what you need, when you need it.

Wednesday, August 10 (Moon in Capricorn)   One foot in front of the other—that's how you proceed today. It's methodical and orderly. Even if it isn't your usual style, even though it lacks flamboyance and drama, it fits the tenor of the day. Keep to yourself; work diligently. By the time you get home this evening, you've earned a vacation.

Thursday, August 11 (Moon into Aquarius, 11:48 p.m.) You and your partner may need some downtime together. It's not that serious stuff is going on. It's just that you need to talk, laugh, and enjoy each other so that you remember why you actually came together. One lesson to take away from this, however, is that even when life is busiest, a phone call or a text message in the middle of the day can prove to be a very nice respite.

Friday, August 12 (Moon in Aquarius)   If you're trying to launch a business, today is a good day to talk with potential partners. But because Mercury is still retrograde, don't sign anything binding unless you don't mind if the deal has to be revisited at a later date.

Saturday, August 13 (Moon in Aquarius)   Today's full moon in Aquarius should be quite nice for your partnerships—romantic or business. Neptune forms a wide and beneficial angle to this moon, indicating that anything romantic begins first in conversation, a meeting of the minds. Neptune has retrograded back into Aquarius, so if there are any loose ends to tie up in the partnership area, Leo, now is the time to do it.

Sunday, August 14 (Moon into Pisces, 8:55 a.m.) Here's that pesky Pisces moon again, the wet towel at your party. That's your initial take, at any rate. But if you're smart—and we know you are, Leo—you'll use this lunar energy in two ways. In the outer world, you'll tackle issues like mortgages, loans, and insurance. In your inner world, you'll allow your intuition and imagination to find the information you're seeking.

Monday, August 15 (Moon in Pisces)   Your interest in things that go bump in the night deepens. Reincarnation, life after death, communication with the dead—these are some of the topics you may be delving into today. Whether you read about these areas or have a personal experience of some kind that prompts you to look for answers, you're now on a quest, Leo.

Tuesday, August 16 (Moon into Aries, 8:03 p.m.) This fire-sign moon ignites your passion and enthusiasm, but may also make you a bit short-tempered or impatient. You may feel that no one around you can do the job as well as you can, so you don't delegate responsibility or gather support. You simply embark on your path and may not be properly equipped for the journey.

Wednesday, August 17 (Moon in Aries)   Midway through August, you're taking stock of where things stand and contrasting it with where you would like things to be by the end of the year. It's a kind of inventory of each area of your life. All the areas probably aren't equal. So focus on the areas where you would like to see improvement, and figure out how to get to where you want to be.

Thursday, August 18 (Moon in Aries)   The Aries moon prompts you to hit the road. But do it virtually and wait until after August 26 when Mercury turns direct again to book your travel plans. Venus is still in your sign—until August 21—and that means your muse is up close and very personal, urging you to dive into your creativity. Plan something special with your partner over the weekend. The stars are lined up nicely for romance.

Friday, August 19 (Moon into Taurus, 8:37 a.m.)
You're grounded today. Any abstract ideas that have been floating around in your head can now be brought down to earth and explained to others. The simplest ideas are often the best—look at the safety pin, the hammer, the shovel. So keep your explanations simple and focused, and illustrate how your ideas can be put to use in daily life.

Saturday, August 20 (Moon in Taurus)   Whenever the moon and Jupiter hook up in your career area, you can expect an opportunity for expansion. But Jupiter doesn't just drop these opportunities in your lap. You have to be alert enough to recognize an opportunity, quick enough to seize it, and then willing to run with it.

Sunday, August 21 (Moon into Gemini, 8:53 p.m.)
Venus enters Virgo and your financial area, where it will be until September 14. Overall, this transit will benefit you—a raise is possible, an unexpected royalty or dividend check arrives, or someone repays a loan. But you may feel like splurging—a bad idea until after August 26, when Mercury turns direct. And if you splurge after that date, be sure you pay with cash. The Virgo part of this component demands accountability.

Monday, August 22 (Moon in Gemini)   You're in the mood to be surrounded by people whose interests and passions are in line with your own. You join or visit such a group and soak up the information it provides. It's as if you're on a hunt for particular kinds of information that may not be available in one place on the Internet. You find what you're looking for through contact with others today and tomorrow.

Tuesday, August 23 (Moon in Gemini)   You're of two minds and two hearts today, and they may not agree on the specifics. So your challenge, Leo, if you choose to accept it, is to decide what you really believe, feel, think. Then make your choice and stand by it. You may have to go with your gut on this one.

Wednesday, August 24 (Moon into Cancer, 6:31 a.m.) A good day to check out your dream journal for clues you got in advance about what's going on in your life now. Or if you keep a journal, look back through it to see if you had any intuitive insights that have come true. You're more psychic than you may think, Leo.

Thursday, August 25 (Moon in Cancer)   You're preparing for two events coming up tomorrow—the moon's transit into your sign and Mercury turning direct. The first transit indicates a power day, so be sure to tie up loose ends today so that you have space in your life to accommodate the new opportunities and new energy this moon will bring. With the second transit, you'll be able to pack your bags and head for the open road!

Friday, August 26 (Moon into Leo, 12:09 p.m.)   Mercury turns direct, so it's time to celebrate. Hold off for another day or two on signing contracts or buying that big-ticket item. Let Mercury stabilize. And since the moon is now in your sign and will be until Sunday afternoon, it could be the perfect getaway weekend for you and a partner or for the entire family.

Saturday, August 27 (Moon in Leo)   Today's moon forms a great angle to Uranus in fellow fire sign Aries. If you seem unpredictable to the people around you, don't adjust your behavior to suit others. You have a right to feel good and optimistic, and anyone who tells you otherwise is simply wrong. You may be most comfortable today with other fire-sign individuals—Leo, Aries, Sagittarius.

Sunday, August 28 (Moon into Virgo, 2:13 p.m.) To-day's new moon in Virgo enjoys a beneficial conjunction from Venus, so you can expect new financial opportunities to surface that will be quite lucrative for you. Also, Pluto forms a strong and beneficial angle to this moon, indicating that the power is in your court. You may be able to negotiate a better deal for yourself.

Monday, August 29 (Moon in Virgo) Read the fine print, read between the lines, and read into what people *don't* say. The Virgo moon enables you to pick up on details and nuances and to string all these bits of information together to gain better perspective on what's actually going on. If your finances are involved in the day's picture, be meticulous about paying bills on time!

Tuesday, August 30 (Moon into Libra, 2:26 p.m.) Jupiter turns retrograde in Taurus until December 25. This movement prompts you to reevaluate your professional goals. Are you happy in your current career? Do you like your job? Are you advancing as quickly as you would like? You don't have to answer all these questions at once, but keep them in mind as you move through the rest of the year.

Wednesday, August 31 (Moon in Libra) A harmless flirtation with someone in your community could lead to something else, particularly if this person shares your values. On other fronts, there's a softness to your personality today that encourages others to share their feelings and thoughts. People trust you.

SEPTEMBER 2011

Thursday, September 1 (Moon into Scorpio, 2:48 p.m.) Ah, here it is again: the intense Scorpio moon that sometimes makes you feel as if as crater has opened in the pit of your stomach. It's the weight of all the excessive emotion racing through you. So just take a few deep breaths and detach from the situation that is causing you to feel like this. Then reach for a more buoyant thought.

Friday, September 2 (Moon in Scorpio)   Keep your own counsel today. No one needs to know your business. If you absolutely have to talk with someone, make sure it's a person whom you trust implicitly. A situation in your personal/domestic environment requires your attention. Forget quick fixes. Get to the root of the issue.

Saturday, September 3 (Moon into Sagittarius, 3:04 p.m.)   Party time, Leo. Here's that wonderful Sadge moon again, lifting you out of yesterday's doldrums, injecting you with some badly needed optimism. You're able to see the big picture today, and things look better than you thought possible. Isn't it good to know that within twenty-four hours, life can flip on a dime?

Sunday, September 4 (Moon in Sagittarius)   Saturn forms a beneficial angle to this moon, suggesting that life unfolds smoothly today and that any projects you initiate are solidly rooted. You're a forceful communicator as well—convincing, charming, capable of changing minds. Sounds like a political narrative of some kind, Leo. Are you running for office?

Monday, September 5 (Moon into Capricorn, 10:04 p.m.) Your focus shifts to your daily work routine. With Jupiter in Taurus forming a nice angle to this moon, you've got the Midas touch, and it happens effortlessly. Your biggest challenge is nonresistance. Go with the flow. See where it leads you.

Tuesday, September 6 (Moon in Capricorn)   Your creative adrenaline is pumping hard and furiously. You and a sibling or a neighbor could be working on a project together. The project may not be traditionally creative—as in the arts—but could lie in your approach to everything you do and say. You're looking for solutions that lie outside the box. Way outside.

Wednesday, September 7 (Moon in Capricorn) You're looking ahead—a month, three months, into 2012. You're attempting to put your short- and long-range goals into perspective so that they fit your world-view or spiritual beliefs. In order to do this, you may have to answer some basic questions. Are you happy in your job/career? Are you satisfied with what you're earning? What would you like to change in your life and how can you best go about doing it?

Thursday, September 8 (Moon into Aquarius, 5:43 a.m.) With the moon opposite your sun for the next couple of days, your focus shifts to professional and personal partnerships. You and a partner may be discussing your individual visions and needs and expectations. With Mercury now moving direct again, the discussion should be clear, with everything spelled out so that you each know where you stand.

Friday, September 9 (Moon in Aquarius) You feel daring today, and people around you pick up on it. They look to you for answers. This is how leaders are chosen, Leo, so whether you're organizing in your community, your business, or your home, act like the leader you are. Uranus is still retrograding in Aries, and it's that fire sign that pushes you to trailblaze.

Saturday, September 10 (Moon into Pisces, 3:27 p.m.) Turn your attention to the mundane—insurance, wills, mortgages, and loans. It's a good day to initiate something in any of these areas. Whether you're looking for new insurance, a loan, or a mortgage, be sure to shop around first for the best prices. Check the Internet. By the time the full moon in Pisces rolls around on Monday, you'll have greater insight into these matters.

Sunday, September 11 (Moon in Pisces)   This moon forms a beautiful angle to Jupiter in Taurus, Mars in Cancer, and Pluto in Capricorn. With this combination of planets in your court, you're in a perfect place to ask for a raise or promotion, or to launch a business, website, blog. So get busy, Leo. You've got your work cut out for you.

Monday, September 12 (Moon in Pisces)   Today's full moon in Pisces brings insight into resources you share with others. This can include anything from your partner's income to mortgages, loans, and insurance. Jupiter forms a wide but beneficial angle to this moon, indicating that professional issues could be involved. The insights you gain or the news that you hear could expand your venues.

Tuesday, September 13 (Moon into Aries, 2:50 a.m.) Aren't you the independent one today? Forget team playing. Today you're a pioneer, an intrepid explorer, fearless in your determination to go where no one else has gone. Just be sure you're well equipped for the journey, Leo. Don't be so cocky about this that you overlook important details.

Wednesday, September 14 (Moon in Aries)   Venus enters Libra, where it will be until October 9. It's traveling with Saturn through your third house, so it's possible that a romance starts up with someone older than you. This person could live in your community or neighborhood or could be someone you meet through a sibling or a neighbor.

Thursday, September 15 (Moon into Taurus, 3:25 p.m.) If you feel out of sorts today, it's only because you got up on the wrong side of the bed. So get back into bed, Leo, shut your eyes, and realign yourself with your higher self. Reach for gentler, more optimistic emotions and a better, more positive frame of mind. It's a great day to expand your professional opportunities.

Friday, September 16 (Moon in Taurus)   Pluto turns direct in Capricorn. The effects of this movement will be subtle, but between now and the end of the year, you should see challenges in your daily work routine begin to dissipate. You'll have to exert some effort of course, but you won't feel as if you're pushing against a concrete wall. The uphill struggle ends.

Saturday, September 17 (Moon in Taurus)   This moon, like your sun sign, is a fixed sign. That can mean stubbornness times two for today, so don't apologize if you're unable to buy into someone else's plan, project, or mission. Stubbornness is probably exactly what the situation needs. Think of it as a survival mechanism. Dig in your heels.

Sunday, September 18 (Moon into Gemini, 4:06 a.m.) Mars enters your sign and will be there until November 11. This transit will energize you physically, giving you terrific staying power. You'll be able to tackle any challenge that comes your way, you may be working longer hours, and you will be more forceful in your dealings with others. This transit also deepens your sexuality.

Monday, September 19 (Moon in Gemini)   You are in a pretty good place today, eager to embrace whatever comes your way, anxious to get out into the larger world and put these good feelings to work for you. In your eagerness, though, you may overlook the obvious. Today's energy favors publicity and promotion, group participation.

Tuesday, September 20 (Moon into Cancer, 2:54 p.m.) Feeling nostalgic for a relationship? A certain time in your life? For the past? This is part and parcel of the Cancer moon. Your mother or another nurturing woman plays into the day's events in a major way. She may need help and support right now, or perhaps she has advice and insights that you should hear.

Wednesday, September 21 (Moon in Cancer)   Allow your emotions to roll through you today. Whether the things you feel are positive or negative, don't resist them or try to scrutinize them. Just feel. You're clearing space for the moon entering your sign tomorrow evening. You may want to try journaling or even updating your blog at the end of the day, when you'll be in a reflective mood.

Thursday, September 22 (Moon into Leo, 9:56 p.m.) Certainly a power day. You're the one others look to for leadership and answers. Even if you don't feel like a leader, act like one. Trust your instincts. With Venus and Saturn in compatible air sign Libra, and Mars and the moon both in your sign, you're able to slice through the PR spin and get down to the real bottom line.

Friday, September 23 (Moon in Leo)   You're in the groove, Leo, and that means lots of flash and drama around you. Or perhaps you're the one who exhibits the flash and drama. However things shake out, put today's energy to good use. You can charm, sell, and talk your way through just about anything.

Saturday, September 24 (Moon into Virgo, 10:50 p.m.) Money, money, money—it's your focus today. You may be shifting your money around. It behooves you to take a close look at your attitudes and beliefs about money. Which beliefs may be holding you back from achieving financial independence?

Sunday, September 25 (Moon in Virgo)   Mercury enters Libra and your solar third house, where it will be until October 13. This transit should galvanize your communication skills—debating, writing, public speaking, sales, blogging. You can convert people today— that's how slick your skills are. So get out there, Leo. Do your thing and bring people to your side.

Monday, September 26 (Moon into Libra, 12:51 a.m.)
The moon joins Venus and Saturn in Libra, a strong combination that's in your favor. You're radiating beauty and certainty today, and other people react to this with warmth and admiration. You may be called upon to arbitrate a discussion or argument or to mediate a situation in your neighborhood, community, or family. Put yourself in the other person's shoes.

Tuesday, September 27 (Moon in Libra)   Today's new moon in Libra ushers in new opportunities for you in terms of communication, travel, your daily life. Five out of ten planets are in Libra today, so the odds are definitely stacked in your favor. Other possibilities? New opportunities for earning money through the arts, for working with others on a project that is important to you, or for making new friends.

Wednesday, September 28 (Moon into Scorpio, 12:06 a.m.)   With Mars still in your sign and the moon in passionate Scorpio, you may be more aggressive in pursuit of what you want. You're a powerhouse now, determined and resolute, and people around you could find this intimidating. But don't worry about what they're saying or thinking. You can't control them. You can only control your own feelings and thoughts.

Thursday, September 29 (Moon in Scorpio)   It's a good day for reflection. Water-sign moons—Scorpio, Cancer, Pisces—are excellent for doing that. So reflect on where you stand in your life right now and where you would like to be in the next three months. Or six months. Or a year from now. Then create your New Year's resolutions so they are in line with what you imagine for yourself.

Friday, September 30 (Moon into Sagittarius, 12:42 a.m.)   In some ways, this moon announces itself like

Saturday Night Live: music, drum rolls, the cast of players, comedy and satire, a reflection of the absurdities and reality of the culture in which we live. So, as you go about your day, do so with a sense of the comedic, with an eye on the big picture.

OCTOBER 2011

Saturday, October 1 (Moon in Sagittarius)   It's the weekend, and yesterday's mood persists. It looks like it's a good day for a party at your place. Keep it small, intimate, limited to the kind of people who share your vision and passions. Today isn't about confrontation. It's about cooperation, team playing, and garnering support and understanding.

Sunday, October 2 (Moon in Sagittarius)   The dots have been connected; you've grasped the larger picture. Now turn this larger scope on a romantic relationship or creative project and decide whether it's right for you. You may not be able to make your decision right away. In fact, wait until the moon enters your sign to see how you feel about things generally.

Monday, October 3 (Moon into Capricorn, 4:16 a.m.) This moon forms a challenging angle to Venus, Mercury, Jupiter, Saturn, and Pluto. Ouch. Okay, it's not going to be a fun day. Your best way to navigate events is to step back, detach, and scoot to the sidelines. Become an observer and absorb.

Tuesday, October 4 (Moon in Capricorn)   The moon is with Pluto, a combination that puts you in the driver's seat, particularly as it relates to your daily work life, your career, and your attitude and beliefs about what you do to earn your daily bread. How self-sufficient are you? Read Naomi Klein's *The Shock Doctrine*. You'll understand what's at stake.

Wednesday, October 5 (Moon into Aquarius, 11:19 a.m.)
There could be some tension today between what you
want and what a partner wants. The easiest way to resolve it is through discussion. It may be time for each of
you to delineate your needs and expectations about the
relationship. Spell it all out.

Thursday, October 6 (Moon in Aquarius)   Someone
close to you thinks he or she has all the answers. This
sort of boorish behavior is exactly what you *don't* need
today. Be patient with this person, and if the behavior
continues, then excuse yourself politely and run in the
opposite direction. You don't want to hang around negative people today or tomorrow. Or ever!

Friday, October 7 (Moon into Pisces, 9:14 p.m.)   Intuition and imagination are highlighted. Trust your
hunches in any decisions you make today. And because you're sensitive to your environment, you could
be absorbing other people's feelings like a proverbial
sponge, so be sure to associate only with upbeat, positive people.

Saturday, October 8 (Moon in Pisces)   Ready to
kick back and relax, Leo? Or have you forgotten how to
relax? If so, then the Pisces moon makes it easier for you
to do just that. You feel sort of dreamy and disconnected
from reality; everything takes on a tone of the surreal.
Your best bet is to find a great novel or to rent some of
your favorite movies.

Sunday, October 9 (Moon in Pisces)   Venus enters
Scorpio, where it will be until November 2. During this
transit, your domestic life should unfold smoothly, but
will be emotionally intense. Your sexuality is heightened during this period. If a relationship begins under
this transit, you can expect an emotionally volatile and/
or powerful several weeks.

Monday, October 10 (Moon into Aries, 8:57 a.m.)
With the moon entering Aries, your entrepreneurial qualities really ramp up. So do your passions. If you're involved right now, be careful that you don't fall into the possessiveness trap. Or the trap called jealousy. Nothing destroys a close relationship faster. Remain optimistic, upbeat, and appreciative.

Tuesday, October 11 (Moon in Aries)   Today's full moon in Aries brings news or insights connected to your personal life and your worldview. You may have an opportunity to travel overseas or to take a course or workshop in something that really interests you. Mars in your sign forms a beneficial angle to this moon, indicating heightened activity.

Wednesday, October 12 (Moon into Taurus, 9:35 p.m.)
If you found yesterday somewhat chaotic, today should be rather quiet by comparison. You will feel more grounded, particularly with professional issues and concerns. Venus opposes this moon, so there could be some tension between your obligations at work and those at home.

Thursday, October 13 (Moon in Taurus)   Mercury enters Scorpio, joining Venus in your solar fourth house until November 2. So now you're able to express all these intense emotions you're feeling. Whether you express yourself verbally or in writing, your communication skills are sharp, intuitive, right on target.

Friday, October 14 (Moon in Taurus)   You dig in your heels about something that really hits your buttons. It's exactly what the situation calls for. Don't allow yourself to bend or change your mind just because you want to be liked. By tomorrow, you'll be in a better position to look at things in a cool, logical light. For today, stick to your script.

Saturday, October 15 (Moon into Gemini, 10:15 a.m.)
This air-sign moon is compatible with your fire-sign sun, so you're feeling very good today. It's an ideal time to update your blog, launch a website, update your client e-mail list, or just hang out with friends. You may need a reprieve from some of the intense emotions you've been experiencing related to your domestic life. So treat yourself to something special.

Sunday, October 16 (Moon in Gemini) Network. However you choose to do this—in person, by phone, through e-mail or blogs—your work is cut out for you today. Groups are part of the day's activities: a team at work, some group that supports your interests, or even a family outing of some kind.

Monday, October 17 (Moon into Cancer, 9:39 p.m.)
Are you hoping to adopt a cat or dog? Perhaps even a bird? Start at the rescue organizations first, then your local Humane Society. Check your local grocery store for postings. In troubled times, animals and pets are often the first to suffer. If you live with a partner or a roommate or within a family structure, be sure to discuss the adoption with others in your household before you go through with it.

Tuesday, October 18 (Moon in Cancer) The next two days are mental and emotional preparation for the moon entering your sign on Thursday morning. And since the universe loves symbolic actions and gestures, clear space in your life for the new opportunities and people that power days can bring. Clean out your car, your desk, your closet, or your attic. But do it with the awareness of *why* you're doing it.

Wednesday, October 19 (Moon in Cancer) If you can embrace change, you're way ahead of the game. But, as you're embracing it, be conscious of what you would like to manifest in your life. What opportunities does change make possible? What opportunities would you like to be offered? Then focus on what you want, and visualize the outcome backed by powerful emotions.

Thursday, October 20 *(Moon into Leo, 6:07 a.m.)* Breathing more easily? You should be. With the moon and Mars both in your sign, you're in rare form and ready to embrace and take on anything that comes your way. So think big, don't hesitate to say what's on your mind, and add all the drama you feel you need to look the part of someone at the top of his or her game.

Friday, October 21 *(Moon in Leo)*   You're able to manifest your desires easily with so many planets in your court. Keep a wish list at your desk, with your deepest desires at the top. Periodically throughout the day, focus on the items at the top of your list. Imagine that they are yours already. This exercise will help you to get into the habit of focusing on what you want—rather than on the *lack* of what you want.

Saturday, October 22 *(Moon into Virgo, 10:42 a.m.)* Keep your criticisms to yourself today, and resist the urge to criticize yourself! You can be harder on yourself than you realize. Don't look to past mistakes and wish that you hadn't made them. Your point of power, Leo, is this instant. Right now. Launch the rest of your life from here.

Sunday, October 23 *(Moon in Virgo)*   Whenever there's activity in your solar second house, money and finances generally are highlighted. Today, pay attention to the details (Virgo) concerning your money—how much you earn and spend, what you buy and why. Are you a spree spender? Do you spend to make yourself feel better? Are you spending more than you earn?

Monday, October 24 (Moon into Libra, 11:50 a.m.)
The moon hooks up with Saturn, and both planets form a beneficial angle to your sun. The combination provides a sturdy, solid venue for expressing your feelings, your creativity, your deepest beliefs. You're very convincing, even to people who don't know you, and can easily change minds today.

Tuesday, October 25 (Moon in Libra) You're in a sociable mood today, and it shows in the way you greet fellow workers, employees, bosses. It's a genuine feeling—something that bubbles up from deep inside of you and then spills out into the larger world. Today, you're an agent for change. Start close to home.

Wednesday, October 26 (Moon into Scorpio, 11:09 a.m.)
The new moon in Scorpio ushers in new opportunities related to your home and domestic situation. You might, for instance, buy or sell your house. The size of your household could increase because of the birth of a child or someone moving in. You may buy property, inherit money, or win the lottery! Pluto forms a beneficial angle to this moon, so any opportunities that surface should put you in a powerful place.

Thursday, October 27 (Moon in Scorpio) Intense feelings swirl the day after the new moon. It's a good thing. Really! All of this powerful emotion is breaking up areas of your life where you may have been stuck. Once the detritus starts moving out of your life, the opportunities promised by the new moon should begin appearing.

Friday, October 28 (Moon into Sagittarius, 10:46 a.m.)
It's not too early to start thinking about the holidays coming up next month and in December. Touch base with relatives, and see who is on which page. If you and your partner prefer spending the holidays alone, with

just your immediate families, then perhaps some sort of compromise can be reached.

Saturday, October 29 (Moon in Sagittarius)   A romantic day overall. Or, if you're not involved, then it's a deeply creative day, when your ideas flow and you can see the proverbial forest through the trees. Either way, you're in the driver's seat, Leo. You've got plenty of enthusiasm and energy to get you through to the end of the month.

Sunday, October 30 (Moon into Capricorn, 12:39 p.m.) If you've got young kids, then do Halloween the fun way. Decorate the house and yard, have your bags of treats ready to give away, carve a pumpkin. You know by now that the Capricorn moon isn't your favorite, but give this moon a specific task—even one like preparing for Halloween—and it's happy.

Monday, October 31 (Moon in Capricorn)   Happy Halloween! Even if you don't have children, get into it. And since this is supposed to be the night when the border between the living and the dead is at its thinnest, give thanks to those you loved who have passed on.

NOVEMBER 2011

Tuesday, November 1 (Moon into Aquarius, 6:08 p.m.) With the moon entering your solar seventh house, you're focused on partnership issues today. A business or romantic partner may need additional support, and you, of course, are glad to give it. You're known as a warm, compassionate individual and always give without reservation.

Wednesday, November 2 (Moon in Aquarius)   Both Venus and Mercury enter Sagittarius, marking the beginning of one of the most romantic and creative periods for you all year. If a relationship begins under this Venus transit, which lasts until November 26, it's apt to be enjoyable, fun, and long-lived. With Mercury also in this sign through the end of the year, the communication between you and your partner should be honest, with each of you clear about your individual needs and expectations.

Thursday, November 3 (Moon in Aquarius) On November 24, Mercury turns retrograde in Sagittarius and turns direct again on December 13. Since this will impact your creative ventures, try to wrap things up before the retrograde begins, or be prepared to revise the project. It will also impact your romantic relationships and your kids, so try to communicate in a clear, concise manner.

Friday, November 4 (Moon into Pisces, 3:18 a.m.) Deal with taxes and insurance matters today. It's not your favorite activity, of course, but you may be able to find deals that lower your bills. Get on the Internet and look for price comparisons. The income that your partner or spouse makes also comes under your scrutiny today.

Saturday, November 5 (Moon in Pisces) Your intuition is right on target today. If you don't like what your intuition is telling you, then back up the intuition with facts. If the facts support your hunches, then use your imagination to forge a new path toward a better outcome.

Sunday, November 6—Daylight Saving Time Ends (Moon into Aries, 2:02 p.m.) It will get darker earlier, which doesn't suit your nature at all. Leo, after all, is ruled by the sun. So, during the next months, if you find yourself feeling somewhat blue or out of sorts, spend a few minutes meditating each day. Paint one of the rooms in your home in a bright, bold color. It will lift your mood.

Monday, November 7 (Moon in Aries)   Your world-view is certainly pushing ahead into new terrain today. This transit triggers your entrepreneurial spirit, and you're utterly fearless in reaching for what you want. Publishing, education, and foreign countries and individuals are part of the day's activities. Your goals in these areas could be changing, or perhaps you're changing the landscape in these areas in some way.

Tuesday, November 8 (Moon in Aries)   This moon is conjunct Uranus retrograde, which triggers unusual emotional responses in you. Your responses don't feel unusual to you—only to the people around you because suddenly you're no longer predictable. And that's a point in your favor. Keep the competition off balance, Leo, and you'll be way ahead of the game.

Wednesday, November 9 (Moon into Taurus, 2:46 a.m.) Neptune turns direct today in Aquarius—its last gasp in that sign. By February 2012, Neptune will be back in Pisces again. So, for the next few months, take a closer look at your partnerships. Do they reflect your highest ideals? If not, why not? Once Neptune enters Pisces again, your spiritual focus will shift, and your ideals will be more heightened and central to who you are.

Thursday, November 10 (Moon in Taurus)   Today's full moon in Taurus joins expansive Jupiter in the career sector of your chart. Expect professional news that will broaden your career opportunities in some way. The opportunities could materialize on or around November 25, with the solar eclipse in fellow fire sign Sagittarius. So, for the next few weeks, focus on what you would like to manifest in your love life, with creative projects, and with your kids.

Friday, November 11 (Moon into Gemini, 3:11 p.m.) Mars enters Virgo and the financial area of your chart and will be there until early 2012. This transit galvanizes everything you do concerning money. You may be spending more, but you're also earning more and working longer to do so. You may, for instance, find a part-time job or start a home-based business. You'll also be looking at a realistic budget. Pay with cash rather than credit card. That's the best place to start your budget.

Saturday, November 12 (Moon in Gemini)   Networking, gathering information, and ideas—those are the day's hallmarks. Sounds like you may be having a party, Leo. Select your guests carefully. Any odd ducks at the gathering could throw a wrench into what would otherwise be a good time.

Sunday, November 13 (Moon in Gemini)   This moon forms a strong and beneficial angle to Saturn in Libra, to Uranus in Aries, to your sun, and to Mercury in Sagittarius. This lineup in your court enables you to achieve success in just about anything you tackle today. So don't hesitate to speak your mind, to reach out to people whose worldview differs from yours, and to express what you feel.

Monday, November 14 (Moon into Cancer, 2:20 a.m.)
For the next two days, you're working up to the moon entering your sign. Remember those symbolic gestures that signal the universe about your intentions to embrace the new? Make some today. If you don't feel like cleaning out your attic or garage, then purge your own psyche of old attitudes and beliefs that may be blocking your success.

Tuesday, November 15 (Moon in Cancer)   It's a good day to embrace the past—and then release it. So dig around all you want in your own psyche today. Uncover the secrets, the power you may have disowned, the issues you have been reluctant to face. Once you expose these things to the light of day, they are easier to deal with and resolve.

Wednesday, November 16 (Moon into Leo, 11:18 a.m.)
Aaahhh. A huge sigh of relief. The moon is in your sign, and are you ever ready for it. You take on more than your share of responsibilities, and you're definitely the one to shoulder it. You're able to zip through your to-do list with plenty of time to spare for enjoyment later in the day. Other fire signs—Sagittarius and Aries—may be a part of the activities after work.

Thursday, November 17 (Moon in Leo) You may be poring over Web sites and blogs today, in search of a particular person or group of people or for specific information of some kind. Possibilities: hunts for a job, house, school or college, an expert in an area that is foreign to you. Remember to hire and buy locally if at all possible.

Friday, November 18 (Moon into Virgo, 5:20 p.m.)
The moon joins Mars in Virgo. While Mars demands action and movement on the financial front today, the moon may caution you to hold back, to keep something in reserve. The Virgo moon is discerning and detailed. You should be too.

Saturday, November 19 (Moon in Virgo) If you're feeling change in the wind, you may be sensitive to the solar eclipse coming up in Sagittarius on November 25, just in time for the long Thanksgiving weekend. Pay close attention to coincidences today. They are signs pointing you in the right direction.

Sunday, November 20 (Moon into Libra, 8:17 p.m.)
The Libra moon brings about another sigh of relief and contentment. It's a gentler moon for you, and even though it's conjunct to stern Saturn, it soothes your soul. And since it's Sunday, it's a perfect time to take in a new art exhibit, to attend a concert, or to settle in with a good book or a movie. In other words, feed your inner artist, Leo.

Monday, November 21 (Moon in Libra)   If you can continue the attention to your artistic side today, you'll be much happier. But if that's not possible, then focus on your people skills. Touch base with employees and coworkers, family and friends. Create a blog if you don't have one already. The idea is to reach out and connect.

Tuesday, November 22 (Moon into Scorpio, 8:59 p.m.) Getting ready for the Thanksgiving holidays? You'd better decide today who is going to host the event. If you're the host, you'll be tending to a lot of last-minute details today, not the least of which is getting your home in order. If you're headed out of town, you probably have your travel plans in place already. Just remember that Mercury turns retrograde on Thursay, so there could be some surprises on your return trip.

Wednesday, November 23 (Moon in Scorpio)   Back up your computer files today. Be redundant. Back up onto a flash drive and an external hard drive. If there's something really sensitive or current on your computer, then send the files to a friend as well. This moon forms a beneficial angle to Mars in Virgo, so you've got plenty of forward movement.

Thursday, November 24 (Moon into Sagittarius, 8:58 p.m.)   Mercury turns retrograde in Sagittarius and remains that way until December 13. You know the drill. It would be smart to postpone your holiday shopping until after December 13, particularly if you're going to be buying electronics or expensive items. For another two days, you're still in that romantic and creative period, so make the best of it!

Friday, November 25 (Moon in Sagittarius)   Today's solar eclipse in Sagittarius attracts new opportunities for romance and for flexing your creative muscles. There could be a pregnancy, or one of your kids could land an incredible opportunity to do something or be involved in something important to him or to her. Read the Big Picture section on eclipses for additional information.

Saturday, November 26 (Moon into Capricorn, 10:05 p.m.)   Venus enters Capricorn, where it will be until December 20. During this transit, your daily work life should improve considerably. If you're looking for a job, you get the leads you need to find work that is satisfying. This transit can also indicate that a flirtation at work becomes something else. Or your creative projects are now folded into your daily work life. Or all of the above!

Sunday, November 27 (Moon in Capricorn)   Today is about earth energy—the moon, Mars, Jupiter, and Venus are in earth signs, and they prompt you to keep things grounded. You won't be inclined to speak abstractly, but if you do, you'll see that others don't understand what you're talking about. So keep things simple and to the point.

Monday, November 28 (Moon in Capricorn)   It's the ideal time to look ahead to the last month of the year and take stock. Have you accomplished what you set out to do this year? If not, why not? Can any of these desires carry over into next year? Are your priorities different now? Brainstorm, Leo.

Tuesday, November 29 (Moon into Aquarius, 2:02 a.m.) The moon joins Neptune in your opposite sign. This will happen only a few more times because in early 2012, Neptune enters Pisces once more. So take a long hard look at your priorities and expectations in partnerships. Do they satisfy your ideals? Don't hesitate to reach outside the box for answers.

Wednesday, November 30 (Moon in Aquarius)   With Mercury retrograde until December 13, be sure to revise and review existing projects rather than launching new ones. This goes for businesses, creative endeavors, even relationships! Saturn forms a beneficial angle to this moon and helps to solidify your ideas.

DECEMBER 2011

Thursday, December 1 (Moon into Pisces, 9:46 a.m.)
If it's almost winter where you are—i.e., cold and gloomy—then today is when you should start to meditate or practice some sort of mind-body activity like yoga. Either activity would appeal to the gentle Pisces moon, which craves the intuitive, the imaginative, the soothing flow of events rather than dramatic events. So ground yourself, Leo, and start making your shopping list!

Friday, December 2 (Moon in Pisces)   So this is where the rubber meets the road, Leo. You stand by what you believe is true, or you cave to the people around you who insist you're wrong. The fixed nature of your sun sign is likely to opt for standing tall. But the Pisces moon is often conflicted, with the head wanting to go one way and the heart another. So what's your stance?

Saturday, December 3 (Moon into Aries, 8:52 p.m.)
If you're traveling abroad today, there could be some snafus in your itinerary, due to the Mercury retrograde. But if you make it through the mix-ups, the traveling should be enjoyable. You're in your element for the next few days, with the moon in a fellow fire sign that encourages you to be daring, to take risks. It's smart to remind yourself, however, that all actions have consequences.

Sunday, December 4 (Moon in Aries)   Imagine, if you can, that the world you live in now is completely different from the world you have known for most of your life. Across the board, this is not the world you knew. Now imagine how you might make your way through this world. How would you earn a living? Where would you live? What would your family look like? This is the visionary part of your sign, Leo. Use it.

Monday, December 5 (Moon in Aries)   You take the reins and lead the troops out of harm's way. At least, that's how it happens in your head. The logistics depend on who the troops are—your family? A friend? A partner? Strangers? If the troops don't want to be led anywhere, then you'll have to forge forward alone.

Tuesday, December 6 (Moon into Taurus, 9:36 a.m.) The moon enters the career sector of your chart, at a time when career may be the furthest thing from your mind. But take care to run ideas past your boss, to do the things you normally do in the course of a day. Don't take shortcuts. In another week, Mercury will turn direct again, and life will look much brighter.

Wednesday, December 7 (Moon in Taurus)   You could be feeling vulnerable and put out about a professional matter. But what you feel shows, and *that* may not be in your best interest. So put on your happy smile, Leo, and lift yourself out of the doldrums so that the people around you are fooled. It's important to look confident and upbeat.

Thursday, December 8 (Moon into Gemini, 9:54 p.m.) This moon is much friendlier for you. Air signs tend to feed the best part of your personality—that part of you that reaches out to people with genuine interest and compassion. With your mood in a much better place than it has been for the last several days, you're content with where you are in your life right this second and have a fairly clear idea of where you would like your life to head throughout the New Year.

Friday, December 9 (Moon in Gemini)   This moon forms a beneficial angle with Saturn in Libra, suggesting that any creative endeavors that you work on now will find the structure they need. This structure could be a group project in which you become involved, or something you and a group of friends initiate. Ideas flow fast and furiously.

Saturday, December 10 (Moon in Gemini)   Uranus turns direct in Aries, and there's a lunar eclipse in Gemini. Uranus's movement should attract idiosyncratic and unusual people whose worldview may differ radically from your own. Consider these individuals to be teachers. Or you will teach them something. Or both. The eclipse brings up emotional issues related to friends or to your own wishes and dreams. It should be quite positive. Sounds like a celebration, Leo!

Sunday, December 11 (Moon into Cancer, 8:27 a.m.) In another two days, Mercury turns direct. Hold off on new projects, the signing of contracts, and firming up travel plans for at least until December 14. For today, go inward for your answers and insight. Request help from your dreams. Meditate.

Monday, December 12 (Moon in Cancer)   How nice that the universe has arranged things so that Mercury turns direct on the same day that the moon enters your sign (tomorrow). Until then, keep backing up your computer files! Spend quality time today with another person or a small group of people whom you trust. It could be that you and a group of old friends wax nostalgic.

Tuesday, December 13 (Moon into Leo, 4:49 p.m.) Another power day and Mercury turns direct as well. You're ready to explode out of the gate, but are advised to open the gate slowly, to look to the right and left, and to move forward with a degree of caution. You know what you want to do and how you want to do it. That won't slip away from you just because you're cautious.

Wednesday, December 14 (Moon in Leo)   You've got plenty to draw from today. Your well isn't just half full—it's nearly brimming over with ideas, support, enthusiasm, and raw, physical energy. Whether you're running a political campaign, doing holiday shopping, or galvanizing the troops at work, you're in charge. So dress for and act the part.

Thursday, December 15 (Moon into Virgo, 10:59 p.m.) The moon enters Virgo late tonight, which means that tomorrow and the next day are ideal for holiday shopping. You'll be more conscious of what you spend and for whom you're buying, and you will be more thrifty. Pay cash and save yourself a credit headache in January.

Friday, December 16 (Moon in Virgo)   There are certain activities that fit a Virgo moon. Pay close attention to details, scrutinize everything as if under a microscope, read the fine print in any legal document, attend to health matters by collecting more information than you need, and work closely with your own beliefs. And that's just for starters. But the bottom line is that the Virgo moon urges you to be present in all that you do.

Saturday, December 17 (Moon in Virgo)   Look ahead to New Year's Eve. What are your New Year's resolutions? With the moon in your solar second house, you are urged to look deeply at your values and priorities. What qualities do you value above all else? Who are the most important people in your life? What would you like to experience or achieve in the next year? Start with questions like those.

Sunday, December 18 (Moon into Libra, 3:07 a.m.) Here comes another air-sign moon that suits you. The Libra moon urges you to be aware of fairness and balance in all your dealings today. With the holidays so close, be sure to have gifts for anyone who performs a service for you. Show your appreciation for the people who make your life easier.

Monday, December 19 (Moon in Libra)   Whether you're leaving town for the holidays or sticking close to home, you've got your work cut out for you. In the midst of the usual chaos in the run-up to the holidays, it seems that you may be called upon to mediate a disagreement in your neighborhood or community or even among your siblings. Your job is to offer an unbiased opinion.

Tuesday, December 20 (Moon into Scorpio, 5:33 a.m.) Venus enters Aquarius and your opposite sign, where it will be until early next year. This transit is wonderful for deepening a commitment in a relationship. You and your partner could move in together or get married. If you're considering launching your own business, then you may encounter the right partner to make it happen.

Wednesday, December 21 (Moon in Scorpio)   Even though emotions are often deeper and more powerful around the holidays, yours are particularly so today. Your focus is entirely on family, roots, and your connections at a collective level to your ancestors. In the Western world, we tend to ignore ancestral roots. Today that won't be possible for you. You'll be swimming at an archetypal level, Leo.

Thursday, December 22 (Moon into Sagittarius, 7:03 a.m.)   If you're doing last-minute holiday shopping, buy for quality rather than quantity. With the Sagittarius moon forming such a beneficial angle to your sun sign and to Uranus in Aries, there will be a quirky quality to gifts you buy for your kids or for the special love of your life. The receivers of these gifts will look back years later and remember that *you* gave a gift that truthfully reflected who they were at that moment.

Friday, December 23 (Moon in Sagittarius) There are ample advantages for you today. If you're trying to push through some last-minute project or idea at work, do it today. You and your family may hit the road early if you're leaving town for Christmas, or you may simply take off early from work to get your home in order for visitors.

Saturday, December 24 (Moon into Capricorn, 8:48 a.m.) Today's new moon in Capricorn will usher in new opportunities between now and the next full moon in January 2012 to realize your goals. Pluto forms a beneficial angle to this new moon, suggesting that you're in a powerful place to bring about profound change. Uranus also turns direct today in Aries, a great portent for the New Year. You can expect unusual and exciting events.

Sunday, December 25 (Moon in Capricorn) Merry Christmas! And just to make sure that the day is actually merry, Jupiter turns direct in Taurus, which will lead to expansion in your life once again. Jupiter in an earth sign like Taurus could help your finances to expand as long as you're willing to pull your weight by sticking to a budget, paying with cash when you can, and working hard to achieve creative satisfaction.

Monday, December 26 (Moon into Aquarius, 12:15 pm) The moon joins Neptune in your opposite sign, injecting a spiritual component into your closest partnerships. You'll be asking yourself if your current partnerships are a true reflection of your higher self or are just business as usual. One challenge with Neptune is that it can dissolve boundaries between your ego and the rest of the world and, in a worst-case scenario, could make you needy. But you're very much your own person so that scenario isn't likely to happen.

Tuesday, December 27 (Moon in Aquarius) Time to come up with your New Year's resolutions. Sit down

237

with a partner, family member, or friend, and brainstorm about the year ahead. Look at different areas in your respective lives—personal, professional, creative, money, family, health—and talk about what you would each like to experience in these areas. Then write it all down.

Wednesday, December 28 (Moon into Pisces, 6:46 p.m.)
Your focus shifts to resources you share with others and vice versa. You have an opportunity today to share your time and expertise, and to simply give your support with someone who needs it. Or the other way around. If you're in the midst of a divorce, this could suggest that you and your partner discuss how to divide your assets.

Thursday, December 29 (Moon in Pisces) Are your New Year's plans in place yet? Get busy. You'll want to bring in 2012 in style, and with the moon in Aries on December 31, that won't be hard to do. Have the party at your place, if you're so inclined, but keep it small, with people you know well.

Friday, December 30 (Moon in Pisces) This moon forms a harmonious angle with Jupiter in Taurus, thus boosting your intuitive grasp of a sticky situation. Best to stay in the background on this one, Leo. Wait until after the New Year to deal with it. You don't have to respond immediately.

Saturday, December 31 (Moon into Aries, 4:49 a.m.)
Celebrate! The moon is in fellow fire sign Aries, Uranus is direct in the same sign, and your head is spinning with possibilities, ideas, what-ifs. Greet the New Year with love in your heart.

HAPPY NEW YEAR!

Sunday, January 1 (Moon in Aries)   You start the year with the moon in fellow fire sign Aries. You're feeling charged, ready to start something new. It's a great day astrologically and as the start of the year the perfect time to write down your goals. They should be dynamic and optimistic, placing yourself right at center stage.

Monday, January 2 (Moon into Taurus, 5:17 p.m.) Okay, it's time to get organized, Leo. Control your impulses. Take care of your obligations. You're building your foundations for the year ahead. Emphasize quality. Tear down the old in order to rebuild.

Tuesday, January 3 (Moon in Taurus)   The moon is in your tenth house today. Your life is more public. You gain an elevation in prestige. You're more responsive to the needs and moods of a group and of the public in general. You're ready to work for the common good, but keep an eye on your own wishes and dreams.

Wednesday, January 4 (Moon in Taurus)   Health and physical activity are highlighted. It's a good day to use common sense and take a down-to-earth perspective on whatever you're doing. Try to avoid stubborn behavior when others question your actions. You could be somewhat possessive now, Leo.

Thursday, January 5 (Moon into Gemini, 5:45 a.m.) It's a number 7 day, your mystery day. You launch a journey into the unknown. Stay alert. You're a searcher, a seeker of truth. Secrets, intrigue, and confidential information play a role. Be aware of decisions made behind closed doors. You work best on your own today.

Friday, January 6 (Moon in Gemini) The moon is in your eleventh house today. That means friends and associates play an important role in your day. You could be working with a group of them. You find strength in numbers, meaning through friends. Focus on your wishes and dreams. Reexamine your overall goals for the year, and make sure those goals remain an expression of who you are.

Saturday, January 7 (Moon into Cancer, 4:06 p.m.) Finish what you've started, and get ready for the new. Clear up odds and ends. Visualize for the future. You're at center stage, Leo! Set your goals and make them so. But don't start anything new today.

Sunday, January 8 (Moon in Cancer)   With Mercury moving into your sixth house today, you'll be methodical and quite efficient the rest of the month. Try not to be too picky with what you do or with what others do around you. Don't spend your time worrying; you're doing fine. It'll all work out.

Monday, January 9 (Moon into Leo, 11:35 p.m.) There's a full moon in your twelfth house today. It's a good day to step back from your busy work schedule and take some time for yourself. Work behind the scenes. That way you'll avoid unwanted influences that could disturb your sense of order. You'll also gain insight and illumination related to whatever or whoever has captivated you.

Tuesday, January 10 (Moon in Leo)   The moon is on your ascendant today. You're recharged for the rest of the month and beyond. You're more appealing to the public. It's a great day for starting something new. Your appearance and personality shine. Your feelings and thoughts are aligned. Dealings with the opposite sex go well.

Wednesday, January 11 (Moon in Leo)   Strut your stuff, Leo. You're at center stage. Drama is highlighted, perhaps involving children. You're searching for ways to improve yourself. You're particularly sensitive to others' feelings now. Your thoughts and feelings are aligned. You're creative and passionate today, impulsive and honest. It's a good day to take a chance.

Thursday, January 12 (Moon into Virgo, 4:44 a.m.) It's a number 5 day. That means you're open to change and variety, and you desire to loosen any restrictions today. You're willing to take a risk and experiment. Variety is the spice of life, and change is good. Think outside the box.

Friday, January 13 (Moon in Virgo)   Expect emotional experiences related to money. You feel best around your favorite possessions. It's not the objects themselves that are important. It's the feelings you associate with them. Look at your priorities in handling your income. Best to put off making any major purchases.

Saturday, January 14 (Moon into Libra, 8:29 a.m.) Venus moves into your eighth house. You profit through partnerships over the next few weeks, Leo. Joint financial affairs work to your benefit. Avoid any tendencies toward jealousies or possessiveness. Seek harmony with your partner, and share your plans before acting on them.

Sunday, January 15 (Moon in Libra)   Your mind is sharp, and you communicate well. Take what you know and share it with others. You send out e-mails or make an entry on a blog. Your thinking is unduly influenced by things of the past. Family members play a role in your day. Do your best to avoid arguing with siblings or neighbors. Better to be competitive and aggressive by playing a video game.

Monday, January 16 (Moon into Scorpio, 11:34 a.m.) It's a number 9 day. Clear your desk for tomorrow's new cycle, but don't start anything today. Use the day for reflection, expansion, and concluding projects. Look for a new approach, a new perspective. Spiritual values surface.

Tuesday, January 17 (Moon in Scorpio)   The moon is in your fourth house today. Spend time with your family and loved ones. Stick close to home, maybe work there, if possible. Attend to a home-repair project in your spare time. You could be dealing with parents now. You feel a close tie to your roots.

Wednesday, January 18 (Moon into Sagittarius, 2:30 p.m.)   The moon is in your fifth house. That means you're innovative, creative, and communicate well. Your artistic talents are highlighted. Enjoy the harmony, beauty, and pleasures of life. Beautify your home. Remain flexible. Your popularity is on the rise.

Thursday, January 19 (Moon in Sagittarius)   Your creativity is highlighted. Look to the big picture now. Are you willing to take a chance to stretch out and reach a goal? Today's the day for it. Take time for romance. Sex for pleasure is the key phrase. Put it to use!

Friday, January 20 (Moon into Capricorn, 5:42 p.m.) You're building foundations for an outlet to expand your creativity. Emphasize quality related to whatever you're working on. Persevere to get things done today. Look for a new approach, a new perspective. Look beyond the immediate.

Saturday, January 21 (Moon in Capricorn)   With the moon in your sixth house today, it's a service day. Others rely on you now. You're the one they reach out to for help. Do what you can—be of service—but don't deny your own needs. Keep your resolutions about exercise, and watch your diet.

Sunday, January 22 (Moon into Aquarius, 9:54 p.m.)
Yesterday's energy flows into your Sunday. Diplomacy is called for in all your interactions. You offer support and advice, but take time to dance to your own tune! Be understanding, and avoid confrontations.

Monday, January 23 (Moon in Aquarius) There's a new moon in your seventh house today. New opportunities arise related to partnerships. You get along well with others. You can fit in just about anywhere. You comprehend the nuances of a situation, but it's difficult to go with the flow. It's a good time to get rid of a bad habit.

Tuesday, January 24 (Moon in Aquarius) Groups and social events are highlighted now. Your individuality is stressed. Your visionary abilities are heightened. You have a greater sense of freedom. You're dealing with new ideas, new options, originality. Your wishes and dreams come true.

Wednesday, January 25 (Moon into Pisces, 4:12 a.m.)
Use the day for reflection, expansion, and concluding projects. Clear up odd and ends. Accept what comes your way now, but don't start anything new. It's all part of a cycle. Strive for universal appeal.

Thursday, January 26 (Moon in Pisces) Your experiences are more intense than usual, especially when dealing with matters related to your home. It's a good day to take time to meditate or study a metaphysical subject, such as life after death or past lives. Other issues of the day could include matters of sex, death, rebirth, rituals, and relationships.

Friday, January 27 (Moon into Aries, 1:29 p.m.) With Mercury moving into your seventh house today, you communicate well over the next couple of weeks, especially with a partner. It's a good time for writing or speaking about whatever interests you. You also could help solve any disputes among others. You're articulate and promote your ideas well.

Saturday, January 28 (Moon in Aries)   You're extremely persuasive now, especially if you're passionate about what you're doing, selling, or trying to convey. It's also a good day for athletics, either participating in or attending a sporting event. Wear bright colors, Leo. Imprint your style. Do something thrilling.

Sunday, January 29 (Moon in Aries)   With the moon in your ninth house today, you're attracted to philosophy or religion, mythology or intellectual interests. You're feeling restless, planning an escape from the routine. Plan a long trip for pleasure, or play a computer game. Role-playing plays a role, Leo! In romance, a flirtation with a foreign-born person could turn serious.

Monday, January 30 (Moon into Taurus, 1:29 a.m.) A change of scenery would work to your advantage. You could be moving to a new location. You're seeking new horizons, travel, and adventure. Promote new ideas, follow your curiosity. You're versatile, changeable. Be careful not to spread out and diversify too much.

Tuesday, January 31 (Moon in Taurus)   The moon is in your tenth house today. It's a good day for sales and dealing with the public. You're more responsive to the needs of others, and you're more emotional and warm toward coworkers. You get a boost in prestige. However, avoid mixing your professional with your personal life now.

FEBRUARY 2012

Wednesday, February 1 (Moon into Gemini, 2:15 p.m.) Start the month by getting everything in order. Be methodical and thorough. Revise, rewrite. You're building foundations for an outlet for your creativity. Persevere to get things done today. Control your impulses. Sorry, Leo. Romance goes onto the back burner for now.

Thursday, February 2 (Moon in Gemini) The moon is in your eleventh house today. Group activities work in your favor now, even if you're a nonjoiner. You assist the group and—surprise—the group helps you in return. You take center stage, Leo. Friends also play an important role. Focus on your wishes and dreams, but make sure that your goals remain an expression of who you really are.

Friday, February 3 (Moon in Gemini) Neptune is in your eighth house today. Joint finances could take an odd twist this year and beyond. There's something secretive or deceptive going on. It could also involve taxes, a mortgage, an inheritance, or insurance. Pay attention to details on these matters. If you're pursuing any metaphysical interests, stay grounded and avoid any groups whose practice might involve manipulation of others, even if they say it's for the common good.

Saturday, February 4 (Moon into Cancer, 1:04 a.m.) It's your mystery day, Leo. You work best on your own today. You investigate, analyze, or simply observe what's going on now. You quickly come to a conclusion and wonder why others don't see what you see. Maintain your emotional balance. Your challenge today is to be independent without feeling isolated.

Sunday, February 5 (Moon in Cancer) The moon is in your twelfth house today, and it's a good day to retreat from public view. Unconscious attitudes can be difficult now. So can relations with women. You feel best working behind the scenes and keeping your feelings to yourself. Follow your intuition, and work on your self-confidence.

Monday, February 6 (Moon into Leo, 8:24 a.m.)   It's a number 9 day. That means it's a good time to complete a project. Clear your desk, and get ready for something new, but don't start it today. Use the day for finishing what you've started and for considering how to expand. Take time to reflect on where things are going in your life.

Tuesday, February 7 (Moon in Leo)   Saturn goes retrograde in your third house today and stays there until June 25. You face misunderstandings from family members, especially siblings. Neighbors could be problematic. You could find yourself feeling depressed, and that could result in some self-doubt about your abilities. Hard work is called for, and you do it best on your own. In addition, there's a full moon in your first house, and that means you gain insight and illumination related to how others see you now. You're sensitive to other people's feelings. Your feelings tend to fluctuate by the moment.

Wednesday, February 8 (Moon into Virgo, 12:33 p.m.) Venus moves into your ninth house today. This month your focus turns to higher learning and/or long-distance travel. You could feel strongly attracted to a philosophy, an art form, or religion. You might also study a foreign country or culture or fall in love with someone born in a foreign land. A trip for pleasure could allow you to make important social contacts or a romantic tryst.

Thursday, February 9 (Moon in Virgo)   The moon is in your second house today. Money issues and your emotions are on your agenda. Put off making any major purchases. Your values play an important role in your decisions. You have a tendency to collect things, and those objects make you feel at home and at peace.

Friday, February 10 (Moon into Libra, 2:55 p.m.) Your organizational skills are highlighted, especially related to financial matters. Fulfill your obligations. Look for an investment, pay your bills, and collect what's owed to you. Persevere to get things done today. This evening you might enjoy getting involved in a challenging mental activity, such as on-line gaming, a debate, or a game of chess . . . anything that engages your mental prowess.

Saturday, February 11 (Moon in Libra) The moon is in your third house today. You'll probably be running around, taking care of chores in your everyday world. You could hear from a sibling, other relative, or neighbor today, and if so, you can expect an invitation. Control your emotions when expressing any opinions, especially on matters related to the past.

Sunday, February 12 (Moon into Scorpio, 5:02 p.m.) It's a number 6 day. Service to others is the theme of the day. You offer advice and support, possibly to a neighbor or family member. Do a good deed. Visit someone who is ill or in need of help. Be sympathetic and kind, generous and tolerant.

Monday, February 13 (Moon in Scorpio) Mercury moves into your eighth house today. You're investigating matters close to home, especially joint resources. You're trying to get to the bottom of a mystery. Insurance, an inheritance, or taxes could be at the heart of the matter. You could also be talking to others about the deeper issues of life, such as life after death and the reality of the spirit world or higher dimensions.

Tuesday, February 14 (Moon into Sagittarius, 7:57 p.m.) This evening, as the moon moves into your fifth house, it's time for romance. There's greater emotional depth to a relationship now. Be yourself; be emotionally honest. Take a chance; experiment. Happy Valentine's Day.

Wednesday, February 15 (Moon in Sagittarius) Your creativity, personal grace, and magnetism are highlighted. But you can be very impressionable today. Be careful about following the advice of others, especially regarding money matters. If there are children in your life, you feel particularly attached to them.

Thursday, February 16 (Moon in Sagittarius)   You see the big picture now, not just the details. Travel is indicated. You're restless, impulsive, and inquisitive. Don't limit yourself. Spiritual values arise. Worldviews are emphasized.

Friday, February 17 (Moon into Capricorn, 12:04 a.m.) Partnerships and cooperative ventures are emphasized now. Use your intuition to get a sense of your day. Don't make waves. Don't rush or show resentment; let things develop. You're diplomatic and capable of fixing whatever has gone wrong.

Saturday, February 18 (Moon in Capricorn)   Yesterday's energy flows into your Saturday. It's a service day. Help others, but don't deny your own needs. It's a good day to clarify any health or work issues. Keep your resolutions about exercise, and watch your diet.

Sunday, February 19 (Moon into Aquarius, 5:29 a.m.) Groups and social events are highlighted now. Take care of your obligations. Emphasize quality. You're building foundations for an outlet for your creativity. Follow your wishes and dreams.

Monday, February 20 (Moon in Aquarius)   The focus turns to relationships, business and personal ones. A legal matter comes to your attention now. You comprehend the nuances of a situation, but it's difficult to go with the flow. Women play a prominent role. Be careful that others don't manipulate your feelings.

Tuesday, February 21 (Moon into Pisces, 12:32 p.m.) There's a new moon in your eighth house today. New moons are about new opportunities, and they give you energy for two weeks. A doorway opens now, especially related to resources shared with a partner. A pursuit of metaphysics could play a role.

Wednesday, February 22 (Moon in Pisces) Imagination is highlighted. Watch for psychic events, synchronicities. Keep track of your dreams, including your daydreams. Ideas are ripe. Universal knowledge, eternal truths, and deep spirituality are the themes of the day.

Thursday, February 23 (Moon into Aries, 9:48 p.m.) It's your power day, your day to play it your way. Unexpected money arrives. Think big and act big! You attract financial success, especially if you open your mind to a new approach.

Friday, February 24 (Moon in Aries) With the moon in your ninth house today, you feel a need to break out of your usual routine, Leo. Travel or higher education plays a role. Plan a trip or sign up for a seminar or workshop. A foreign country or person of foreign birth could play a role. Be bold and adventurous in your pursuits. Your higher mind plays a role.

Saturday, February 25 (Moon in Aries) It's a great time for initiating projects, launching new ideas, and brainstorming. You're passionate but impatient. You're extremely persuasive now, especially if you feel strongly about what you're doing, selling, or trying to convey. Pisces and Virgo play extraordinary roles with the Aries moon.

Sunday, February 26 (Moon into Taurus, 9:30 a.m.) You prefer center stage, Leo, but let's face it, sometimes sharing the limelight with a partner works to your benefit. Today is one of those days. You excel in working with others now. Be honest and open. You're playing the role of the visionary.

Monday, February 27 (Moon in Taurus)   Your focus turns to professional matters, whether it's your career or education. You could be dealing with a matter related to your reputation. You get a boost in prestige today. You're received well by others now, but avoid making an emotional display in public.

Tuesday, February 28 (Moon into Gemini, 10:28 p.m.) It's a number 4 day, so your organizational skills are emphasized. Clear your desk or clean a closet. Tear down the old in order to rebuild. Be methodical and thorough. Revise, rewrite. You're at the right place at the right time.

Wednesday, February 29 (Moon in Gemini)   The moon is in your eleventh house today. Thanks to your friends, you get a nice break, a new opportunity. Your sense of security is tied to your relationships. You work well with a group now, especially if you're working for the common good.

MARCH 2012

Thursday, March 1 (Moon in Gemini)   Friends play an important role in your day and help you in surprising ways. You work well with a group of like-minded people. Focus on your wishes and dreams, and watch how many of them come true this year.

Friday, March 2 (Moon into Cancer, 10:09 a.m.) Mercury moves into your ninth house today. You communicate well about your philosophy of life. Mythology or religions could capture your interest. You also might be talking a lot this month about plans for a long trip. You have many ideas now, and you express them well. It's a good time to learn a foreign language.

Saturday, March 3 (Moon in Cancer)   The moon is in your twelfth house today. Think carefully before you act, Leo. There's a tendency now to undo all the positive actions you've taken. Avoid any self-destructive tendencies. It's best to work behind the scenes and stay out of the public view. Be aware of hidden enemies.

Sunday, March 4 (Moon into Leo, 6:19 p.m.)   It's a number 8 day, your power day, and your day to play it your way. You're recharged now for the month ahead. You can go far with your plans and achieve financial success. You have a chance to expand, to gain recognition, even fame and power. You focus on how the public relates to you. You're playing with power, so be careful not to hurt others.

Monday, March 5 (Moon in Leo)   With Venus moving into your tenth house today, it's a month for focusing on a career matter related to the arts, fashion, beauty, or entertainment. You can stay grounded now and move ahead. Career opportunities come through a marriage or partnership.

Tuesday, March 6 (Moon into Virgo, 10:28 p.m.)   It's a number 1 day, and you're at the top of your cycle. You attract creative people now. So don't bother with those who have closed minds. Stress originality. You take the lead, Leo. You get a fresh start, and you're at center stage. Get out and meet new people, have new experiences, do something you've never done before.

Wednesday, March 7 (Moon in Virgo)   Stick close to home today, if possible. Focus on tidying up the house; attend to the details and loose ends. You may exhibit some perfectionist tendencies. Relax. Take time to write in a journal. You write from a deep place now with lots of details.

Thursday, March 8 (Moon into Libra, 11:50 p.m.) There's a full moon in your second house today. You hear news about money; your finances are on your mind.

You also have greater insight into your values, or what you value. It's a good time to set up a doctor or dentist appointment. You're a stickler for details now.

Friday, March 9 (Moon in Libra)   The moon is in your third house today. You're busy keeping your mind occupied with new information coming your way. You're excited and want to share what you know. However, keep conscious control of your emotions, especially when dealing with family members and neighbors. Don't let matters from the past cloud your thinking.

Saturday, March 10 (Moon in Libra)   Relationship issues figure prominently in your day. Romance is highlighted. It's a good day to go out on the town. Museums, art, music, and creativity all figure in. Your personal grace and magnetism allow you to keep everyone around you in balance.

Sunday, March 11—Daylight Saving Time Begins (Moon into Scorpio, 1:25 a.m.)   Service to others is the theme of the day. You offer advice and support. Be diplomatic, especially when dealing with a situation at home. A change in the home, an adjustment or readjustment, might be needed now. Don't put off the situation. That will only aggravate the problem.

Monday, March 12 (Moon in Scorpio)   Mercury goes retrograde in your ninth house today and stays there until April 4. It's a great time for a long-distance journey or preparing for one. Learning a foreign language comes easily for you now. Matters dealing with the law or publishing could come to your attention this month.

Tuesday, March 13 (Moon into Sagittarius, 2:54 a.m.)
It's another power day, so focus on a power play. Business discussions go well. You attract financial success,

especially if you open your mind to a new approach. Be aware that fear of failure or fear that you won't measure up will attract tangible experiences that reinforce the feeling.

Wednesday, March 14 (Moon in Sagittarius)   It's a good day to take a chance. Express your creativity. Get out there and do something unexpected, especially if it's about helping others. Children play a role. In love, there's greater emotional depth to a relationship now, especially if you're emotionally honest.

Thursday, March 15 (Moon into Capricorn, 6:24 a.m.) You're at the top of your cycle today. You're inventive and make connections that others overlook. You're determined and courageous. In romance, something new is developing. Be independent, creative, and refuse to be discouraged by naysayers. Express your opinions dynamically.

Friday, March 16 (Moon in Capricorn)   It's your service day again. You improve, edit, and refine the work of others. But don't ignore your own needs or fall into the trap of martyrdom. Have you made that doctor or dentist appointment yet? It's best if you follow a regular schedule now.

Saturday, March 17 (Moon into Aquarius, 12:12 p.m.) You're innovative, creative, and communicate well, Leo. You're at center stage and quite comfortable there. Spread your good news, and take time to listen to others. Ease up on routines. Your attitude determines everything today.

Sunday, March 18 (Moon in Aquarius)   The moon is in your seventh house today. Friends and partners play an important role in your day. You and your partner could be working with a group, and the collective energy works to your benefit. That's especially true if you're working for the common good. It's a good day to make a donation to a worthy cause.

Monday, March 19 (Moon into Pisces, 8:05 p.m.)   It's a number 5 day. Change and variety are highlighted now. Promote new ideas; follow your curiosity. Approach the day with an unconventional mind-set. Release old structures; get a new point of view. Variety is the spice of life.

Tuesday, March 20 (Moon in Pisces)   With the moon in your eighth house today, your experiences intensify. You could be dealing with a matter related to shared belongings or resources. It could involve an inheritance, insurance, a mortgage, or taxes. Avoid becoming overly possessive or greedy. Alternately, an interest in metaphysical subjects—astrology, ghosts, or past lives—plays a role in your day.

Wednesday, March 21 (Moon in Pisces)   It's a day for deep healing. You respond emotionally to whatever is happening now. Your imagination is strong; your fantasy life is vivid. Turn inward for inspiration, universal knowledge, eternal truths. Remember and record your dreams.

Thursday, March 22 (Moon into Aries, 5:58 a.m.) There's a new moon in your ninth house today. New opportunities come your way related to higher education or long-distance travel. A new beginning, a new doorway opens for you. Your thoughts run wild. You're a dreamer and a thinker, and your thoughts tend to rattle the status quo.

Friday, March 23 (Moon in Aries)   Yesterday's energy flows into your Friday as you launch something new. It's a good time for brainstorming fresh ideas or initiating a new project. You're extremely persuasive now, Leo. Wear bright colors. Imprint your style. Have an adventure.

Saturday, March 24 (Moon into Taurus, 5:44 p.m.)
It's a number 1 day, and so you're at the top of your cycle again. You get a fresh start, a new beginning. In romance, a flirtation could turn serious, if that's what you want. Get out and meet new people, have new experiences, do something you've never done before. Explore and discover.

Sunday, March 25 (Moon in Taurus) The moon is in your tenth house today. Even though it's a weekend, your thoughts turn to your career or profession. You gain attention or recognition from coworkers now. You're also appealing to the public. You're feeling grounded and stable.

Monday, March 26 (Moon in Taurus) It's a good day to cultivate new ideas. You're opinionated and highly sensual. Try to avoid stubborn behavior when others question your actions. Use common sense; take a down-to-earth perspective on whatever you're doing. Health and physical activity are highlighted.

Tuesday, March 27 (Moon into Gemini, 6:44 a.m.)
It's time to get organized. Clean out your garage, attic, or a closet. Tear down in order to rebuild. Be methodical and thorough. Missing papers are found. Revise and rewrite. You're building a creative base.

Wednesday, March 28 (Moon in Gemini) Friends play an important role in your day, Aries and Sagittarius in particular. You work well with others, especially in a group. Focus on your wishes and dreams. Examine your overall goals, and make sure that they're still an expression of who you are.

Thursday, March 29 (Moon into Cancer, 7:08 p.m.)
A domestic adjustment works out for the best. You could face emotional outbursts or someone making unfair demands. Be understanding, and avoid confronta-

tions. Offer advice and support, but do it in a diplomatic way.

Friday, March 30 (Moon in Cancer)   The moon is in your twelfth house today. It's a good day to withdraw and spend time in private. Relax and meditate. Keep your feelings to yourself, unless you're confiding to someone close to you. It's a great day for pursuing a mystical or spiritual discipline.

Saturday, March 31 (Moon in Cancer)   Stay close to home and tend to family matters today, Leo. Snuggle with your loved one. Beautify your home; take care of repairs. You're intuitive and nurturing now. Hide any moodiness. Stay positive.

APRIL 2012

Sunday, April 1 (Moon into Leo, 4:37 a.m.)   You begin the month on a service day. Diplomacy wins the day. Focus on making people happy. Do a good deed for someone. Visit someone who is ill or in need of help. Your feelings and thoughts are aligned today.

Monday, April 2 (Moon in Leo)   The moon is in your first house today. You're sensitive to other people's feelings. You may feel moody one moment, happy the next, then withdrawn and sad. It's all about your health and your emotional self: how you feel and how you feel about yourself. You focus on how the public relates to you and how you can improve yourself.

Tuesday, April 3 (Moon into Virgo, 9:54 a.m.)   Venus moves into your twelfth house today. You're feeling introspective now and enjoy working behind the scenes. It's a good month to spend time on your own, especially if you're recovering from a relationship that has recently ended. Alternately, you could be getting involved in a secret romance. You have compassion for those who have less than you.

Wednesday, April 4 (Moon in Virgo)   Mercury goes direct in your eighth house today. That means any confusion and miscommunication related to shared resources recede into the past. Things move more smoothly now. You get your message across, and everything works better, including computers and other electronic equipment. Any delays you experienced related to taxes, insurance, a mortgage, or inheritance are over.

Thursday, April 5 (Moon into Libra, 11:33 a.m.) It's a number 1 day, and you're at the top of your cycle again. You're inventive and make connections that others overlook. You're determined and courageous today. You can take the lead now and get a fresh start. Don't be afraid to turn in a new direction. Trust your hunches. Intuition is highlighted.

Friday, April 6 (Moon in Libra)   There's a full moon in your third house today, and that means you gain insight and illumination related to matters of the past. Your mental abilities are strong now, and you have an emotional need to reinvigorate your studies, especially in history or archaeology. A short trip works to your benefit. You reap what you have sown.

Saturday, April 7 (Moon into Scorpio, 11:18 a.m.) Some of yesterday's energy flows into your Saturday. You're innovative and creative and communicate well. You keep everyone in balance today. Your artistic talents are highlighted.

Sunday, April 8 (Moon in Scorpio)   The moon is in your fourth house today. Spend time with your family and loved ones. Stick close to home. You're dealing with the foundations of who you are and who you are becoming. Take time to retreat to a private place for meditation. It's also a good day to recall, record, and closely consider your dreams.

Monday, April 9 (Moon into Sagittarius, 11:13 a.m.)
Change and variety are highlighted now. Think freedom, no restrictions. Find a new point of view that fits current circumstances and what you know. Release old structures; get a new point of view. It's a good day to take a risk, experiment. Promote new ideas.

Tuesday, April 10 (Moon in Sagittarius)   Pluto goes retrograde in your sixth house today and stays there until September 17. If you're planning to help others in the workplace, things might not go exactly as you hoped. Likewise, if you're dealing with a health issue, you could encounter some delays keeping you from finding out a diagnosis or proceeding with any other medical procedure.

Wednesday, April 11 (Moon into Capricorn, 1:02 p.m.)
It's a mystery day, and you're a seeker of truth. Look beneath the surface for the reasons others are shifting their points of view, "changing their tune." Knowledge is essential to success. Gather information, but don't make any absolute decisions until tomorrow. Make sure that you see things as they are, not as you wish them to be.

Thursday, April 12 (Moon in Capricorn)   With the moon in your sixth house today, the emphasis turns to your daily work and service to others. Try to keep a regular schedule now. Attend to all the details. Be careful not to overlook any seemingly minor matters that could take on importance. Keep up with your exercise plan, and watch your diet.

Friday, April 13 (Moon into Aquarius, 5:48 p.m.)
It's a number 9 day, your day to finish up what you've been working on and get ready for something new. Take

time to reflect on what you've been doing and look for a way to expand. Visualize the future; set your goals, then make them so.

Saturday, April 14 (Moon in Aquarius)   The moon is in your seventh house today. You communicate well with a spouse or partner. It's all about working together. A contract or a lawsuit could play a role. You get along well with others now. You can fit in anywhere, but it's a challenge to remain detached and objective.

Sunday, April 15 (Moon in Aquarius)   Groups and social events are highlighted now. Friends play an important role in your day. Help others, but dance to your own tune. You have a greater sense of freedom. You're dealing with new ideas, new options, originality. You get a new perspective. Play your hunches.

Monday, April 16 (Moon into Pisces, 1:38 a.m.) Mercury moves into your ninth house today. Your writing and speaking abilities are strong now. You teach others what you know. You could have an interest in law or publishing, philosophy or religion. It's a good time to learn a foreign language, to prepare yourself for a long trip, or even launch such a journey.

Tuesday, April 17 (Moon in Pisces)   An interest in metaphysics plays a role in your day. You could be looking into shamanism and power animals or learning more about contact with spirits. Alternately, you're dealing with shared resources now. If you are planning on making a major purchase, make sure that you and your partner are in agreement. Otherwise you could encounter intense emotional resistance.

Wednesday, April 18 (Moon into Aries, 12:00 p.m.) You're seeking new horizons now. Approach the day with an unconventional mind-set. You're versatile and changeable. Release old structures, and find a new point of view. Be careful not to spread out and diversify too much. Freedom of thought and action is key.

Thursday, April 19 (Moon in Aries)   Yesterday's energy flows into your Thursday. You're a dreamer and a thinker. You're keenly perceptive, and you understand how others feel. You yearn for a new experience, an escape, possibly with a special friend. You could be looking at a foreign destination, or maybe that friend is foreign-born. You can create positive change through your ideas.

Friday, April 20 (Moon in Aries)   The energy of the past two days moves into your Friday. You're open to new ideas now and highly self-motivated. You take on the day as if it were an adventure. Emotions could be volatile. You're passionate but impatient.

Saturday, April 21 (Moon into Taurus, 12:06 a.m.) There's a new moon in your tenth house today, and the high energy of recent days keeps on flowing. New opportunities come your way now related to your profession. It's a good time to begin a new project. You get a fresh start, a new beginning.

Sunday, April 22 (Moon in Taurus)   Once again, cultivate new ideas, but make sure that they're down-to-earth. Use your common sense when making any major decisions. Health and physical activity are highlighted. Try to avoid stubborn behavior if others question your actions. Be practical with your money.

Monday, April 23 (Moon into Gemini, 1:06 p.m.) Your high-powered surge continues. Be independent, creative, and refuse to be discouraged by naysayers. Don't be afraid to turn in a new direction. Trust your hunches; intuition is highlighted. Stress originality. In romance, a flirtation turns more serious.

Tuesday, April 24 (Moon in Gemini)   The moon is in your eleventh house today. You have deeper contact with friends now. You join a group of like-minded individuals. Focus on your wishes and dreams. Examine your overall goals, and make sure those goals should be an expression of who you are.

Wednesday, April 25 (Moon in Gemini)   You're restless and communicate well now. You see two sides of an issue. You're feeling creative and have an urge to express yourself in writing. A change of scenery is good. It's a good time to take a trip to visit relatives.

Thursday, April 26 (Moon into Cancer, 1:43 a.m.) Your organizational skills are highlighted. Be methodical and thorough. You're building a creative base for your future. Do things like clean your closet, clear your desk, straighten up your garage. It's not a day for experimentation or new approaches.

Friday, April 27 (Moon in Cancer)   With the moon passing through your twelfth house today, you might feel a need to work behind the scenes. You could feel moody, and you tend to hide your emotions. Take time to reflect and meditate. It's a great day for a mystical or spiritual discipline. Your intuition is heightened.

Saturday, April 28 (Moon into Leo, 12:11 p.m.)   It's time to clear up a situation at home that has lingered too long. Don't put off the situation. You could face emotional outbursts or someone making unfair demands. Be understanding and diplomatic, but know when to say enough is enough.

Sunday, April 29 (Moon in Leo)   The moon is on your ascendant today. The way you see yourself now is the way others see you. You're recharged, and this makes you more appealing to the public. You're physically vital, and you're attractive to the opposite sex.

Monday, April 30 (Moon into Virgo, 7:03 p.m.) It's a number 8 day, your power day, and a great day for finances. A business meeting goes well. Unexpected money comes your way. Expect a windfall. It's a good day for buying a lottery ticket.

MAY 2012

Tuesday, May 1 (Moon in Virgo) You could be somewhat picky today, focusing on all the details. Expect emotional experiences related to money. Dig deep for information, especially related to finances. Stop worrying and fretting. Take time to exercise, and watch your diet.

Wednesday, May 2 (Moon into Libra, 10:04 p.m.) It's another power day, Leo, and you're in the power seat. Open your mind to a new approach that could bring in big bucks. You're being watched by people in power. Be courageous. Be yourself; be honest.

Thursday, May 3 (Moon in Libra) The moon is in your third house today. Lots of information is coming your way. You study the details, especially those that relate to the past. Tell others what you know, but try not to get overly emotional.

Friday, May 4 (Moon into Scorpio, 10:20 p.m.) You can take the lead today in whatever you're doing. Trust your hunches; intuition is highlighted. You're inventive and make connections that others overlook. You're determined and courageous. Avoid people who have closed minds. In romance, something new is developing.

Saturday, May 5 (Moon in Scorpio) There's a full moon in your fourth house today. You gain new insight and illumination related to whatever you've been inves-

262

tigating. You reap what you've sown related to matters of your home or home life. Forgive and forget; try to avoid going to extremes. Control issues might arise.

Sunday, May 6 (Moon into Sagittarius, 9:40 p.m.) Your attitude determines everything today. You communicate well. You're warm and receptive to what others say. Ease up on routines. Spread your good news, and take time to listen to others. Take time to relax, enjoy yourself, and recharge your batteries.

Monday, May 7 (Moon in Sagittarius) The moon is in your fifth house today. Be yourself; be emotionally honest. In love, there's greater emotional depth to a relationship now. It's a good time to expand on a creative project. You're restless, impulsive, and inquisitive.

Tuesday, May 8 (Moon into Capricorn, 10:01 p.m.) Freedom of thought and action is key. But so is moderation; avoid excess in whatever you're doing. Change and variety are highlighted. It's a good time to take a risk. You can overcome obstacles with ease. Look for adventure. Get out and meet new people.

Wednesday, May 9 (Moon in Capricorn) Mercury moves into your tenth house today. Your speaking and writing abilities are strong now. You communicate effectively, especially related to your profession. Your ideas catch the interest of the public now and the support of coworkers.

Thursday, May 10 (Moon in Capricorn) The moon is in your sixth house today. It's a service-oriented day. You improve, edit, and refine the work of others. You're well grounded now, and your responsibilities increase. Be conservative; don't speculate or take any unnecessary risks. Maintain emotional balance. It's a good day to clarify any health or work issues. It's best if you follow a regular schedule.

Friday, May 11 (Moon into Aquarius, 1:04 a.m.)   It's another power day, Leo, and you're in the driver's seat. Business dealings go well. Be aware that you're playing with power, so try not to hurt anyone. Think big and act big! You can go far with your plans and achieve financial success.

Saturday, May 12 (Moon in Aquarius)   The moon is in your seventh house today. You get along well with others now. Loved ones and partners are more important than usual. You feel a need to be accepted. You're looking for security, but have a hard time going with the flow.

Sunday, May 13 (Moon into Pisces, 7:43 a.m.)   It's a number 1 day, and you're at the top of your cycle again. You get a fresh start, a new beginning. You can take the lead now, and don't be afraid of turning in a new direction. You attract creative people to your cause. Emphasize originality. Meanwhile, a flirtation could turn serious, if that's what you want.

Monday, May 14 (Moon in Pisces)   The moon is in your eighth house today. Your experiences are more intense than usual. You have a strong sense of duty and feel obligated to fulfill your promises. Security is an important issue with you right now. You could be involved in controlling or managing someone else's finances. An interest in metaphysics, such as life after death, plays a role in your day.

Tuesday, May 15 (Moon into Aries, 5:47 p.m.)   Venus goes retrograde in your twelfth house today and stays there until June 27. You feel best working behind the scenes now. Old issues, probably related to a relationship from the past, surface. Alternately, something that you thought was over is back on the table for consideration.

Wednesday, May 16 (Moon in Aries)   The moon is in your ninth house today. You're a dreamer and a thinker, Leo. You yearn for a new experience, and whatever it is, you want to take center stage. You have a strong curiosity now about foreign cultures. A foreign-born person could play a role. It's a good time to sign up for a workshop or seminar.

Thursday, May 17 (Moon in Aries)   You're extremely persuasive now, especially if you're passionate about what you're doing, selling, or trying to convey. Do something thrilling today; have an adventure. You're passionate but impatient. Avoid reckless behavior. Fellow fixed signs Scorpio, Aquarius, and Taurus play a role in your day, Leo.

Friday, May 18 (Moon into Taurus, 6:04 a.m.)   It's a service day, a day for being diplomatic with others. Offer your assistance but dance to your own tune. Be understanding, and avoid confrontations. Focus on making people happy. Domestic purchases are highlighted.

Saturday, May 19 (Moon in Taurus)   The moon is in your tenth house today. You're thinking about your career or profession now. You're looking for a new opportunity, an advancement or raise. Your life is more public. You get along well with fellow workers, but be careful if you're mixing your personal and private lives.

Sunday, May 20 (Moon into Gemini, 7:06 p.m.) There's a solar eclipse in your eleventh house today. That's the same as a double new moon or new opportunities times two! Your friends play a role. It's the beginning of something new for you or the end of something, so you might have to give something up in order to take advantage of your opportunities. Social consciousness plays a role.

Monday, May 21 (Moon in Gemini)　　Yesterday's energy flows into your Monday. You find strength in numbers. You find meaning through friends and groups. Your wishes and dreams can come true now, especially if your goals are a true expression of who you are.

Tuesday, May 22 (Moon in Gemini)　　You're feeling restless today and sending text messages to friends and associates to pass the time. You see both sides of an issue and feel a need to communicate through writing. Your mind moves quickly from one thought to another. You get your message across, maybe through e-mail or on Facebook. A change of scenery is a good idea now.

Wednesday, May 23 (Moon into Cancer, 7:32 a.m.) Partnerships are highlighted today. The spotlight is on cooperation. Your intuition focuses on relationships. Your emotions and sensitivity play a role. Don't make waves. Don't rush or show resentment; let things develop.

Thursday, May 24 (Moon in Cancer)　　Mercury moves into your twelfth house today. Your thinking now is strongly influenced by matters of the past or subconscious influences. Feeling rather than logic dominates the day. You tend to be secretive and work behind the scenes. Confide to a close friend, but otherwise it's best to keep your thoughts to yourself. Write them down instead of shouting them out.

Friday, May 25 (Moon into Leo, 6:12 p.m.)　　Hard work is called for today. Get organized; stay focused. Control your impulses. Put off any romantic notions for the time being. Fulfill your obligations. Tear down the old in order to rebuild. Be methodical and thorough.

Saturday, May 26 (Moon in Leo)　　With the moon on your ascendant, you're recharged for the coming month. You're physically vital, and relations with the opposite sex go well. The way you see yourself now is the way others see you. Your face is before the public.

Sunday, May 27 (Moon in Leo)   Your self-image is on your mind now. You're sensitive to other people's feelings. You may feel moody—withdrawn one moment, happy the next, then sad. It's all about your emotional self. Your feelings and thoughts are aligned. You're dealing with the person you are becoming.

Monday, May 28 (Moon into Virgo, 2:07 a.m.) There's an air of mystery in your day, Leo. Look beneath the surface, investigate. Secrets, intrigue, and confidential information play a role. Knowledge is essential to success. See things as they are and not how you wish them to be. You work best on your own now.

Tuesday, May 29 (Moon in Virgo)   The moon is in your second house today. Take care of your bills, and collect what's owed to you. You feel better when your checkbook is balanced. Material assets make you feel secure. It's a good day to pursue a real estate transaction or simply to look for a good place to invest.

Wednesday, May 30 (Moon into Libra, 6:46 a.m.)   It's a number 9 day. Visualize for the future. Set your goals, then make them so. Strive for universal appeal. You're up to the challenge. Complete a project, and get ready for something new coming up. But wait until tomorrow to begin a new project.

Thursday, May 31 (Moon in Libra)   You have an emotional need to pursue ideas and subjects that interest you. Your intellectual curiosity requires continual nurturing. Meanwhile, you're dealing with the everyday world. Expect a lot of running around, short trips here and there. Keep your cell phone turned on.

Friday, June 1 (Moon into Scorpio, 8:32 a.m.) It's a number 8 day, and you're in the power seat. Think big and act big, Leo! You can go far with your plans and achieve financial success, especially if you open your mind to a new approach. Joint finances could play a role in your day.

Saturday, June 2 (Moon in Scorpio) The moon is in your fourth house today. You're dealing with the foundations of who you are and who you are becoming. Spend time with your family and loved ones. Take time to retreat to a private place for meditation. It's a good day for dream recall.

Sunday, June 3 (Moon into Sagittarius, 8:33 a.m.) It's a number 1 day, and you're at the top of your cycle again. It's a good day to get out and meet new people, have new experiences, or do something unexpected. Explore and discover. Creativity is emphasized. In romance, something new is developing, if that's what you're looking for.

Monday, June 4 (Moon in Sagittarius) Neptune goes retrograde in Pisces, your eighth house, today and stays that way until November 10. There could be some difficulties related to a partner's finances. Something secretive and deceptive is going on. Move with care when dealing with financial matters or taxes. Meanwhile, there's a lunar eclipse in your fifth house, and that means you could have an emotional reaction related to a romantic relationship, children, or a creative project.

Tuesday, June 5 (Moon into Capricorn, 8:32 a.m.) You're creative and express yourself well today, Leo. You can influence people now with your upbeat attitude. Your popularity is on the rise. Take time to relax, enjoy yourself, recharge your batteries. Have fun in preparation for tomorrow's discipline and focus.

Wednesday, June 6 (Moon in Capricorn) Service to others is the theme of the day. Help others, but don't deny your own needs. Take time to exercise, and watch your diet. Self-discipline and structure are key. It's best if you follow a regular schedule now.

Thursday, June 7 (Moon into Aquarius, 10:18 a.m.) Mercury moves into your twelfth house today. Subconscious influences affect your thinking and play an important role in your day. You're secretive about your thoughts and ideas and more reserved than normal. You've got a lot on your mind now, but you tend to avoid speaking about it.

Friday, June 8 (Moon in Aquarius) The moon is in your seventh house of partnerships and contracts today. The focus turns to relationships, business and personal ones. You get along well with others now. You can fit in just about anywhere. Loved ones and partners are more important than usual. A legal matter comes into play.

Saturday, June 9 (Moon into Pisces, 3:23 p.m.) It's your mystery day, Leo. Secrets, intrigue, confidential information play a role. Gather information, but don't make any absolute decisions until tomorrow. Go with the flow. Maintain your emotional balance. Avoid confusion and conflicts.

Sunday, June 10 (Moon in Pisces) Your experiences are more intense than usual. Security is an important issue with you right now. It can affect your feelings about your possessions, as well as things that you share with others, such as a spouse. Alternately, you pursue mystical matters today. You could be reading about shamanism, power animals, and spirit contact.

Monday, June 11 (Moon in Pisces)   Jupiter moves into your eleventh house today and stays there for a year. That means you'll have luck making friends who will help you fulfill your wishes and dreams. You see the big picture now and have the chance to expand. Friends and associates play an important role.

Tuesday, June 12 (Moon into Aries, 12:22 a.m.)   The moon is in your ninth house today. You may feel a need to get away now, a break from the usual routine. You yearn for a new experience. You're a dreamer and a thinker. Plan a long trip. Sign up for a workshop or seminar. A foreigner or a foreign country plays a role.

Wednesday, June 13 (Moon in Aries)   It's a great time for initiating projects, launching new ideas, brainstorming. Imprint your style. You're passionate, but you can be reckless as well. Thrills and spills are highlighted. Have an adventure, but take care to avoid accidents.

Thursday, June 14 (Moon into Taurus, 12:22 p.m.)   It's a number 3 day. Your attitude determines everything today. Spread your good news, and take time to listen to others. Play your hunches, and remain flexible. In romance, you're an ardent and loyal lover.

Friday, June 15 (Moon in Taurus)   You communicate your feelings well to coworkers, who are sympathetic. You get along well with others in the workplace. But it's best to avoid getting too personal with a colleague. Your life is more public now, so avoid emotional displays. Use your common sense, and stay grounded.

Saturday, June 16 (Moon in Taurus)   Use your common sense today, especially when dealing with matters related to your career. It's a good day for cultivating ideas. You're more responsive to the needs and moods of a group and of the public in general. Take a down-to-earth perspective on any plans to ask for a raise or an advancement.

Sunday, June 17 (Moon into Gemini, 1:24 a.m.) Service to others is the theme of the day. Adjust to the needs of loved ones. You offer advice and support. Romance and love are highlighted. You're creative and passionate today. Focus on making people happy.

Monday, June 18 (Moon in Gemini) The moon is in your eleventh house today. You get along better with friends and associates. You find strength in numbers. Your sense of security is tied to your relationships. Work for the common good with a group, but keep an eye on your own wishes and dreams.

Tuesday, June 19 (Moon into Cancer, 1:34 p.m.) It's another power day Leo, and your day to play it your way. You have a chance to expand, to gain recognition, fame, and power. You pull off a financial coup. Be aware that fear of failure or fear that you won't measure up will attract tangible experiences that reinforce the feeling. You're being watched by people in power.

Wednesday, June 20 (Moon in Cancer) Unconscious attitudes and relations with women can be difficult, Leo. Keep your feelings secret. It's a great day for a mystical or spiritual discipline. Your intuition is heightened. It's a good time to discuss matters with a therapist or close friend who is empathic and empathetic.

Thursday, June 21 (Moon into Leo, 11:48 p.m.) You get a fresh start, a new beginning. Express your opinions dynamically. You're determined and courageous today. If you stress originality, you attract creative people. A flirtation turns more serious.

Friday, June 22 (Moon in Leo) You're creative and passionate today. Impulsive and honest. Theatrics and

271

drama are highlighted. Be wild, imaginative; be the person you always imagined you might be. Play with different personas. Showmanship is emphasized.

Saturday, June 23 (Moon in Leo) With the sun remaining on your ascendant, yesterday's energy flows into your Saturday. Your appearance and personality shine. Your feelings and thoughts are aligned today. You're physically vital, and relations with the opposite sex go well. You're already recharged for the summer months.

Sunday, June 24 (Moon into Virgo, 7:43 a.m.) It's a good day to restore order out of chaos. That could mean straightening up your house after your Saturday partying. Maybe you clean a closet or the garage or organize your attic. Get your desk in order for the week ahead. Tear down the old in order to rebuild. Keep your goals in mind; follow your ideas.

Monday, June 25 (Moon in Virgo) Mercury moves into your first house today, and that means you're especially talkative. You get your ideas across and are understood. You also adapt quickly to changing circumstances. Meanwhile, Saturn goes direct in your third house. That gives you more mental discipline this year. You also start to take a more practical outlook on matters. Keep your spirits up. Think positive!

Tuesday, June 26 (Moon into Libra, 1:16 p.m.) It's your mystery day, Leo. You work best on your own today. Secrets, intrigue, or confidential information plays a role. You investigate, analyze, or simply observe what's going on now. You quickly come to a conclusion and wonder why others don't see what you see. You detect deception and recognize insincerity with ease. Maintain your emotional balance.

Wednesday, June 27 (Moon in Libra) Venus goes direct in your eleventh house today. That means you can achieve success through the help of friends and social contacts. You work well with others, especially on a joint project emphasizing the common good. Your artistic talents are highlighted and supported by friends, many of whom are quite artistic themselves.

Thursday, June 28 (Moon into Scorpio, 4:33 p.m.)
You're at the top of your cycle, Leo. Be independent and creative and refuse to be discouraged by naysayers. You can take the lead now, and don't be afraid to turn in a new direction. Express your opinions dynamically. Do something you've never done before.

Friday, June 29 (Moon in Scorpio)   It's a good day to stick close to home and spend time with your family. You're dealing with your foundations. A parent plays a role. Do something to beautify your home. But take time to breathe deep and meditate.

Saturday, June 30 (Moon into Sagittarius, 6:05 p.m.)
The month ends on a power day for you. Financial gain is at hand; expect a windfall. Be courageous. Be yourself; be honest. Appear successful now, even if you don't feel that way.

JULY 2012

Sunday, July 1 (Moon in Sagittarius)   The moon is in your fifth house today. You like to flaunt and celebrate, Leo. Your creativity is highlighted. You might be somewhat possessive of loved ones. You're more protective and nurturing toward children. Animals could play a role in your day.

Monday, July 2 (Moon into Capricorn, 6:52 p.m.)   It's a number 1 day, and you're at the top of your cycle again. You get a fresh start, a new beginning. You can play a leadership role, especially if you emphasize creativity.

Don't let the naysayers bother you. You're on top of your game today.

Tuesday, July 3 (Moon in Capricorn)   Mars moves into Libra, your third house, today and stays there for most of the month. You're aggressive in pursuing a community activity that could involve neighbors and family. You have a strong will to get your message across. Be aware that there's a tendency now to get into arguments, especially with siblings. Best to avoid a confrontation by taking a short trip or writing down your thoughts. With the full moon in your sixth house, you have an opportunity to gain insight and illumination related to your workplace. You reap what you've sown.

Wednesday, July 4 (Moon into Aquarius, 8:26 p.m.) You're innovative and creative and communicate well. Ease up on routines. Your attitude determines everything today. Spread your good news, and take time to listen to others.

Thursday, July 5 (Moon in Aquarius)   You're open and responsive to others, especially partners. However, you might have trouble now getting in touch with your own feelings because the partnership dominates your awareness. Try to avoid being overly dependent. A legal matter could come to your attention.

Friday, July 6 (Moon in Aquarius)   With the moon remaining in your seventh house, yesterday's energy flows into your Friday. Lovers and partners are highlighted. Women play a prominent role in your day. You feel a need to be accepted. You're looking for security, but you have a hard time going with the flow.

Saturday, July 7 (Moon into Pisces, 12:29 a.m.)   Service to others is the theme of the day. You have a sense of duty and respond emotionally to whatever is happening now. Diplomacy wins the way. Do a good deed for someone. Visit someone who is ill or in need of help. Focus on making people happy.

Sunday, July 8 (Moon in Pisces)   Turn inward for inspiration, universal knowledge, eternal truths. It's a day for deep healing. Keep track of your dreams, including your daydreams. Ideas are ripe. You can tap into the collective unconscious for inspiration. Your imagination is strong.

Monday, July 9 (Moon into Aries, 8:14 a.m.)   It's your power day, Leo. Open your mind to a new approach. Unexpected resources arrive. You can go far with your plans and achieve financial success. But be aware that you're playing with power, so try not to hurt anyone.

Tuesday, July 10 (Moon in Aries)   The moon is in your ninth house today. You're a dreamer and a thinker. You yearn for a new experience, a new adventure. You may feel a need to get away, a break from the usual routine. Foreigners or a foreign country plays a role in your day.

Wednesday, July 11 (Moon into Taurus, 7:30 p.m.) It's a number 1 day. You're inventive and make connections that others overlook. You're determined and courageous today. Stress originality. In romance, something new is developing. A flirtation turns more serious. Explore, discover, create.

Thursday, July 12 (Moon in Taurus)   With the moon in your tenth house today, professional concerns are the focus of the day. You're ready for a boost in prestige, possibly a raise. You could be looking for a more public position now. Friendly coworkers are on your side.

Friday, July 13 (Moon in Taurus)   Uranus goes retrograde in your ninth house today and stays there until December 13. You could experience some delays related to a long-distance trip or pursuing higher education. Expect some erratic behavior by people around you, if not your own actions. You could have some difficulty making up your mind. Everything seems somewhat uncertain.

Saturday, July 14 (Moon into Gemini, 8:27 a.m.) Mercury goes retrograde in your sign, Leo, and stays there until August 8. Expect some confusion in your communication with others over the next three weeks. If you need to talk to the public, whatever you say should be simple and straightforward to avoid misunderstandings. Others might misinterpret your intentions. You could be feeling uncertain or insecure about your ability to communicate effectively.

Sunday, July 15 (Moon in Gemini) Friends play an important role in your day, especially Sagittarius and Aries. You get together with a group of like-minded individuals and work toward a common goal. Focus on your wishes and dreams, and make sure that they still reflect who you are.

Monday, July 16 (Moon into Cancer, 8:32 p.m.) Diplomacy is called for now, especially if you need to clear up a situation at home that has lingered too long. Don't put off the situation. That will only aggravate the problem. Be understanding, and avoid confrontations.

Tuesday, July 17 (Moon in Cancer) With the moon in your twelfth house today, you tend to withdraw from public view. Unconscious attitudes can be difficult. So can relations with women. Keep your feelings secret. Work behind the scenes, and follow your intuition.

Wednesday, July 18 (Moon in Cancer) It's a good day to work at home, if possible. Tend to loved ones; do something with your children, if you have any at home. Beautify your home; take care of repairs. Your psychic abilities are enhanced, and you're sensitive to other people's moods. Best to keep things to yourself to avoid conflict.

Thursday, July 19 (Moon into Leo, 6:14 a.m.) There's a new moon in your twelfth house today. That means you have opportunities to work on your own or behind the scenes. It's a good time to start meditating or pursue a past-life regression. If you record your dreams, read over some of your entries now to get a new perspective.

Friday, July 20 (Moon in Leo) With the moon in your first house, your self-awareness and appearance are more important now than usual, Leo. You're dealing with the person you are becoming. You may feel moody—withdrawn one moment, happy the next, then sad. It's all about your emotional self. Your feelings and thoughts are aligned.

Saturday, July 21 (Moon into Virgo, 1:25 p.m.) Relationships play a major role in your day. You need to balance your outgoing nature with a sense of cooperation now. Use your intuition to get a sense of the day. Be aware that you could be feeling moody or picky from time to time. Best advice: don't make waves. Don't rush or show resentment; let things develop.

Sunday, July 22 (Moon in Virgo) With the moon in your second house today, money and material goods are important to you now and give you a sense of security. You identify emotionally with your possessions or whatever you value. Watch your spending. Look at your priorities in handling your income. You have a tendency to collect things, and those objects make you feel at home and at peace.

Monday, July 23 (Moon into Libra, 6:39 p.m.) Take care of your obligations today. Stay grounded and control your impulses. Romance takes a back seat. Remain focused, and you can solve any problem you face. Be methodical and thorough.

Tuesday, July 24 (Moon in Libra)   The moon is in your third house today. Your mental abilities are strong now, and you have an emotional need to reinvigorate your studies, especially regarding matters of the past. You're attracted to historical or archaeological studies or other matters from the deep past. Alternately, you could be getting involved in a challenging mental activity, such as online gaming, a debate, or a game of chess—anything that engages your mental prowess.

Wednesday, July 25 (Moon into Scorpio, 10:30 p.m.) It's a number 6 day, a service-oriented day. Offer your advice and support. Do a good deed for someone. Be generous and tolerant. Diplomacy wins the way. An adjustment in your domestic life works out for the best. Be helpful, but dance to your own tune.

Thursday, July 26 (Moon in Scorpio)   The moon is in your fourth house today. It's a good day to stick close to home and spend time with your family and loved ones. But also find time to focus inward in quiet meditation. You feel a close tie to your roots. You could be dealing with your parents.

Friday, July 27 (Moon in Scorpio)   Expect intense, emotional experiences today. You're passionate, and your sexuality is heightened. Be aware of things happening in secret and of possible deception. You can dig deep for information now. Best to avoid making any major purchases.

Saturday, July 28 (Moon into Sagittarius, 1:18 a.m.) It's a good time to complete a project. Clear your desk for tomorrow's new cycle, but don't start anything today. Visualize the future; set your goals, then make them so.

Use the day for reflection, expansion, and concluding projects.

Sunday, July 29 (Moon in Sagittarius)   Your emotions tend to overpower your intellect today, but you're in touch with your creative side. Take a chance, experiment. Your personal grace and magnetism are highlighted. You also might be more possessive of loved ones and protective of children. Animals play a larger role than usual.

Monday, July 30 (Moon into Capricorn, 3:30 a.m.) It's a number 2 day. Partnerships take center stage, Leo. Your intuition comes into play as you focus on relationships. Don't make waves. Don't rush about or show resentment. Cooperation is stressed now.

Tuesday, July 31 (Moon in Capricorn)   It's another service-oriented day. You improve, edit, and refine the work of others. Offer assistance, but don't deny your own needs. You could be feeling emotionally repressed now. Keep your resolutions about exercise, and watch your diet.

AUGUST 2012

Wednesday, August 1 (Moon into Aquarius, 5:56 a.m.) There's a full moon in your seventh house today. That means you gain insight and illumination related to a partnership, either personal or business. You get along well with others now, especially if you share your place at center stage, Leo. You can fit in just about anywhere.

Thursday, August 2 (Moon in Aquarius)   Today your camaraderie expands from partnerships to friendships. You work with a group and benefit from the association, especially if you're working for the common good. Your individuality is stressed. Your visionary abilities are heightened. Friends play an important role.

Friday, August 3 (Moon into Pisces, 9:58 a.m.) It's a number 3 day. Your attitude determines everything today, Leo. Your popularity is on the rise. You communicate well. You're curious and inventive. Ideas bubble forth. Your imagination is keen.

Saturday, August 4 (Moon in Pisces) Security is an important issue with you right now. It's a good day to deal with finances, insurance, taxes, or a mortgage. You could be dealing with a partner's resources. A mystery of the unknown, such as life after death, comes into play.

Sunday, August 5 (Moon into Aries, 4:59 p.m.) You're feeling lighter today, as if anything is possible. Change and variety are highlighted now. Think freedom, no restrictions. Release old structures; get a new point of view. You're versatile and changeable.

Monday, August 6 (Moon in Aries) You could be launching a long trip now or at least dreaming of one. You feel good about pursuing higher learning. Ideas, philosophies, religion, and art interest you. A foreign country or a foreign-born person could play a role.

Tuesday, August 7 (Moon in Aries) With Venus moving into your twelfth house today, there's nothing better than solitude. Secrecy plays a role, possibly involving an affair, so you crave time alone to think things over, especially related to this romance. You might be wondering if someone special in your life now was also a friend in a past life.

Wednesday, August 8 (Moon into Taurus, 3:28 a.m.) Mercury goes direct in your first house. Any confusion, miscommunication, and delays start to recede into the past. Things move more smoothly now, especially related to your appearance and your place in front of the public. You get your message across and attract more attention than usual. Everything works better, including computers and other electronic equipment.

Thursday, August 9 (Moon in Taurus) Business dealings are highlighted. You get an elevation in prestige, Leo. You're at center stage now. Your life is more public today, and you're more emotional and warm toward coworkers. But don't blur the boundary between your personal and professional lives.

Friday, August 10 (Moon into Gemini, 4:12 p.m.) You're inventive and make connections that others overlook. You're determined and courageous today. Explore, discover, create. Express your opinions dynamically. You can certainly do that, Leo! Get out and meet new people, have new experiences, do something you've never done before.

Saturday, August 11 (Moon in Gemini) The moon is in your eleventh house today. Your sense of security is tied to your relationships and friends. Focus on your wishes and dreams. Examine your overall goals. Those goals should be an expression of who you are. Your interests are so diverse that others might think you lack depth. Social consciousness plays a role in your day, especially related to a group activity.

Sunday, August 12 (Moon in Gemini) You communicate well and get your ideas across. It's a good day to get out and meet friends, maybe over coffee at a bookstore. Challenge your mind with new ideas. A change of scenery works well for you today. In dealing with siblings, you see two sides to every story.

Monday, August 13 (Moon into Cancer, 4:29 a.m.) As the work week begins, it's a great day to get everything in order. You can overcome any bureaucratic red

tape. You're in the right place at the right time. Emphasize quality. Revise and rewrite. Tear down the old in
order to build the new. You're building a creative base.

Tuesday, August 14 (Moon in Cancer)   You could
be feeling somewhat moody. You're intuitive and nurturing, and feel best at home now. Work there today, if
possible. Beautify your home or take care of repairs.
Find time to snuggle with your loved one.

Wednesday, August 15 (Moon into Leo, 2:06 p.m.)
Service to others is the theme of the day. Offer advice
and support, but dance to your own tune, Leo. Diplomacy wins the way. Do a good deed for someone. Visit
someone who is ill or in need of help. You tend to search
for ways to improve yourself while trying to make others
feel good. Your feelings and thoughts are aligned today.

Thursday, August 16 (Moon in Leo)   Your face is
in front of the public or maybe all over Facebook. Your
appearance and personality shine. Your self-awareness
and appearance are important now. You're dealing with
the person you are becoming.

Friday, August 17 (Moon into Virgo, 8:34 p.m.)   With
a new moon in your first house today, yesterday's energy
flows into your Friday. Now you find new opportunities
through your appearances before the public. You're recharged for the rest of the month and beyond, and this
makes you more appealing to a love interest. New opportunities expand your possibilities in business and
romance.

Saturday, August 18 (Moon in Virgo)   With the
moon in your second house, it's a good day to deal with
money matters. Your financial picture improves. Pay
your bills, and collect what's owed you. Take a close
look at how you're spending your income, and decide on
your priorities.

Sunday, August 19 (Moon in Virgo)   You attend to details today, and you can skillfully handle any problems that·come up. However, don't worry about getting it all perfect. Stick close to home, and clear up loose ends.

Monday, August 20 (Moon into Libra, 12:46 a.m.) Yesterday's energy flows into your Monday. You're diplomatic and capable of fixing whatever has gone wrong. Marriage or a partnership plays a key role now. Use your intuition when dealing with others. Don't make waves. Don't rush or show resentment; let things develop.

Tuesday, August 21 (Moon in Libra)   It's a good day for journaling or working on any writing project. You get your ideas across, but you could be overly influenced by past events. A female relative plays a role. Stay in control of your emotions when talking with others, especially family members or neighbors.

Wednesday, August 22 (Moon into Scorpio, 3:54 a.m.) Your organizational skills are highlighted now, but try not to wander off task. Emphasize quality; you're building a creative foundation for your future. Tear down the old in order to rebuild. Be methodical and thorough.

Thursday, August 23 (Moon in Scorpio)   Mars moves into your fourth house today. There's a lot of energy in the home over the next three weeks. You move very aggressively to take care of domestic matters. Be aware that your actions could cause some dissension. It's a good time for remodeling, refurbishing, or cleaning your house. People will be coming and going.

Friday, August 24 (Moon into Sagittarius, 6:50 a.m.) It's a number 6 day, a service day. Do a good deed for someone. Visit someone who is ill or in need of help. Focus on making people happy. Be diplomatic, understanding, and generous with your time.

Saturday, August 25 (Moon in Sagittarius) You see the big picture today, Leo. You're creative and romantic. There's greater emotional depth to a relationship now. Pleasure and fun are highlighted, express your joy. Children and pets play a role.

Sunday, August 26 (Moon into Capricorn, 9:59 a.m.) It's your power day again and your day to play it your way. You're in the power seat. You can go far with your plans and achieve financial success. You have a chance to expand, to gain recognition, fame, and power. Be aware that you're playing with power, so try not to hurt anyone.

Monday, August 27 (Moon in Capricorn) The moon is in your sixth house today. It's another service day, so it's best to maintain structure and self-discipline. Help your coworkers, but don't overlook your own needs. Make appointments that you've been putting off.

Tuesday, August 28 (Moon into Aquarius, 1:39 p.m.) It's a number 1 day. Don't be afraid to turn in a new direction. Trust your hunches. Get out and meet new people, have new experiences, do something you've never done before. Explore and discover; creativity is highlighted. Express your opinions dynamically.

Wednesday, August 29 (Moon in Aquarius) The moon is in your seventh house today. The focus turns to relationships, business and personal ones. You get along well with others now. You comprehend the nuances of a situation, but it's difficult to go with the flow. It's a challenge to remain detached and objective.

Thursday, August 30 (Moon into Pisces, 6:32 p.m.) Think positive, stay optimistic. Others look to you for inspiration. You can influence people now with your upbeat attitude. In business dealings, diversify. Insist on all the information, not just bits and pieces.

Friday, August 31 (Moon in Pisces)   Mercury moves into your second house today. It's a great day to come up with moneymaking ideas, Leo. Your mind is sharp now, especially when it comes to finding ways to boost your income. Meanwhile, with the full moon in your eighth house, you reap what you've sown related to taxes, insurance, or an inheritance. You gain insight about someone with whom you share resources or possessions.

SEPTEMBER 2012

Saturday, September 1 (Moon in Pisces)   Security is an important issue with you right now. It can affect your feelings about your possessions, as well as things that you share with others, such as a spouse. An inheritance could play a role. Other issues of the day could include matters of sex, death, rebirth, rituals, and relationships. You take a renewed interest in past lives or contact with the spirit world.

Sunday, September 2 (Moon into Aries, 1:38 a.m.) Your attitude determines everything today. You communicate well. You're warm and receptive to what others say. Your popularity is on the rise, Leo. Take center stage, and spread your good news. But take time to listen to others. Expect an invitation from a friend.

Monday, September 3 (Moon in Aries)   Higher education and the higher mind are highlighted. You feel a need to get away now, a break from the usual routine. You're a dreamer and a thinker, and you could be dreaming about a long trip to a foreign land. You're playing the role of adventurer, Leo.

Tuesday, September 4 (Moon into Taurus, 11:42 a.m.) Promote new ideas; follow your curiosity. Look for adventure. It's a good time to pursue self-employment. You're courageous and adaptable. A change of scenery would work to your advantage. You could be moving to a new location.

Wednesday, September 5 (Moon in Taurus)   Professional concerns dominate your thoughts today. You're looking for an advancement or a boost in prestige. You get along well with coworkers, but avoid emotional displays in public. It's a good day for sales and dealing with the public.

Thursday, September 6 (Moon in Taurus)   Venus moves into your first house today. Your personal grace is noticed and appreciated now. You're more outgoing than usual and maintain a positive outlook. You can develop relationships that will work to your advantage. Stay grounded, and use your common sense.

Friday, September 7 (Moon into Gemini, 12:11 a.m.) It's your power day, so go for a power play. Think big and act big! You can go far with your plans and achieve financial success. Unexpected money arrives. Open your mind to a new approach that could bring in big bucks. You're playing with power, so be careful not to hurt others.

Saturday, September 8 (Moon in Gemini)   You get along especially well with friends and members of a group. You work for the common good, but keep an eye on your own wishes and dreams. Your sense of security is tied to your relationships and friends.

Sunday, September 9 (Moon into Cancer, 12:50 p.m.) Be independent and creative. Don't let others tell you what to do. Get out and meet new people, have new experiences, do something you've never done before. Express your opinions dynamically.

Monday, September 10 (Moon in Cancer)   The moon is in your twelfth house today. Think carefully before you act. There's a tendency now to undo all the positive actions you've taken. Avoid any self-destructive tendencies. Be aware of hidden enemies. You might feel a need to withdraw and work on your own.

Tuesday, September 11 (Moon into Leo, 11:01 p.m.)
You're warm and receptive to what others say. Your imagination is keen now. You're curious and inventive. Enjoy the harmony, beauty, and pleasures of life. You have a strong sense of duty and feel obligated to fulfill your promises

Wednesday, September 12 (Moon in Leo)   You're recharged for the rest of the month, and this makes you more appealing to the public. You're physically vital, and relations with the opposite sex go well. Your appearance and personality shine. Your feelings and thoughts are aligned today.

Thursday, September 13 (Moon in Leo)   You're sensitive to other people's feelings. You may feel moody one moment, happy the next, then withdrawn and sad. It's all about your health and emotional self now. You tend to search for ways to improve yourself.

Friday, September 14 (Moon into Virgo, 5:31 a.m.)
It's a number 6 day. You could face emotional outbursts or someone making unfair demands. Be understanding and avoid confrontations. Offer advice and support, but do it in a diplomatic way. A domestic adjustment works out for the best.

Saturday, September 15 (Moon in Virgo)   There's a new moon in your second house today. New financial opportunities come your way. You get a raise or find a better investment for your money. You find new opportunities to explore your values or anything you consider important in your life. New communication opportunities come your way.

Sunday, September 16 (Moon into Libra, 8:55 a.m.)
Mercury moves into your third house today. You have more communication with friends, siblings, and other relatives. Your communication abilities are heightened for the rest of the month. You get out more, socialize, and exchange ideas. It's a good time to start a blog, build a Web site, or publish a newsletter.

Monday, September 17 (Moon in Libra) Yesterday's energy flows into your Monday. Now there is more emotion in your interactions with friends, family members, or neighbors. Share what you know, but avoid becoming overly emotional in making your points. Meanwhile, Pluto goes direct in your sixth house today, where it will stay until 2024. That means your daily work life will undergo profound change over the next twelve years.

Tuesday, September 18 (Moon into Scorpio, 10:46 a.m.) You're at the top of your cycle again. You're inventive and make connections that others overlook. You're determined and courageous today. You get a fresh start, a new beginning. Don't be afraid to turn in a new direction. Trust your hunches; intuition is highlighted.

Wednesday, September 19 (Moon in Scorpio) With the moon in your fourth house today, it's a good day to stick close to home. You're dealing with the foundations of who you are and who you are becoming. Retreat to a private place for meditation. It's a good day for dream recall.

Thursday, September 20 (Moon into Sagittarius, 12:34 p.m.) Ease up on routines today. Take time to relax, enjoy yourself, recharge your batteries. Have fun in preparation for tomorrow's discipline and focus. Your charm and wit are appreciated. You can influence people now with your upbeat attitude.

Friday, September 21 (Moon in Sagittarius)   Yesterday's energy flows into your Friday. Your creativity, personal grace, and magnetism are highlighted. Be yourself; be emotionally honest. It's a good day to take a chance, experiment. You see the big picture, but stay focused. Persevere to get things done today. Be methodical and thorough.

Saturday, September 22 (Moon into Capricorn, 3:21 p.m.)   It's a number 5 day. You're seeking new horizons now. Look for variety. You're versatile, changeable. Freedom of thought and action is key. But so is moderation; avoid excess in whatever you're doing. Release old structures; get a new point of view.

Sunday, September 23 (Moon in Capricorn)   The moon is in your sixth house today. It's a service day. You're the one others go to for help. You improve, edit, and refine their work. But don't deny your own needs. Attend to details about your health. Keep your resolutions about exercise, and watch your diet.

Monday, September 24 (Moon into Aquarius, 7:33 p.m.)   It's your mystery day, Leo, as you venture into the unknown. Secrets and intrigue play a role. Be aware of decisions made behind closed doors. Knowledge is essential to success. You work best on your own today. Gather information, but don't make any absolute decisions until tomorrow.

Tuesday, September 25 (Moon in Aquarius)   The moon is in your seventh house today. Partnerships play a key role in your day. You tend to get along well with others now. You comprehend the nuances of a situation, but it's difficult to remain detached and objective. Be careful that others don't manipulate your feelings.

Wednesday, September 26 (Moon in Aquarius)   Group activities and social events are highlighted now.

Your individuality is stressed. Your visionary abilities are heightened. You're dealing with new ideas, new options, and originality. You get a new perspective. Play your hunches, and look beyond the immediate.

Thursday, September 27 (Moon into Pisces, 1:25 a.m.)
It's a number 1 day. That means you can take the lead now, and don't worry about turning in a new direction. Explore and discover. Get out and meet new people. Express your opinions dynamically. In romance, make room for a new love. A flirtation turns more serious.

Friday, September 28 (Moon in Pisces) The moon is in your eighth house today. Your experiences are more intense than usual, especially related to shared possessions or resources. Security is an important issue with you right now. You could find yourself managing or controlling someone else's assets. You also could be exploring metaphysical ideas, possibly past lives or life after death.

Saturday, September 29 (Moon into Aries, 9:15 a.m.)
There's a full moon in your ninth house today. Growth and expansion are keywords. You harvest what you've sown. You yearn for a new experience. You can create positive change through your ideas. You're a dreamer and a thinker.

Sunday, September 30 (Moon in Aries) Yesterday's energy flows into your Sunday. You may feel a need to get away now, a break from the usual routine. It's a great time for initiating projects, launching new ideas, or brainstorming. You're extremely persuasive, especially if you're passionate about what you're doing or trying to convey.

Monday, October 1 (Moon into Taurus, 7:27 p.m.)
Your attitude determines everything today. You're creative and express yourself well. Your artistic talents are highlighted. Remain flexible, open to new ideas. Spread your good news, and take time to listen to others.

Tuesday, October 2 (Moon in Taurus) The moon is in your tenth house today. Professional concerns are the focus of the day. You're more open and accessible now, but take care to avoid emotional displays, especially in public. You get a boost in prestige.

Wednesday, October 3 (Moon in Taurus) With Venus moving into your second house today, you're especially aware of your appearance this month. You love dressing up and looking good. You're also seeking security, especially financial stability. You like the social status that money brings. If you're artistic, you could make money this month through your creative endeavors.

Thursday, October 4 (Moon into Gemini, 7:47 a.m.)
Diplomacy wins the day. You offer advice and support. You need to clear up a situation at home that has lingered too long. Don't put off any such matter. That will only aggravate the problem. Be understanding, and avoid confrontations. Friends and associates are supportive now.

Friday, October 5 (Moon in Gemini) With Mercury moving into your fourth house today, there could be some changes taking place in your home. There's lots of talk and activity in your home life. Meanwhile, Saturn also moves into your fourth house, where it will stay for two and a half years. That means you have better structure and stability in your home life. There could be some delays, especially if you try to take shortcuts on a home repair. If you're looking for a romance, you don't have to go far. It might be right in your home.

Saturday, October 6 (Moon into Cancer, 8:46 p.m.) Mars moves into your fifth house today. It's time to take action regarding a creative project or romance. There's greater emotional depth in whatever you're pursuing. You're aggressive and willing to take a chance. You have an opportunity to expand and grow. However, be careful about getting into arguments over the next three weeks.

Sunday, October 7 (Moon in Cancer) The moon is in your twelfth house today. Unconscious attitudes can be difficult. Keep your feelings secret. You might feel a need to withdraw and work on your own. Take time to reflect and meditate. It's a great time for pursuing a spiritual discipline.

Monday, October 8 (Moon in Cancer) You're intuitive and nurturing today. It's a good day to stay home. Take the day off or work at home, if possible. You could be feeling somewhat moody, so it's best to keep things to yourself. Water plays a prominent role in your day. Beautify your home, or take care of home repairs.

Tuesday, October 9 (Moon into Leo, 7:55 a.m.) Use your intuition to get a sense of the day. Relationships are important now. Don't make waves. Don't rush or show resentment. Let things develop. You're diplomatic and capable of fixing whatever has gone wrong. Your emotions and sensitivity are highlighted.

Wednesday, October 10 (Moon in Leo) Yesterday's energy flows into your Wednesday. You're sensitive to other people's feelings. You might feel moody one moment, happy the next, then withdrawn and sad. It's all about your emotional self. Your feelings and thoughts are aligned. You're dealing with the person you are becoming.

Thursday, October 11 (Moon into Virgo, 3:24 p.m.)
Your organizational skills are highlighted. Persevere to get things done today. Don't get sloppy. Tear down the old in order to rebuild. Be methodical and thorough. Revise, rewrite.

Friday, October 12 (Moon in Virgo) Money issues and your emotions are on your agenda. You equate your financial assets with emotional security now. Look at your priorities in handling your income. Collect what's owed you, and pay what you owe. Put off making any major purchases.

Saturday, October 13 (Moon into Libra, 7:02 p.m.)
It's another service day. You could face emotional outbursts or someone making unfair demands. Help others, but do it your own way. A domestic adjustment works out for the best. Purchases for your home are highlighted.

Sunday, October 14 (Moon in Libra) You're quite opinionated today and ready to tell others what you think. That's fine, Leo, but keep conscious control of your emotions when communicating. Your thinking is unduly influenced by things of the past. A short trip to visit a sibling or other relatives works to your benefit.

Monday, October 15 (Moon into Scorpio, 8:07 p.m.)
There's a new moon in your third house today, and that means you find new opportunities in your everyday world. Relatives and siblings or neighbors could play a role. It's a good time to begin a new project or end one. Your communication skills are emphasized now.

Tuesday, October 16 (Moon in Scorpio) The moon is in your fourth house today. The domestic scene takes on more importance. It's a good day to work at home or work on a home-repair project. You feel closer to your roots. You could be dealing with parents.

Wednesday, October 17 (Moon into Sagittarius, 8:26 p.m.) It's a number 1 day, so you're at the top of your cycle. You get a fresh start, a new beginning. You're inventive and make connections that others overlook. You're determined and courageous today. Stress originality. You attract creative people.

Thursday, October 18 (Moon in Sagittarius) The moon is in your fifth house today. You're emotionally in touch with your creative side now. Be yourself; be emotionally honest. In love, there's greater emotional depth to a relationship. You might be somewhat possessive of loved ones, particularly children.

Friday, October 19 (Moon into Capricorn, 9:42 p.m.) You communicate well now. You're curious and inventive. Ideas bubble forth. Your imagination is keen. Your popularity is on the rise. You can influence people with your upbeat attitude. Take time to relax, enjoy yourself, recharge your batteries.

Saturday, October 20 (Moon in Capricorn) It's another service day. Others come to you for help. So what else is new, Leo! Offer assistance, but don't deny your own needs. Visit someone who is ill; do a good deed. But pay attention to your own health matters. Exercise, and watch your diet.

Sunday, October 21 (Moon in Capricorn) Your ambition and drive to succeed are highlighted. You're at center stage, Leo, but your responsibilities increase, and that could cause some drama. You could be feeling stressed, overworked. Be conservative; don't speculate or take any unnecessary risks. Maintain emotional balance.

Monday, October 22 (Moon into Aquarius, 1:03 a.m.) Diplomacy wins the way today. Do a good deed for someone. Focus on making people happy. Be sympathetic, kind, and compassionate, even if you face angry outbursts. A domestic adjustment works out for the best.

Tuesday, October 23 (Moon in Aquarius) You have a greater sense of freedom now. You're dealing with new ideas, new options, originality. You get a new perspective. Play your hunches. Look beyond the immediate. Bust old paradigms. Your wishes and dreams come true.

Wednesday, October 24 (Moon into Pisces, 7:01 a.m.) It's your power day, Leo, and that means you're in the driver's seat. Business discussions go well, especially if you open your mind to a new approach. You're being watched by people in power.

Thursday, October 25 (Moon in Pisces) With the moon in your eighth house today, your experiences are more intense than usual. Your emotions could affect your feelings about belongings that you share with others. Finances or an inheritance could play a role. An interest in metaphysical topics, such as sympathetic magic, grabs your attention.

Friday, October 26 (Moon into Aries, 3:32 p.m.) You're at the top of your cycle again, Leo. Stress originality now as you get a fresh start. Get out and meet new people, have new experiences, do something you've never done before. Don't be afraid to turn in a new direction. Trust your hunches. You're inventive and make connections that others overlook. You're determined and courageous today.

Saturday, October 27 (Moon in Aries) The moon is in your ninth house today. You're a dreamer and a thinker. Your thoughts run wild. You may feel a need to get away now, a break from the usual routine. You yearn for a new experience. A publishing venture goes well. Publicity and advertising are emphasized.

Sunday, October 28 (Moon in Aries)   With Venus moving into your third house today, the next couple of weeks should be interesting, especially if you're involved in a creative project or an education program. You really enjoy what you're doing. You also get along well with family members and neighbors. You stay socially active, and you can easily convince others to follow your suggestions.

Monday, October 29 (Moon into Taurus, 2:16 a.m.) Mercury moves into your fifth house today, and that means your writing and speaking skills are enhanced. You express yourself in a dramatic and forceful manner, Leo. There's also a full moon in your tenth house, suggesting that you reap whatever you've sown related to your career goals. You gain better understanding of and insight into your career goals.

Tuesday, October 30 (Moon in Taurus)   Yesterday's energy flows into your Tuesday. Your career is about to take a new turn. You could gain a boost in your prestige now. You're well regarded by fellow workers, and your warmth toward them is appreciated. However, avoid any emotional displays in public.

Wednesday, October 31 (Moon into Gemini, 2:41 p.m.) Domestic matters are highlighted today. A change in the home—an adjustment or readjustment—is needed now. Don't put off the situation. That will only aggravate the problem. Clear up any situation at home that has lingered too long. Domestic purchases are highlighted. Help others, but dance to your own tune.

NOVEMBER 2012

Thursday, November 1 (Moon in Gemini)   The moon is in your eleventh house today. That means you have deeper contact with friends. You find strength in numbers and could join a group of like-minded individuals. Focus on your wishes and dreams. Examine your overall goals. Those goals should be an expression of who you are. Social consciousness plays a role.

Friday, November 2 (Moon in Gemini) Your mind is busy today as you communicate with friends and associates, in person or in writing. You make calls, send e-mails or text messages, or address your Facebook friends. You're feeling restless and looking for a change in scenery. It's a good day to get together with friends for lunch or maybe visit a bookstore for new ideas.

Saturday, November 3 (Moon into Cancer, 3:43 a.m.) Service to others is the theme of the day. Clear up a situation at home that has lingered too long. Adjust to the needs of loved ones. Diplomacy wins the day. Be sympathetic and kind, generous and tolerant.

Sunday, November 4—Daylight Saving Time Ends (Moon in Cancer) The moon is in your twelfth house today. Think carefully before you act. There's a tendency now to undo all the positive actions you've taken. Avoid any self-destructive tendencies. You might feel a need to withdraw and work behind the scenes.

Monday, November 5 (Moon into Leo, 3:40 p.m.) It's a number 8 day, your power day and your day to play it your way. You're recharged for the month ahead, and this makes you more appealing to the public. Focus on a power play. Unexpected money arrives. You can go far with your plans and achieve financial success.

Tuesday, November 6 (Moon in Leo) Mercury goes retrograde in your fifth house today and remains retrograde until November 26. That means there could be some miscommunication or misunderstanding over the next three weeks related to romance or a creative project. There could be delays with travel plans, glitches with electronics, and confusion with any gamble or speculation.

Wednesday, November 7 (Moon in Leo)   With the moon in your first house today, your appearance and personality shine. Your feelings and thoughts are aligned. You're physically vital, and relations with the opposite sex go well. However, your feelings tend to fluctuate by the moment. You could spend time either procrastinating or changing your plans.

Thursday, November 8 (Moon into Virgo, 12:36 a.m.) The spotlight is on cooperation today. Help comes through friends, loved ones, and especially a partner. Take a close look at your finances, and stop worrying. Take time to consider the direction you're headed and your motivation for continuing on this path.

Friday, November 9 (Moon in Virgo)   The moon is in your second house today, boding well for financial matters. Look at your priorities in handling your income. Take care of payments, and collect what's owed to you. You equate your financial assets with emotional security now.

Saturday, November 10 (Moon into Libra, 5:36 a.m.) Neptune goes direct today, where it stays for fourteen years. It's in your eighth house, where it can create confusion over mortgages, insurance, or taxes. Make sure you gather all the facts before you make any final decisions on such matters. However, Neptune in Pisces also creates a good situation for developing your psychic abilities. You could be pursuing a spiritual quest or enhancing one over these years.

Sunday, November 11 (Moon in Libra)   The moon is in your third house today. Take what you know and share it with others. However, keep conscious control of your emotions when communicating. Your mental abilities are strong now, and you have an emotional need to reinvigorate your studies, especially regarding matters of the past.

Monday, November 12 (Moon into Scorpio, 7:11 a.m.)
It's another service day. Be aware that you could face emotional outbursts or someone making unfair demands. Adjust to the needs of loved ones. Be as diplomatic as possible. Help others, but dance to your own tune. Domestic purchases are highlighted. Be understanding, and avoid confrontations.

Tuesday, November 13 (Moon in Scorpio) There's a solar eclipse in your fourth house. That means you can expect new opportunities in your domestic and personal environment. There could be a move coming, or you set up a new home office. An older child might move out or return to the house. It's also a good time for research and investigation.

Wednesday, November 14 (Moon into Sagittarius, 6:53 a.m.) Mercury moves back into your fourth house today as it continues its retrograde movement, which temporarily stymies those opportunities that came your way yesterday. There could be confusion related to domestic matters and delays linked to any plans to carry out repairs or renovations to your house. Likewise, any plans to sell or buy a house or to move could be put on hold for a time.

Thursday, November 15 (Moon in Sagittarius) Your emotions tend to overpower your intellect today. You feel strongly attached to loved ones, particularly children. There's greater depth to a relationship now. Romance is highlighted. It's also a good day to take a chance, experiment.

Friday, November 16 (Moon into Capricorn, 6:36 a.m.)
With Mars moving into your sixth house today, you're

energetic and hard-working. You're so committed and such a perfectionist that coworkers could get annoyed by your aggressive behavior. Best to keep your thoughts to yourself and control your temper.

Saturday, November 17 (Moon in Capricorn)   Even though it's a weekend, yesterday's energy flows into your Saturday. Others rely on you now. You're the one they go to for help. You improve, edit, and refine their work. Keep your resolutions about exercise, and watch your diet. Attend to details related to your health.

Sunday, November 18 (Moon into Aquarius, 8:11 a.m.)   It's a number 3 day, and everything eases up now. The intensity you've been feeling evaporates. Be happy, positive, upbeat. Your attitude determines everything. You're well liked and receive a social invitation. Your charm and wit are appreciated. Spend time in conversation. Hobbies are accented.

Monday, November 19 (Moon in Aquarius)   The moon is in your seventh house, and partnership issues are the focus of your day. Expect some related drama. A legal matter comes to your attention now. Women play a prominent role. You comprehend the nuances of a situation, but it's difficult to go with the flow.

Tuesday, November 20 (Moon into Pisces, 12:55 p.m.) Promote new ideas; follow your curiosity. Look for adventure. Freedom of thought and action is key. But so is moderation; avoid excess in whatever you're doing. Be aware that there could be some miscommunication today with a spouse, partner, or sweetheart. A change of scenery works to your advantage.

Wednesday, November 21 (Moon in Pisces)   Venus moves into your fourth house today. Happy home, domestic bliss! At least until mid-December. You're also feeling artistic and enjoy redecorating or beautifying your home. You get along well with others in your "love nest."

Thursday, November 22 (Moon into Aries, 9:12 p.m.) It's your mystery day, Leo. You launch a journey into the unknown. You're a searcher, a seeker of truth. You investigate, analyze, or simply observe what's going on now. You quickly come to a conclusion and wonder why others don't see what you see. You work best on your own today. Knowledge is essential to success. Go with the flow.

Friday, November 23 (Moon in Aries) The moon is in your ninth house today. You may feel a need to get away now, a break from the usual routine. You yearn for a new experience. Higher education or long-distance travel plays a role. It's also a good day to pursue a publishing project. You might sign up for a workshop or seminar on a topic that interests you. A foreign country or foreign-born person could play a role.

Saturday, November 24 (Moon in Aries) Be aware that emotions can be volatile today. Be careful about accidents and reckless behavior. The time is ripe for initiating projects, launching new ideas. Athletics are highlighted. It's a good day to attend a sports event. Wear bright colors. Imprint your style.

Sunday, November 25 (Moon into Taurus, 8:18 a.m.) Yesterday's energy rolls into your Sunday. You get a fresh start, a new beginning. You're inventive and make connections that others overlook. You're determined and courageous today. Get out and meet new people, have new experiences, do something you've never done before. Explore and discover. Express your opinions dynamically.

Monday, November 26 (Moon in Taurus) Mercury goes direct today in your fourth house. Confusion, miscommunication, and delays recede into the past. Things move more smoothly now, especially domestic matters. You're mentally alert and quick witted, and family members and others in your home setting instantly understand. You and others in the home get along better. You can move ahead on any plans to remodel, renovate, or repair your home. Everything works more smoothly, including computers and other electronic equipment.

Tuesday, November 27 (Moon into Gemini, 8:59 p.m.)
You're creative and express yourself well today. Your artistic talents are highlighted. Use your intuition in whatever decisions you're making. Your attitude determines everything now. You're warm and receptive to others. Spread your good news, and take time to listen to others. Look for hidden messages in their words.

Wednesday, November 28 (Moon in Gemini) There's a lunar eclipse in your eleventh house today. News comes your way regarding friends or associates that affects your feelings. You react emotionally to whatever you've heard. You could also gain insight about a group, or members of a group, in which you are involved.

Thursday, November 29 (Moon in Gemini) Yesterday's energy flows into your Thursday. You find strength in numbers. Friends and group associations play an important role in your day. A project supporting the common good finds favor. Focus on your wishes and dreams. Examine your overall goals.

Friday, November 30 (Moon into Cancer, 9:56 a.m.)
It's a number 6 day, a service day. You're the one others come to for help. You improve what they're doing. You offer advice and support. Be sympathetic and kind, generous and tolerant. It's time to resolve any unsettled situation in your home.

Saturday, December 1 (Moon in Cancer)   The moon is in your twelfth house today. It's a good day to withdraw, work behind the scenes, and keep your thoughts to yourself. Think carefully before you act, and avoid any actions that might undo all the positive steps you've taken. Be aware that hidden enemies could be lurking about, waiting for you to make the wrong move.

Sunday, December 2 (Moon into Leo, 9:58 p.m.) Drama is highlighted today. You could face emotional outbursts or someone making unfair demands. Offer advice and support, but do it in a diplomatic way. Be understanding and avoid criticizing, condemning, and complaining.

Monday, December 3 (Moon in Leo)   The moon is in your first house today, Leo. Spread your wings and fly. Don't limit yourself. You could easily change your mind now about an important matter. You're restless and uncertain what to do. You are sensitive to the thoughts and feelings of others, so you are easily influenced by those around you.

Tuesday, December 4 (Moon in Leo)   The moon is on your ascendant today. You're recharged for the rest of the year, and this makes you more appealing to the public. You're physically vital, and relations with the opposite sex go well. Your appearance and personality shine, especially if that's the way you see yourself. It's all about your health and emotional self.

Wednesday, December 5 (Moon into Virgo, 7:53 a.m.) It's a number 9 day. Finish what you started, Leo. Visualize the future; set your goals, then make them so. You'll probably find that old ways have outlived their usefulness. Look for a new approach, a new perspective. Spiritual values surface.

Thursday, December 6 (Moon in Virgo)   The moon is in your second house today. Money and material goods are important to you now and give you a sense of security. You identify emotionally with your possessions or whatever you value. Watch your spending.

Friday, December 7 (Moon into Libra, 2:37 p.m.) Use your intuition to get a sense of your day. Cooperation, especially with partners, is highlighted. Don't make waves. Don't rush or show resentment; let things develop. Marriage plays a key role.

Saturday, December 8 (Moon in Libra)   Your mind is sharp, and you communicate well. Take what you know and share it with others. Your thinking is unduly influenced by things of the past. Family members play a key role in your day. Do your best to avoid arguments with siblings or neighbors.

Sunday, December 9 (Moon into Scorpio, 5:52 p.m.) It's a good day to get organized. Clean out a closet or straighten up your desk. Keep your goals in mind, follow your ideas. Be tenacious. You tend to stay with the tried and true. It's not a day for experimentation or new approaches.

Monday, December 10 (Moon in Scorpio)   Mercury moves into your fifth house today. You express yourself dramatically and forcefully through speech or writing. You draw attention to yourself, Leo, and any creative endeavors. You may have an analytical outlook on romance and life.

Tuesday, December 11 (Moon into Sagittarius, 6:22 p.m.)   Clear up a situation at home that has lingered too long. Do a good deed for someone. Visit someone who is ill or in need of help. Be sympathetic and kind, generous and tolerant. Focus on making people happy. Avoid scattering your energies. A domestic adjustment works out for the best.

Wednesday, December 12 (Moon in Sagittarius)   The moon is in your fifth house today. You feel a sudden surge of inspiration, a creative urge that helps you break through a block. In romance, there's more depth and understanding in a relationship. Children play an important role in your day.

Thursday, December 13 (Moon into Capricorn, 5:43 p.m.)   There's a new moon in your fifth house, indicating that you find new opportunities in your creative life. It's a good day to take a gamble. With Uranus going direct in your ninth house today, you're likely to develop an unconventional philosophy of life. You could be erratic in your pursuit of higher education. Your ideas about religion, the higher mind, and the law become more unusual over time. Regarding travel, you prefer to take the road less traveled. You seek adventure in exotic locales. Rather than traveling with a group, you prefer more independence.

Friday, December 14 (Moon in Capricorn)   It's a service day. Help others in the workplace, but don't deny your own needs. Keep your resolutions about exercise, and watch your diet. Make any needed doctor or dentist appointments.

Saturday, December 15 (Moon into Aquarius, 5:53 p.m.)   With Venus moving into your fifth house today, you're more attractive to the opposite sex. It's a good month for making money related to the arts. You also have a strong affection toward children. You make an excellent parent now. If there are no children in your life, pets play an important role. You could be getting a new animal this month.

Sunday, December 16 (Moon in Aquarius)   Marriage and partnerships take on new importance. There's harmony in a relationship. You might be socializing with associates from the workplace today. You get along well with your partner. You're looking for security, but be careful that others don't manipulate your feelings.

Monday, December 17 (Moon into Pisces, 8:48 p.m.) You're creative and express yourself well today. Your artistic talents are highlighted. Your attitude determines everything now. Avoid becoming caught up in the collective muck related to fears of the upcoming end of the Mayan Calendar this Friday.

Tuesday, December 18 (Moon in Pisces) You may feel a need to get away now, a break from the usual routine. Plan a long trip. Sign up for a workshop or seminar. Publicize and advertise whatever you're doing. If you're involved with a publishing project, expect some answers—positive ones.

Wednesday, December 19 (Moon in Pisces) Imagination is highlighted. Watch for psychic events, synchronicities. Keep track of your dreams, including your daydreams. Ideas are ripe. You can tap deeply into the collective unconscious for inspiration. It's a time for deep healing.

Thursday, December 20 (Moon into Aries, 3:44 a.m.) Service to others is the theme of the day. You offer advice and support. Do a good deed for someone. Be sympathetic and kind, generous and tolerant. You're passionate but impatient. You're extremely persuasive now.

Friday, December 21 (Moon in Aries) The Mayan Calendar ends today! The old world ends, the new one begins. Look for transformation on a large scale as the old paradigm fades. Your mind is receptive, and you're open to many ideas and concepts. Your thoughts run wild today. You're a dreamer and a thinker, and your ideas tend to rattle the status quo. You jump easily from one idea to another.

Saturday, December 22 (Moon into Taurus, 2:26 p.m.)
It's a number 8 day, your power day. Expect a financial coup. Open your mind to a new approach that will pay off. You have a chance to expand, to gain recognition, fame, power. Look and act successful, even if you don't feel that way. Be aware that fear of failure or fear that you won't measure up will attract tangible experiences that reinforce the feeling.

Sunday, December 23 (Moon in Taurus) Cultivate new ideas, but make sure that they're well grounded in reality. Try to avoid stubborn behavior when others question your actions. While you maintain a common-sense, down-to-earth perspective on life, you also long for the good life with its material rewards. You could be somewhat possessive now. Avoid stubborn behavior. Health and physical activity are highlighted.

Monday, December 24 (Moon in Taurus) With the moon in your tenth house today, professional concerns take priority. Your prestige is elevated; business is highlighted. You get an end-of-year bonus, a raise, or an advancement. You're warm toward fellow workers, but make sure you don't let your professional life mix with your personal life now.

Tuesday, December 25 (Moon into Gemini, 3:14 a.m.)
With Mars moving into your seventh house today, the key phrase now is "think before you act." That's especially true over the next three weeks. Control your temper, and avoid confrontations with a spouse, sweetheart, or partner. You tend to exhibit aggressive behavior. Merry Christmas!

Wednesday, December 26 (Moon in Gemini) The moon is in your eleventh house today. As the year comes to an end, examine your overall goals. Make sure that they remain an expression of who you are. Revise and rewrite as needed. Friends play a key role in helping you fulfill your wishes and dreams. You get along well with groups, especially when everyone is of like mind. You help the group's goals, and you benefit in return.

Thursday, December 27 (Moon into Cancer, 4:08 p.m.) Take care of obligations now. Get everything organized. Be methodical and thorough. Don't get sloppy. You're building foundations for an outlet for your creativity. You're at the right place at the right time.

Friday, December 28 (Moon in Cancer) There's a full moon in your twelfth house today. Opportunities come your way to work behind the scenes or explore your own unconscious. It's a good time to start meditating or pursue a past-life regression.

Saturday, December 29 (Moon in Cancer) Yesterday's energy flows into your Saturday. You could feel moody, and you tend to hide your emotions. Take time to reflect and meditate. It's a great day for a mystical or spiritual discipline. Your intuition is heightened.

Sunday, December 30 (Moon into Leo, 3:47 a.m.) It's your mystery day, Leo. Look beneath the surface for the reasons others are shifting their points of view, "changing their tune." Keep any secrets entrusted to you. Gather information, but don't make any absolute decisions until tomorrow. Maintain your emotional balance. Go with the flow.

Monday, December 31 (Moon in Leo) Mercury moves into your sixth house today. You're very methodical and efficient in whatever you're doing over the next couple of weeks. You're concerned about your duties, your health, and following a proper diet. Stop worrying. Relax this evening; have good time.

HAPPY NEW YEAR!

Locate your date of birth, find the sign of your North Node, then read the description in chapter 11.

07-04-1930 NN Taurus
12-29-1931 NN Aries
06-25-1933 NN Pisces
03-09-1935 NN Aquarius
09-14-1936 NN Capricorn
03-04-1938 NN Sagittarius
09-11-1939 NN Scorpio
05-23-1941 NN Libra
11-19-1942 NN Virgo
05-13-1944 NN Leo
12-01-1945 NN Cancer
12-10-1945 NN Cancer
12-14-1945 NN Cancer
07-31-1947 NN Gemini
01-22-1949 NN Taurus
07-26-1950 NN Aries
03-29-1952 NN Pisces
10-10-1953 NN Aquarius
04-02-1955 NN Capricorn
10-04-1956 NN Sagittarius
06-16-1958 NN Scorpio
12-15-1959 NN Libra
06-08-1961 NN Virgo
12-21-1962 NN Leo
08-25-1964 NN Cancer

02-18-1966 NN Gemini
08-20-1967 NN Taurus
04-20-1969 NN Aries
11-04-1970 NN Pisces
04-27-1972 NN Aquarius
10-27-1973 NN Capricorn
07-11-1975 NN Sagittarius
01-08-1977 NN Scorpio
07-04-1978 NN Libra
01-11-1980 NN Virgo
09-23-1981 NN Leo
03-16-1983 NN Cancer
09-13-1984 NN Gemini
04-01-1986 NN Taurus
04-14-1986 NN Taurus
04-22-1986 NN Taurus
11-30-1987 NN Aries
05-24-1989 NN Pisces
11-19-1990 NN Aquarius
08-03-1992 NN Capricorn
02-01-1994 NN Sagittarius
08-01-1995 NN Scorpio
01-25-1997 NN Libra
10-19-1998 NN Virgo
04-12-2000 NN Leo
10-11-2001 NN Cancer
04-11-2003 NN Gemini
12-24-2004 NN Taurus
06-19-2006 NN Aries
12-15-2007 NN Pisces
08-22-2009 NN Aquarius
02-28-2011 NN Capricorn

SYDNEY OMARR

Born on August 5, 1926, in Philadelphia, Pennsylvania, **Sydney Omarr** was the only person ever given full-time duty in the U.S. Army as an astrologer. He is regarded as the most erudite astrologer of the twentieth century and the best known, through his syndicated column and his radio and television programs (he was Merv Griffin's "resident astrologer"). Omarr has been called the most "knowledgeable astrologer since Evangeline Adams." His forecasts of Nixon's downfall, the end of World War II in mid-August of 1945, the assassination of John F. Kennedy, Roosevelt's election to a fourth term and his death in office . . . these and many others are on the record and quoted enough to be considered "legendary."

ABOUT THE SERIES

This is one of a series of twelve *Sydney Omarr®
Day-by-Day Astrological Guides* for the signs of
2012. For questions and comments about the book,
go to www.tjmacgregor.com.

COMING SOON

SYDNEY OMARR'S® ASTROLOGICAL GUIDE FOR YOU IN 2012

These expert forecasts for 2012 offer valuable insights about the past and extraordinary predictions for the future. Brimming with tantalizing projections, this amazing guide will give you advice on romantic commitment, career moves, travel, and finance. Along with year overviews and detailed month-by-month predictions for every sign, you'll learn everything that's new under the stars, including:

- What to expect from relationships with family and partners
- New career opportunities for success in the future
- Global shifts and world forecasts
- New information about the 13th zodiac sign
- And much more!

Available wherever books are sold or at penguin.com